DENTISTRY:

BUILDING YOUR MILLION DOLLAR SOLO PRACTICE

Edward L. Silker, DDS

Original Edition
April, 1995

SILK PAGES PUBLISHING, Lakeshore, Minnesota 56468

DENTISTRY:

BUILDING YOUR MILLION DOLLAR SOLO PRACTICE

Published by:

SILK PAGES PUBLISHING
7030 Gullwood Road
Lakshore, Minnesota 56468
United States of America

Permission to use cover photograph granted by
STAR DENTAL / DEN-TAL EZ, Inc.

Copyright© 1995, by Edward L. Silker, DDS
First Printing April, 1995
Printed in the United States of America

Library of Congress Cataloging-in-Publication Data
Silker, Edward L.
>   Dentistry: Building Your Million Dollar Solo Practice

>   Includes Bibliographical references
>   ISBN 0-9645815-0-7: $59.95

FOREWORD

When first approached by Dr. Edward L. Silker to write a foreword to this most remarkable text, I thought he must have mistaken me for someone else. Most of my confreres correctly believe that when it comes to understanding business, I would have great difficulty making change in a drugstore. However, I carefully digested the contents and wished that I had had the opportunity to learn even a small fraction of the wisdom contained within these pages when I was in dental school. It wasn't in the curriculum then, and it barely is now, almost 50 years later.

In spite of good intentions, most of the authors of texts of dental practice management have not been effective communicators. This vade mecum is designed to open the lines of communication between the dentist and his or her patients and between the dentist and his or her support staff. The new graduate and the not-so-recent graduate dentist cannot fail to learn from Dr. Silker's expository. It's all there: how to be efficient in all branches of dentistry, how to schedule, how to deal with difficult patients, how to communicate, how to market, and how to run your practice - all 31 chapters are gems.

While Dr. Silker may not have provided an answer to every question that might be proposed, he has, I believe, gone a long way in answering many of the most common ones.

Dr. Robert J. Gorlin
Regents' Professor Emeritus
University of Minnesota
Health Science Center

DEDICATION

This book is dedicated to all of the teachers in my life, my family, my professors, my staff and my peers -- but most of all to those loving patients from whom I continually learn so very much.

PROFESSIONAL ECONOMICS BUREAU OF AMERICA

279 North Medina Street • Loretto, MN 55357 • Phone Twin Cities Area (612) 479-6166 • Toll Free 1-800-328-2925 • Fax (612) 479-1210

January 9, 1995

Ed Silker, DDS
265 North, Box 385
Deerwood, MN 56444

Dear Dr. Silker:

Congratulations on attaining a ONE MILLION DOLLAR PRACTICE in 1994! This is a very rare accomplishment for a solo practitioner.

Your practice - building skills are truly impressive. I was pleased to hear that you are authoring a book on your strategies for growth and success. Many of your colleagues could benefit from your experiences.

Sincerely,

Dick Kallio
PEB President

INTRODUCTION

This text is intended to reveal to fellow dentists and/or dental field personnel as much information as possible about how a new start up dental practice in a town of 524 population (Deerwood, Minnesota) grew from zero (0) patients in May of 1990 to a Million Dollar Annual Solo Practice in 1994.

This text's intention is to describe how this occurred. Your author is not so naive or presumptuous to suggest this is the only way of doing any of the following procedures or that this is the only way to construct the physical plant or the only way to equip it.

However, this is what worked and if you can benefit in any way from our climb up the elusive learning curve it would fulfill the purpose of this book.

If you have some things which are working for you -- great! If you are making all the money you want -- wonderful! If you have your own way of doing things -- Terrific! Our only desire is that from our experience you can glean some information which will be of help to make your day more fun, more flexible, more profitable, or more efficient so you might finish sooner, or serve more patients, whichever is your preference.

However, if it is your desire to increase your production, collections, profit, number of patients, office size or staff; or if you are a dental student or a dentist thinking of building a new facility or leasing a new facility, here is a system which has been proven to be able to function as a million dollar per year solo practice in a town of less than 1000 people.

Although some details will be shown, the general underlying principles will perhaps be more important and applicable to your particular unique situation.

unique situation.

As was stated in dental school -- whatever works in your hands -- or, on a more global scale - whatever works for your dental practice.

The transition from dental school to high productivity or the transition from a slow or stagnant practice to high productivity can be very difficult and time consuming. In fact, it may be impossible if you do not know how. This writing is designed to make it not only possible, but quicker and easier than you anticipated. An alternate title consideration was "What They Didn't Teach You In Dental School" which also might have been appropriate. This book is based upon empirical evidence derived from a massive barrage of clinical experiences. In any situation in which it conflicts with academic beliefs, findings or teachings, apologies are extended in advance. However, these are the findings observed clinically.

In any event utilize everything which will help you attain your goals. Good Luck -- Make a Million!

Edward L. Silker, DDS

FOOTNOTE: Your author has had male dental assistants and male dental hygienists and has been very pleased with both. However, since the majority of the dental assistants and dental hygienists as of this writing are female, we will speak of dental assistants and dental hygienists in the feminine gender. For simplicity of writing only, dentists will be assigned the masculine gender. This eliminates approximately 1,000 he/she's throughout the text and is only for simplicity in my writing and your reading and certainly does not rule out or discriminate against either. Patients, for variety, will be referred to in the feminine, masculine and collective gender.

TABLE OF CONTENTS

CHAPTER 1

BUILDING YOUR MILLION DOLLAR SOLO PRACTICE

"You can get everything in life that you want -- if you'll just help enough other people get what they want."

Zig Ziglar

Congratulations! You have in your hands all the information necessary to create your own million dollar per year solo dental practice!

This book reveals how a start-up practice in a village of 524 residents in a sparsely populated area of northern Minnesota grew to a million dollar per year solo practice in its fourth full year!

My approach worked in a sparsely populated rural area. My methods likely would work even better in an urban area.

Not only did the practice prosper, but this fourth full year, which saw the million dollars, was a year in which 1760 new patients were added to the practice.

The following chapters will explore how this goal was attained and how you can develop your own very successful dental practice. By gradual increases in efficiency, flexibility and effectiveness the dental team can treat more and more patients daily -- these consistent increases are reflected in skyrocketing production per unit of time as profits soar to exceptional levels. And this all takes place because one is working smarter -- not harder!

Successfully building a dental practice is like trying to pick up a dropped raw egg. The harder you try to grab it, the more it escapes you. Or, to put it another way, it's like attempting to get your forceps on that marble-shaped third molar...the tighter you squeeze, the faster it slips out of your grasp.

Sometimes the harder we try to achieve our goal by the direct approach the more it eludes us -- the extra effort seems counterproductive. The direct approach is not working.

Similarly, the more you focus on achieving *financial success* the more *financial success* evades you. How can this be? Possibly because our intuitive patients can feel when a dentist is sincerely and totally interested in what is best for them. If the dentist is more concerned with the business of dentistry than with the patient's well-being a successful practice will not be realized.

The dentist's perspective, which naturally will dominate his thought process, is a legitimate starting point for discussion with the patient for dental treatment needed. However, the patient's reactions to your proposal must be closely monitored and observed.

MAXIM

**STRIVE TO DISCOVER YOUR PATIENT'S
PRIORITIES AND VALUE SYSTEM AND
INTEGRATE THEIR DESIRES WITH YOUR
BROAD KNOWLEDGE OF DENTISTRY
TO DEVELOP A TREATMENT DECISION
WHICH IS IN YOUR PATIENT'S BEST INTEREST
AND YOUR PRACTICE WILL FLOURISH**

One of the most important elements in the rapid building of a successful dental practice is establishing a solid rapport with your patient. Once you have earned your patient's trust your continual concern for his well-being will keep you bonded for life. This patient is the one who tells family and friends, "Go to my dentist. My dentist will take good care of you." This patient often is responsible for a significant percentage of the patient base of the practice.

The key is to respect your patient's perspective. Recognize that he may have different value systems, different priorities, and different socio-economic conditions. These factors are important in reaching his preferred treatment decision. Once the dentist understands the patient's priorities, treatment decisions can be made and the needed dental treatment begun.

It is very rewarding to be given these votes of confidence on a daily basis. But these votes of confidence don't just happen; they are earned by fully implementing this concept of understanding the patient, communicating clearly and always acting in the patient's best interest.

Therefore, you begin to build a very successful practice -- not by focusing on building the successful practice, but by focusing your attention instead on "Serving each patient from the patient's perspective." When you take good care of the patient, the patient will take good care of you by providing referrals.

15

Some may choose not to put forth the effort necessary to achieve a $1,000,000 goal. That is your choice! Some may far exceed this achievement. That is admirable! Some may be willing only to put forth sufficient effort to attain a 10% or a 25% increase in production. That is a substantial increase! Some may choose to use this text in order to work fewer hours or perhaps one fewer day per week -- and there is certainly nothing wrong with that.

In order to attain your goals you must realize that a dental practice is a constantly evolving phenomenon and it must be watched and guided continually to keep it headed in the desired direction.

The practice described throughout this book began four years ago with the four present operatories plumbed and only two equipped. It started with one full-time receptionist and one part-time assistant working 1-1/2 days a week.

The current four-operatory practice consists of two full-time receptionists, four full-time assistants and two full-time hygienists. The staff grew as the patient flow increased. By having ample staff during this growth period one can constantly look for and discover ways to become more efficient.

Ultimate efficiency is a goal to work toward constantly. While one can get closer and closer to ultimate efficiency, one can never quite "arrive", so improvement will always be possible. As your dental team becomes more efficient, it should be possible to serve more and more patients with quality dental care while your patients feel special and well-cared for.

One way to assist in accomplishing this goal of making people feel less apprehensive and well-cared for when they come to the dental office is to utilize qualified, well-trained dental assistants to spend time with the patients prior to the dentist's arrival answering any questions, preparing the patients, confirming the day's procedures and in general, making the patient feel welcome.

When your dental office is well-organized and everything is efficiently in place, the dentist can appear and spend a minute or two chatting with the patient about something other than their teeth. This small time expenditure is enjoyable and relaxing for the dentist and allows the patient to feel good as it neutralizes any tendency for a rushed feeling.

On our journey together through the following pages of this book, we will explore the dental office through the patient's eyes, and then discover the learning curve and how it applies to the dental office.

We will go on to examine the principles of efficiency, and then proceed to put efficiency into action. Once we have a grasp of the use of efficiency we will be ready to learn how flexible we can be due to our increased efficiency.

Next we will look at the importance of scheduling and how the dentist's attitude influences the way his receptionist(s) schedules. Then we will explore the affect the patient factor has on scheduling, stress, and longevity of the dental team.

We then will discover what the dental team can do to facilitate efficiency prior to the dentist's arrival in the operatory. We will examine tray set-ups for operative and surgery as well as how the dental assistants set up for root canal treatment, fixed and removable prosthetics and denture patients.

Then we will address the benefits of using nitrous oxide/oxygen analgesia and discuss treating the primary dentition without local anesthesia.

The next chapter is dedicated to the Modified Rubber Dam Technique and will demonstrate a technique of placing the rubber dam without the time and frustration factors many of us have experienced.

As Art Linkletter says, "Kids say the darnedest things." In our Pedodontics chapter we will learn how little patients can be like a breath of fresh air in our busy schedules and how to make going to the dentist less frightening and ultimately enjoyable for them.

17

A discussion of root canal treatment will follow after which we will look into removable prosthetics and explore how, with streamlining techniques, we can get great results.

We will venture into fixed prosthetics and discuss how crown and bridge services are in the patient's best interest and how effective the dentist can be in communicating this fact to the patient, once the dentist is totally convinced himself. We will address how important it is to "do it right the first time." The following chapter will explain why we should love the dental laboratory we send our cases to.

Operative dentistry, the bread and butter of dentistry, will be addressed and we will find that maximum organization and steady increases in efficiency of the dental team pay big dividends.

We will discuss personality and the role it plays in the successful dental team -- how auxiliary personnel can complement the dentist's personality. We will even take a look at technical skills v. social skills in a successful dental practice.

Following will be a look at third party payments and their effects on the dental practice finances.

Dental office expenses are always a captivating subject - we will take a close look at this area of a successful dental practice.

Marketing -- and how it applies to dentistry -- is the next topic of discussion, followed by accounting and the business of dentistry where we will look into criteria for selecting an accountant to be on your team.

Then we will discover how to make a trip to the banker an enjoyable experience.

The importance of a mission statement and your role in helping your staff develop their mission statement, followed by the all important chapter on goal setting will prove that preparing a mission statement, setting goals, inspiration and motivation are Essentials for Success.

We will take a look at the physical plant and choosing a location for your dental office, along with the advantages of a free standing building and the layout for a facility which has been proven capable of becoming a million dollar solo practice. In this chapter we will look at the actual building floor plans including electrical, plumbing, landscaping and outdoor signage. We will address the telephone system and what to look for in a telephone number. Then the super important open operatory concept, how it increases efficiency and its psychological effect on the patients.

Next we discuss dental equipment and detail a list of dental equipment which may be helpful when you visit your banker.

Chapter 30 gives you some ideas on sample Chalk Talks for you to have with your staff which will make staff meetings more enjoyable and educational.

The In-House Laboratory chapter will detail an equipment list and give some hints on how denture repairs are completed while the patient waits.

In the back of the book you will find 52 quotes to remember - one for each week of the year, along with a summary of Maxims from the text of the book, and a list of toll-free 800 #s for your convenience in calling dental suppliers.

Whatever goals you establish for yourself and your dental practice, this book will provide the tools! However, you must *PICK UP THE TOOLS AND USE THEM!* No quick fix, no shortcut to success -- but we will offer suggestions from empirically proven methods for realizing your goals!

CHAPTER 2

THE NEW PATIENT'S FIRST TRIP TO THE DENTAL OFFICE

(as seen through the eyes of the new patient)

You only get one chance at a first impression.

The patient often drives by the dental office and notices the logo on the sign, the neatly trimmed lawn, attractive building, sidewalk, well-kept shrubs, and cars always in the parking lot.

The patient has a tooth which hasn't felt quite right for some time so she decides to call for an appointment. The patient gets a friendly greeting on the 2nd ring of the telephone: "The Smile Center -- this is Jan. How may I help you?" The receptionist's warm greeting as she answers the telephone provides welcome reassurance.

The patient is able to get an appointment at her preferred time. Her first contact with the office has been positive! Had the patient been in pain, she would have received an immediate appointment -- OUR POLICY!

When the patient arrives for the appointment she drives to the facility, parks near the front door, enters and is greeted with a friendly smile and a warm welcome. She is asked to fill out a chart (one page only). Inside the office everything is clean, neat and bright, cheerful -- and busy -- this is a good sign!

After her chart is completed she is greeted and escorted to the operatory by a smiling dental assistant. When the patient sees the clean, bright open operatory setting she is further impressed with the state of the art equipment and is more relaxed once she sees other patients being treated in the same large room with no immediate sounds of discomfort. The patient is escorted to an operatory and a friendly dental assistant inquires about which tooth is bothering her. The empathetic assistant further inquires as to the severity of discomfort and confirms that the tooth has not been waking the patient up at night. X-rays are taken by the dental assistant and the patient is offered a magazine to look at while the film is being processed. Once the film is processed the dentist takes a look at the film to confirm the tentative diagnosis. The assistant chats with the patient while setting up the operatory for the procedure. The dental assistant places topical anesthetic on a Q-tip in the patient's mouth in preparation for the local anesthetic "...so it will be more comfortable for you."

By the time the dentist arrives, the patient is comfortable and has decided she likes this dental office. Therefore, the dentist's task has been made easier with this pre-conditioning.

The dentist reviews the x-rays, does the emergency examination and dictates the diagnosis to a dental assistant. The dentist excuses himself after the examination has been completed. The assistant gives the information to a receptionist, then chats with the patient while the receptionist prepares an estimate for her treatment. The estimate is presented in duplicate -- one copy stays in the chart, the patient keeps the original. When the patient agrees with the anticipated procedure the dentist returns to commence treatment. After the procedure is completed, the assistant escorts the patient to the front desk where the receptionist schedules her next appointment.

When one observes this initial visit through the eyes of the patient one sees the importance of the physical plant, the support staff, the modern equipment, and the prompt, effective treatment in affecting the impression on the patient.

State-of-the-art dental equipment appears space-age to individuals who haven't been exposed to it previously. Patients strongly prefer to have the most modern dental equipment available so that the procedure can be effectively completed in the minimum time and with minimum discomfort.

Our practice is in a rural and remote part of the state and we regularly see patients who have retired to our area from the Twin Cities (Minneapolis and Saint Paul) area. Their former dentists apparently have equipment purchased upon graduation from Dental School because when patients step into our brightly lit four-operatory setting we regularly hear comments like --- "This looks like an operating room (hospital)." "Wow, this is neat!" "Oh, I love the brightness." "Yes! My favorite color." (All chairs, stools and countertops in our office are the color of raspberry yogurt.)

Add to this routine trip, our policy that any patient who is in pain gets an appointment right away and you come up with an impressive scenario.

On her first visit the patient is impressed with our facility, our staff, and our professional treatment.

Once she has had a positive experience she anticipates that her subsequent visits will be pleasant. This patient will return and will tell many of her friends about her wonderful experience. This makes your task much less challenging the next time.

THIS IS THE BEST ADVERTISING OF ALL! WORD OF MOUTH!!

MAXIM

WORD OF MOUTH -- YOUR BEST ADVERTISING!

HAPPY PATIENTS

We insist that every patient be happy -- wow, what an ambitious undertaking!.

Absolutely whatever it takes.

Right or wrong - the patient always gets the benefit of any misunderstanding. This is sometimes hard, sometimes tough, but in the long run pays off handsomely.

Anyone can get along with the good natured, reasonable patients. The real test is dealing with a patient who is having a bad day or even possibly a bad life.

Realize they are in a troubled state -- do what you can to help! If you give your best effort but feel that you are not making progress, let the patient know you feel it is not working, offer to cancel any charges and let them move on. This often causes the patient to re-evaluate the situation; frequently they will become loyal patients.

Some of our initially grouchiest patients have turned into some of our best patients. If you can just break the ice with them they will often warm up nicely.

Generally, grouchy patients are not accustomed to being treated in a kindly way. Just keep it up and they will usually transform into great patients!

As the patients leave they are given a helium-filled balloon for being such a "good patient."

Do everything you can to make the patient's first visit an enjoyable one -- from the telephone lines being open -- to good visibility from the street -- to convenient parking -- to being greeted by a smiling face the moment they enter. And by having your facility clean and neat with well-trained friendly staff organized for prompt and efficient delivery of dental treatment.

In the next Chapter we will have the opportunity to explore the Learning Curve and how it applies to your dental practice.

CHAPTER 3

THE LEARNING CURVE

"O! This Learning, What a Thing It Is!"

Wm. Shakespeare

"Repetition is the Mother of Skill."

Anthony Robbins

A Learning Curve is basically nothing more than a graphic depiction of changes in performance or output during a specified time period. The phrase 'learning curve' is also used to refer to mathematical equations which describe the relationship between practice and performance. Learning curves provide a concrete measure of the rate at which an individual or group of individuals are learning a task. In their simplest forms, learning curves are generally depicted in Figures 3-1 and 3-2 below.

27

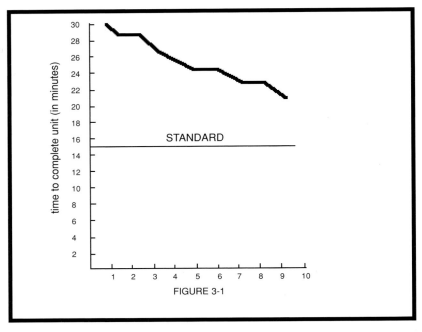

FIGURE 3-1

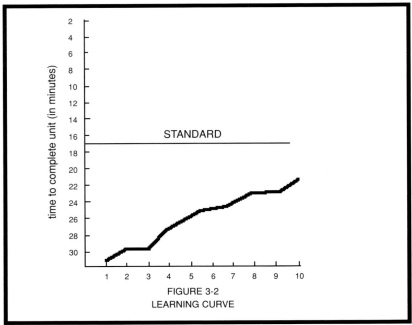

FIGURE 3-2
LEARNING CURVE

"It is important to note that both figures are based on the same data. However, as is readily apparent, one curve slopes downward while the other curve slopes upward. Both are correct. But in most cases, the upward sloping curve with the X (horizontal) and Y (vertical) axes depicted as shown is preferred because it is generally regarded as less confusing. People tend to assume that improvement in performance should be associated with an upward swing in a graph.

"The Boeing Company is perhaps best known for having recognized the 80% learning curve effect for the manufacture of airframes. This effect is based on their own research which indicated that for this specific activity, each time unit output is doubled, there is a corresponding 20% decline in labor input or the time needed to produce the end product.

"For example, if 10,000 hours are needed to produce the first airframe (1 unit), it can be projected with the use of the 80% learning curve, that only 8,000 hours will be needed to produce the second unit, 6,400 hours to produce the 3rd unit and so on, until the curve begins to level off."

"A Guide to Learning Curve Technology to Enhance Performance Prediction in Vocational Evaluation."

Paul McCray, Thomas Blakemore Research Utilization Report, Stout Vocational Rehabilitation Institute, School of Education and Human Services, UNIVERSITY OF WISCONSIN-STOUT Menomonie, WI 54751

THE LEARNING CURVE (by definition): "A graph that depicts rate of learning, especially a graph of progress in the mastery of a skill against the time required for such mastery." The American Heritage Dictionary of The English Language, Third Edition, 1992.

THE LEARNING CURVE IN DENTISTRY:

The more times we have opportunity to repeat a given procedure the less time each consecutive procedure requires on the average.

Sounds pretty straightforward.

Your last filling in dental school hopefully required less time than your first, or have you intentionally forgotten your first filling?

After your 1,000th filling your time requirement, on average, was less. After your 12,000th filling, less time yet was required.

The more you do the more efficient you become.

The individual who does only a few dentures per year may well have sufficient time between dentures to forget what he learned from his last effort.

Therefore, it is essential that the young dentist get the maximum possible experience in those years immediately following dental school if he is to advance up the learning curve and become efficient in his skills.

So, get into a busy, busy situation!

Financial reward for the young dentist should be less of a priority than gaining experience. Through experience will come efficiency in treating patients. And with increased efficiency the dentist is better prepared to serve more patients.

When you DRIVE your car you likely know how to get there the next time. When you RIDE with someone you are probably much less aware.

Jump in with both feet! Get active with patients! When you have questions or challenges consult with your mentor.

One learns very little by watching.

One learns much by doing.

One learns even more by doing and sweating a little.

Get active. Get busy!

HOW TO GET THE MAXIMUM EXPOSURE
TO LEARNING OPPORTUNITIES

- practice a lot of hours - you worked long hours in dental school for minimal rewards. Work a few more years of long hours. Advance up the learning curve and rewards will be abundant.

- practice in a busy office, long hours

- practice in the military

- practice as an associate with a buy-in agreement

- practice as an associate with a buy-out agreement

The greater number of experienced dentists with whom you practice and the more varied are their experiences, the more the potential for you to learn.

REMEMBER, you learn by stretching; not by doing only what is totally comfortable. Those who take the path of least resistance do not grow!

The more frequent the repetition of a given procedure the greater the advancement on the learning curve. Constant repetition with little time lapse between the exposures is the most beneficial for learning.

OTHER FACTORS BESIDES LEARNING
WHICH AFFECT PERFORMANCE

ENVIRONMENT - a comfortable enjoyable environment promotes performance. Comfortable temperature and ventilation as well as compatible background music can improve performance.

DENTAL ASSISTANT - a well trained dental assistant with a great attitude has a phenomenal effect on performance.

SECOND DENTAL ASSISTANT - a second well trained, happy dental assistant can increase performance far beyond most dentist's expectations.

EFFICIENCY INCREASES PERFORMANCE - state-of-the-art equipment standardized and positioned strategically for optimal time/motion efficiency will further improve performance. Everything which is usually needed is at your fingertips. Keep everything which could possibly be needed within easy reach. Cover all bases. Additional staff to provide anything you could possibly need without interrupting the six-handed team further increases performance.

PATIENT ATTITUDE - the patient with whom great rapport has already been established prior to the dentist's appearance is a further aid to increased performance --

The patient who:

- Has had an initial positive contact with the office via telephone.

- Has driven up to the front door for convenient parking.

- Has been welcomed into the office with a big smile, a friendly greeting and conversation.

- Has been taken into the operatory by a friendly, smiling assistant who chats with the patient until the dentist arrives.

- When arriving in the operatory the dentist recognizes the comfortable, loving environment and is automatically much more likely to perform well.

Advancing up the learning curve is important in dentistry. The best way to advance rapidly is to get lots of practice in all phases of dentistry and to observe astutely what is working, what is getting the project finished more efficiently. Improve on those factors which facilitate efficiency. Note what slows the procedure, for that is where efficiency can be improved.

Evaluate, then address the needed changes in techniques, equipment, supplies, procedures, instruments, tray set-up, dental assistant drawer arrangement or mobile cart stocking. Discuss potential changes with dental assistants and reap the benefits of their suggestions, because their focus and concentration is on the immediate environment while the dentist's focus is on one tooth at a time.

Fine tuning is a constant process -- not a destination! This is fortunate because you will continue improving through astute observation and well planned modifications.

Whatever will make the procedure smoother, do it!

Then watch for further potential improvements.

There are many learning curves in dentistry. Each of us advances at our own pace which is determined by aptitude, motivation, intuition, dexterity, determination and the frequency of exposure.

As the dentist gains more and more experience in a specific phase of dentistry -- let's say full dentures -- he becomes more efficient, confident and comfortable. The more he does, the better he becomes, the more referrals, the more happy patients, and it just snowballs. More experience in a specific phase breeds more and more efficiency in that phase.

The more learning curves you ascend and the faster you ascend them the more successful you will become. Get going...Get growing!

MAXIM

ADVANCE ON AS MANY DENTAL LEARNING CURVES AS POSSIBLE AS SOON AS POSSIBLE

In order to produce one million dollars of dentistry per year one must either be able to accomplish a lot of dentistry per hour, or work a lot of hours - like around the clock. Since we know around the clock is not practical or possible one must become more efficient to attain such a goal.

We all started out at the pace of a two surface filling per half day in dental school.

Unfortunately, this is not an acceptable level for a successful practice.

In order to produce $1,000,000 per year one must produce $83,333.33 per month or $20,000 per week or $4,000 per day (assuming a 5-day week).

If one is to produce $4,000 per day, one must average $500 an hour for eight hours or $400 per hour for 10 hours and so on.

The discrepancy between the $500.00 per hour and the 2-surface per half day filling is approximately a factor of 40. This transition from the dental school pace to high efficiency is one which requires both effort and time.

Efficiency in performing dental procedures is improved through repetition and observation. Repetition without observation does not significantly contribute to improvement or efficiency.

Observe each procedure and each motion of each procedure as if you were a third party. From this vantage point one is often able to discover areas which lend themselves to further improvement in efficiency.

TIME/MOTION STUDIES REVEAL MUCH

As dental school students, several of us attended a time/motion seminar put on by Dr. Hugo Wolf.

Dr. Wolf showed a video tape of THE OLD STAND UP-DO-IT-ALONE DENTIST. The dentist was taped doing an amalgam filling for a patient. The film was shown at many times its original speed. We nearly rolled on the floor with laughter. The dentist's eyes were everywhere EXCEPT in the patient's mouth.

His entire body was not even near the patient a large part of the time. He was across the room looking for an instrument in his cabinet. Back to the patient. Next he went across the room to mix the amalgam, then came back, loaded the carrier, and plugged the amalgam. Then he looked for a carver. It was wonderful -- the dentist's eyes were focused in the mouth only 14% of the time the patient was in the chair.

With a couple of trained assistants we strive for 90% to 95% of our chair time with our eyes focused on the dentition.

High production occurs only after one has progressed sufficiently far along the learning curve.

MAXIM

LEARN TO BE FLEXIBLE ENOUGH TO SERVE THE PATIENT SPONTANEOUSLY

Patients appreciate prompt service whether they require help for a broken tooth (new crown), an extraction, a restoration replacement or a denture.

They almost always prefer treatment when they present with the problem rather than being rescheduled at a later date.

For example, after establishing rapport and agreeing to make the patient a denture, if the patient is ready to proceed, we make impressions at the initial visit. An assistant pours the models with slurry water before the patient gets out of the chair, we construct base plates and bite rims, have the patient back in an hour for the vertical dimension, take a bite and have their models in the mail for set-up the same day. Being flexible enough to be able to provide this service. This is what the patient appreciates!

We will explore flexibility in depth in Chapter 6 but first let's review our next Chapter where we will take a serious look at efficiency and how it affects your dental practice.

CHAPTER 4

EFFICIENCY

Efficiency -- your Key to Success.

DENTISTRY has historically been lucrative enough that dentists could survive or even prosper moderately without being very efficient. Therefore, they did just that!! And it is often still the case.

An efficiency or time-motion expert from industry would likely walk out shaking his head in disbelief if he were to observe most dental offices for a day.

To become efficient is to radically increase production (we assume an unlimited supply of patients; see Chapter 21 on Marketing). If the patients are not there yet, use this time to improve efficiency so you can handle the flow when it arrives.

Efficiency means to complete the procedure (restoration) (extraction) (root canal treatment) quickly, correctly and precisely. It should be pleasant for the patient, the staff and the dentist in a stress-free environment with the optimal end product.

This is not to be confused with speed alone which implies doing it fast at the expense of the end product, or at the expense of patient comfort or at the expense of the staff.

Becoming efficient means working smarter rather than harder. It means the dentist does only what the dentist *must do* because no one else is allowed to do it.

IT MEANS:

> • **Being organized!**
>
> • **All staff members are well trained!**
>
> • **All staff members work together as a team!**

IT MEANS:

> • **All procedures are standardized!**
>
> • **All tray set-ups are standardized!**
>
> • **Procedures flow smoothly!**
>
> • **Stress is reduced by working efficiently!**

You say, "It sounds great--but how do I do it?"

You start by getting everything standardized.

STANDARDIZATION IS:

> • **Every operatory is equipped and supplied in exactly the same way right to the most minute**

detail.   Efficiency starts with organization -- for maximum efficiency it is mandatory that all operatories are equipped the same.

All dental equipment is the same.

All delivery systems are the same.

When operatories are equipped identically and supplied identically, any and all possible procedures can be performed in any and all operatories.

- All operatories are totally equipped with ...

    -- 3 high speed fiberoptic handpieces

    -- 1 slow speed handpiece

    -- Condensaire Pneumatic Amalgam Plugger Footnote below*

    -- Sonic scaler

    -- Ultrasonic scaler

    -- X-ray capability

    -- Nitrous oxide/oxygen capability

    -- Ultraviolet light

    -- 2 air/water syringes

    -- 2 high volume evacuators -- when one high volume evacuator plugs the assistant picks up the other and the procedure goes on smoothly.

> **After the patient is dismissed the obstacle is dislodged.**

--   **Saliva ejector**

--   **Amalgamator with high efficiency 2 to 3 second mix time**

--   **Carpule warmer**

--   **Full complement of supplies, medicaments, back-up instruments and cements**

FOOTNOTE:

AMALGAM PLUGGER - Condensaire Pneumatic Plugger (not to be confused with the Ultrasonic Amalgam Packers which received negative publicity.) This is a PLUGGER AND A POINTER. We use one tip only - the 1.1mm Round tip. For overpacking we use the ELBOW of the tip. See Chapter 17 for research report on Condensaire Pneumatic Plugger.)

STANDARDIZATION INCLUDES:

- **All instrument trays signed by the assistant who sets up the tray in the sterilization area for use in the operatory. No more extra matrix bands in the Toffelmeier Retainer or missing instruments.**

- **All bur blocks are the same.**

- **All assistants are trained the same for all procedures.**

While state-of-the-art equipment may appear expensive, it is much more costly to attempt to get by with anything obsolete. Antiques belong in museums not in highly efficient dental offices.

All procedures performed consistently in the same fashion allow the procedures to go like clockwork.

40

This allows the dentist and the staff to chat about the upcoming County Fair or Sam's new puppy while breezing through the procedure.

Efficiency often means six-handed dentistry.

One dental assistant can keep the aspirator in place and/or the cheek retracted while her assistant stays one step ahead of the procedure and does not allow a single pause in the entire procedure. The assistant's assistant mixes and places materials and changes burs, if necessary, and keeps the tray set up neatly arranged and whatever else facilitates the smooth operation. She selects temporary crowns, spins the amalgam, gets the cavity varnish ready, assembles Bard Parker blades, passes suture scissors to the number one assistant, and on and on. The moment a bur is not melting through tooth structure effortlessly the number one assistant requests a new bur in the handpiece as soon as the dentist puts it down. Never, never, never use even slightly dull instruments. The strain on the handpieces is much more costly than the cost of a new bur --- sharp means efficient!

Next, all staff are trained to the most minute detail in preparing the operatory for each procedure. This means specified burs in all 4 handpieces, anticipated procedure confirmed with the patient or preliminary diagnosis if the patient presents in pain and topical anesthetic in place. The instrument tray and medicaments are ready, the rubber dam clamp is in the rubber dam, forceps are in the clamp and the dental assistant is chatting with the patient until the dentist arrives.

By being efficient we are able to produce more dentistry in a given period of time. Also, because many of our overhead costs are fixed much of the added income goes right to the bottom line.

Do all four quadrants when the patient is in agreement and the schedule permits. You might be able to do all four quadrants in two hours, one sitting. An alternative would be to schedule four one-hour appointments. It is 100% more efficient to do all four quadrants in one sitting. Obviously, this is not for all patients, but many people

41

prefer one sitting.

> "I see you came a long distance today!" "I suppose you would like to get as much done today as possible?" "Would you like to get it all completed today if we can or would you rather come back several times?"

<u>The way you structure the question determines to a very large extent the response you get.</u>

The difference in expense incurred between doing two restorations per hour and doing eight restorations per hour is only pennies, but the profit difference changes from barely making a living to a very affluent practice.

And in most cases the patient is most grateful when he spends the least possible amount of time in the dental chair.

We routinely hear remarks like, "Boy, you are really fast." And respond "Thank you. We have been working on that for a long, long time and are pleased you appreciate it!"

This efficiency does not happen all of a sudden; it is gradually attained over the years by constantly looking for more efficient ways of doing procedures.

Even though efficiency is difficult to teach in written form, here are some clues which may help:

MOUTH MIRROR - pick up the mouth mirror at the beginning of the procedure and do not lay it down until the patient is dismissed. Learn to operate with the mouth mirror handle tucked in the palm of your non-dominant hand. **NEVER** lay it down!

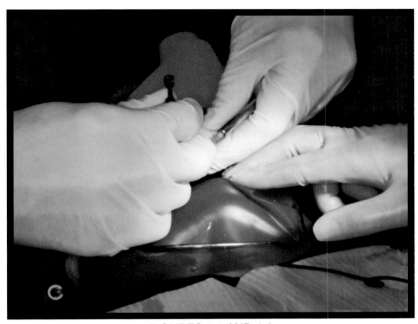

FIGURES 4-1 AND 4-2
Learning to work with the mouth mirror tucked in the non-dominant
hand will eliminate the need to ever waste time or motion
looking for it again.

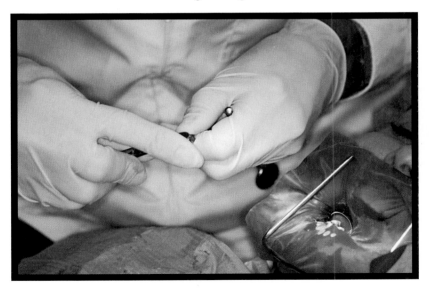

EFFICIENCY IS:

•   **Minimizing the number of hand transfers (passing of instruments) by:**

     --   **Utilizing each instrument to the maximum prior to giving it back. FOR EXAMPLE: if you have just packed four amalgams, let's say, 2-mo, 3-do, 4-o, and 5-o, when the dental assistant passes you the carver, carve all four restorations prior to giving up the carver.**

     --   **Having the dental assistant place the amalgam where you point. She has hold of the amalgam carrier and you have hold of the amalgam condenser....Keep it that way!**

     --   **Dental assistant placing articulating paper. You have the carver in your hand. The dental assistant places the articulating paper. Have the patient close, open, carve, paper in, close, open, carve, paper in, close, grind, open, carve, paper in, close, grind, open, completed ....! ALL WITH NO PASSING OF INSTRUMENTS -- THAT'S EFFICIENCY!**

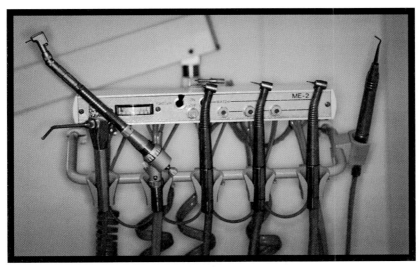

FIGURE 4-3
Condensaire Pneumatic Amalgam Plugger
mounted on end of handpiece arm so tubing does
not tangle with four handpiece tubings

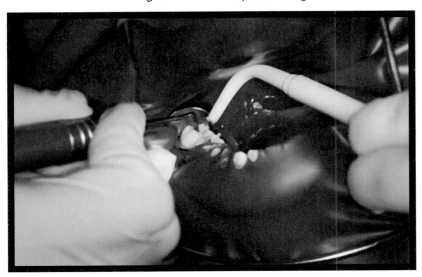

FIGURE 4-4
Dental Assistant placing amalgam in the preparation

"REPETITION IS THE MOTHER OF SKILL!"

EFFICIENCY - is having the STAFF do all it can to support the dentist. The dentist does only what the dentist *must* do.

EFFICIENCY - is having everything required for the routine procedure out and ready and everything for the exceptional procedure within reach.

EFFICIENCY - is having backup instruments at your fingertips.

EFFICIENCY - is having the dental assistants trained to do everything that they can legally do in your location that does not require the dentist..

EFFICIENCY - is keeping paperwork to a minimum.

EFFICIENCY - is *always* working with sharp instruments.

EFFICIENCY - is going into a procedure briskly with positive expectations.

EFFICIENCY - is visualizing the desired result prior to starting the procedure.

EFFICIENCY - is operating with no wasted motions.

EFFICIENCY -   is minimizing the number of instrument transfers required to complete a procedure.

EFFICIENCY -   is encouraging maximum dental assistant participation.

The primary purpose of maximum dental assistant participation is to allow all procedures to go more quickly and smoothly to get through the procedure as proficiently as possible while attaining the best possible result. The secondary purpose is to have a participating dental assistant who is alert and involved because she realizes she is an important member of the dental team.

EFFICIENCY -   is having additional dental assistants trained to get the next patient into the operatory, confirm the anticipated procedure with the patient, verify that everything is ready, get the patient's chair positioned, get topical anesthetic in place and chat with the patient until the dentist arrives (this is a great time buffer for the dentist).

EFFICIENCY -   is having a trained dental assistant clean up the patient, give post treatment instructions, (i.e., no smoking for 24-hours, don't chew anything hard the rest of the day, stay away from drinking anything extremely hot until the anesthetic effect is gone); answer any questions that your assistant is qualified to answer, and escort the patient to the front desk for scheduling the next appointment.

EFFICIENCY - is having two off-angle hatchets (The American Dental 15-8-14, 10-10) for planing all distal proximal walls and distal gingival seats, and the counterpart (The American Dental 15-8-14, 10-11) for all mesial proximal walls and mesial gingival seats.

These two instruments replace a whole drawer of hoes, hatchets and chisels formerly required for the same purpose.

EFFICIENCY - is having the distal off-angle hatchet marked with a band so either the distal or mesial hatchet (unbanded) can be identified at a glance.

EFFICIENCY - is having an open operatory concept (See Chapter 28) so the dentist is able to keep informed of the progress and/or challenges the assistants and hygienists are experiencing in the other operatories where they are:

-- making impressions

-- taking x-rays

-- pre-diagnosing pain symptoms

-- questioning patient about motivation to save the troublesome tooth in order to make an educated guess as to how to set up the operatory.

       -- set up for a root canal treatment when the tooth can be saved and the patient wants to save the tooth.

--   set up for an extraction
when the tooth is beyond
saving or if the patient
insists the tooth be removed.

Even though the dentist always has the option of changing directions, the experienced assistant can calculate correctly 90% to 95% of the time. When in a gray area the assistant can have both trays available with the operatory set up for the procedure she thinks is most likely, while still being flexible to switch, if necessary.

Assistants often are able to learn much about the patient during pre-treatment chats while waiting for the dentist to arrive. When interesting information is obtained, it is recorded by the assistant in the upper right margin of the back of the patient chart.

This may be about --

--   Her twin daughters

--   His winters in Arizona

--   Her new puppy

--   His business ventures

or any other topic the patient is interested in.

This kind of information is very valuable when the dentist arrives to chat with the patient prior to treatment.

EFFICIENCY – is preparing the denture patient prior to the dentist's arrival:

While working on one patient, a dentist can instruct an assistant in the adjacent operatory to dry out the denture, coat it with pressure indicator paste, and have the patient bite on articulating paper. By having the assistants doing this, the dentist's time with the patient may be reduced by as much as 80%, yet your patient will feel well cared for.

When the dentist arrives he can check the occlusion as well as any marks inside the denture from the pressure indicator paste and make adjustments efficiently. Following the adjustment the assistant cleans the pressure indicator paste from the full denture, cleans the patient's face, if necessary, and escorts the patient to the front desk.

EFFICIENCY – is having auxiliary personnel do all for which a dentist is not required and which they are allowed to do in your location. For example, a receptionist can present an estimate of the dental work needed and make financial arrangements with the patient just as well and oftentimes better than the dentist.

EFFICIENCY – is having assistants trained to stop in and chat with the patient when the dentist gets delayed...his two minute extraction that takes 20 minutes instead of 2 minutes...while patient A is getting numb (sound familiar)?

EFFICIENCY – is not having to wait for ANYTHING...by the time the preparation is completed the

Cavity varnish, matrix band, wedge and restorative material are there...just like clockwork!

EFFICIENCY - is amalgamators that titurate in two (2) seconds instead of the classic twenty (20) seconds.

EFFICIENCY - is keeping the number of instruments on the set-up trays to a minimum for the desired result. THE FEWER INSTRUMENTS THE MORE EFFICIENT.

EFFICIENCY - is keeping the number of burs on the bur block to a minimum. The fewer burs the more efficient.

EFFICIENCY - is having designated dental auxiliary personnel call in prescriptions as opposed to using the dentist's time writing prescriptions.

EFFICIENCY - is having the dental assistant place the amalgam from the amalgam carrier (where the dentist points with the tip of the Condensaire Pneumatic Amalgam Plugger). No more hand transfers. Plugger to carrier, to plugger, to carrier, and so on, saves dozens of transfers per quadrant. Efficiency is having the assistant handle the articulating paper while the dentist has a grasp on the carver. She never puts the articulating paper down until the dentist is satisfied with the occlusion, saving many more hand transfers.

EFFICIENCY - is having auxiliaries do all that is legal to do in your location. If they don't do it well enough at first, train them. Remember - "Repetition is the Mother of Skill!"

EFFICIENCY - is having the dental assistant blow a stream of air in one side of the cavity preparation with the aspirator on the other side during caries removal with the slow speed round bur. She keeps the preparation clean and all you have to do is remove the caries.

EFFICIENCY - is six-handed dentistry.

EFFICIENCY - is doing complete quadrant dentistry while the patient is anesthetized - we rarely do less than a quadrant at a time. Just ask the patient "Would you like to complete all the work in the upper right while you are numb up there?" Often we will offer to save them several trips back and finish up all four quadrants that day if they would like. The question to ask is "You have seven restorations that need to be completed. Would you prefer to get all your restorations completed today, if possible, or would you rather come back several times?" The response is overwhelmingly in favor of finishing today...you must be efficient to commit to something like this in a busy schedule scenario!

EFFICIENCY - is having your dental assistant remove the wedge(s).

EFFICIENCY - is planning ahead...let's say your patient presents with the lingual cusp of #20 fractured. You observe #21 has a hugh mod amalgam.

Suggest crowning both teeth while she is numb.

Rather than doing one crown now and having the patient return with the adjacent tooth fractured two months later (a road we all know too well), offer to do them both that day. Explain carefully what could happen to number 21 and get the patient's response and feelings on doing them both at one time. This approach will very likely save the patient not only additional trips to the dentist but also is the best way to repair a mouth in this condition. This, of course, must be coordinated with their insurance and financial situation. Your front office will be happy to check that part out and make those arrangements for you.

Thanks front office!

Since you are now becoming more efficient you are capable of preparing the two teeth in approximately the same time it used to take for a single crown preparation.

This is exciting!

As well, you will be saving your patient from having to be numb twice and having to hold open for an extended period of time twice. You are also possibly saving her from a fracture involving the root which could not be salvaged.

GOOD DENTISTRY MAKES GOOD SENSE!

Now that we have LEARNED some of the principles of efficiency let's move on to Chapter 5 which deals with Efficiency in Action!

CHAPTER 5

EFFICIENCY IN ACTION

Put what you have learned into action -- knowledge without action is of little value.

MAXIMIZING THE DENTIST'S UTILIZATION:

<u>EFFICIENCY OF THE DENTAL TEAM</u>

By keeping the entire staff flexible in trying to best utilize the dentist's available time, much more can be accomplished in a given time period. Assume, for instance, that the dentist has cemented a crown or bridge more quickly than average. The dental assistant routinely takes over, waiting for the cement to begin to gel to clean off the excess cement. The dentist is then free to move on to the next patient. If the hygienist and her dental assistant have just seated two patients - B & C, the dentist may choose to examine patient B while

55

the bitewing x-rays are being taken on patient C even though we usually have the teeth clean and x-rays developed prior to the dentist's examination.

A dental assistant records the dentist's clinical diagnosis on Patient B, i.e., 3-ol, 10-m, 14-ol, 19-f and so on. The dentist may next move on to examine Patient C who has now had x-rays taken but the x-rays are not yet through the automatic developer.

After examining Patient C the dentist moves on to anesthetize Patient D for an extraction and the hygienist and her dental assistant proceed with the prophylaxis, x-rays, and fluoride treatments, if indicated.

During the time after the films from patients B and C are out of the developer, mounted and returned to the patient's operatory, the dentist may return and view the patient's films and finalize the diagnosis by adding 4-mo, 13-do and 30-mo for the dental assistant to integrate into her clinical diagnosis list. The dental assistant then records the findings on the chart in numerical sequence (1-------->32).

If, when the hygienist and her assistant are finished with patients B and C, the dentist has not yet returned, the hygiene assistant takes the films and clinical diagnosis notes to an area where the dentist can view them.

The dentist reviews the films and the hygiene assistant supplements the clinical diagnosis with the radiographic findings. Patients B and C may then be escorted to the front desk for rescheduling or set up for restorations at this appointment if the dentist's schedule permits and the patients so desire...about 80% of the patients, when approached properly, would like to "finish today and not have to come back for 6 months, if possible." This is valuable information which can increase production exponentially, as well as creating very happy patients who tell their friends about their experience of having all of their dental work completed in one visit.

THE STAFF CAN:

1. Welcome the patient - the reception-ist greets the patient first. The dental assistant brings the patient into the operatory and chats with the patient until the dentist arrives.

2. A dental assistant can anticipate the emergency patient's needed treat-ment so she can make an educated guess on how to set up the operato-ry. Only the dentist can diagnose, of course, but a highly trained dental assistant can usually make a pretty good estimate for purposes of set-ting up the operatory.

3. Call in the dentist's prescriptions, with the dentist's supervision, sav-ing the dentist time (this will depend, of course, on whether or not your auxiliaries are able to perform this function in your location). We tend to avoid written prescriptions because they can be duplicated and a whole gamut of other abuses are possible. An additional benefit is that call-in prescriptions are not a burden on the dentist's time.

4. Monitor the patient after nitrous oxide/oxygen analgesia, rinse the patient's mouth, clean the patient's face, and escort the patient to the front desk for the next appointment. Don't forget the balloon for being such a good patient!

5.   Pour the models from impressions and make bite rims for dentures.

6.   Listen to patient's concerns and interpret them to the dentist. Often patients are more comfortable explaining their symptoms to dental assistants, and assistants can at times condense five or ten minutes of explanation into five or ten seconds. The dentist then just confirms his understanding of the symptoms with the patient.

7.   Help the patient select the shade for their prosthetic teeth. *We invite our patients to make the shade selection with the dental assistant's help.* If it is good the dental assistants compliment the patient. If it is not so good the dental assistants suggest considering other possibilities until they agree on one they both like. When the dentist arrives the dental assistant shows the dentist the shade "Mary" picked out. Since everyone's eyes interpret colors and shades slightly differently and since the patient is the one we are striving to please, it makes sense to arrive at a shade which is comfortable with their interpretation of a match.

8.   Make alginate impressions for opposing models.

9.   Fit and place temporary crowns with the supervision of the dentist.

10.   Prepare and package laboratory cases for mailing to the dental laboratory.

EFFICIENCY IN CHARTING:

Our current record keeping system evolved through many less efficient stages.

While we don't claim ours to be the most efficient it is much improved over its predecessors.

Here's how it works --

At the time of the initial examination, the exam and the date are recorded on the chart. The treatment that needs to be completed is listed under the column heading DIAGNOSIS.

Those services performed today are so designated with the date and an arrow descending from today's date in the column headed DATE. On subsequent visits the assistant simply fills in the date on which the remaining procedures were completed. The dentist fills in any notes he desires in the "COMMENTS" section on the same horizontal line as the recorded treatment. See Sample:

"SPARKLE"

SCHNAUZER

NAME: _____JILL HILL_____ **D.O.B.** _7-19-80_

DIAGNOSIS	DATE COMPLETED	COMMENTS
EX 4 BW	9-30-94	Pt to start flossing
PANO, P+FL	⬇	
3-ol		
5-o		
14-ol		
19-PFS		
30-PFS		

WINTERS IN
BROWNSVILLE, TX

NAME: _CANDY COATES_ **D.O.B.** _7-04-54_

DIAGNOSIS	DATE COMPLETED	COMMENTS
EX 4BW	9-07-94	PT flosses daily
PANO		
2 PA's	◁▷	
4 PFM		
13 PFM		

Also, at this time all work to be completed on this patient (the diagnosis) is listed and recorded in numerical sequence beginning with tooth #1 and concluding with tooth #32.

In the mixed dentition stage as well as all stages the sequence starts with the upper right posterior progressing around the arch to the upper left posterior thence the lower left around the arch to the lower right: numerically 1 through 32.

Therefore we may have 3-ol, A-mo, C-f, J-mo, 14-ol, 19-o, 30-f...in the mixed dentition.

Or we may have 3-ol, 3-f, 4-RCT 1-1, 4-RCT 1-2, 4-RCT 1-3, 4-bu-up, 4-PFM, 4 cement PFM, 8-m-14-ol, 19-o, 30-f.

The chart is filled in under the diagnosis column at the time of the examination.   The examination date is filled in and an arrow descends to the extent of the day's services. See next sample charts.

Ballet / Dance
Piano Lessons

NAME: _____SARA SACHS_____ **D.O.B.**___7-4-86___

DIAGNOSIS	DATE COMPLETED	COMMENTS
CX 4BW	9-07-94	Brushes well
PANO	↓>	
3-ol		
A-mo		
C-f		
J-mo		
14-ol		
19-0		
30-f		

"BUZZ"

NAME ROCKY POND   **D.O.B.** 6-05-41

DIAGNOSIS	DATE COMPLETED	COMMENTS
EX 4 BW	9-30-94	PT desires to keep
PANO		teeth as long as poss.
P	⟨|⟩	
4-MO		
7-M		
9-d		
10-m		
14-f		
31-o		
P/		Replacing 2,5,8, 12
/P		Replacing 19,20,21,29,30

Raises Sled Dogs

NAME: Minnie (Marlene) Houser   **D.O.B.** 1-14-69

DIAGNOSIS	DATE COMPLETED	COMMENTS
EX 4 BW	9-30-94	Pt home care is excellent
PANO, P	‹›	

"FLIP" - *CHAMPAGNE*
COCKER

NAME: JOHN TOLATE **D.O.B.** 1-14-69

DIAGNOSIS	DATE COMPLETED	COMMENTS
EX 4BW	9-30-94	PT wants F/ - Dr. agrees
PANO	))	
2-TR		
5-TR		
7-TR		
8-TR		
9-TR		
10-TR		
11-TR		
13-TR		
14-TR		
F/		
19-o		
21-o		
28-do		
30-f		
PROPHY		

When the patient returns for further treatment, the treatment date is noted and an arrow descends to the extent that it is completed. No rewriting, no charting. (No coloring book.) If you did an MO on #4 you write 4-mo - no colored pencils, no pictures.

You write it once at the time of the examination (your assistant does this as you dictate), and you fill in the date when the procedures are completed (your assistant also does this).

The right half of the page is for comments pertaining to the day's procedures.

If you have a better idea, go for it! If not, give this a try until a better idea presents.

CODING (ABBREVIATIONS)
AND THEIR
INTERPRETATION

We use certain coding and/or abbreviations. A copy is on our front desk at all times. This allows us to function and communicate more efficiently (from the operatory to the front desk) on our patient charts.

Some of these coding/abbreviations are as follows:

(There are only six surfaces which our computer recognizes - one letter per surface - for EASY communication and billing):

ABBREVIATION		INTERPRETATION
m	-	Mesial
d	-	Distal (small "d" does not get confused with an o)
o	-	Occlusal
L	-	Lingual (large "L" does not get confused with an "I" for incisal or a #1)
f	-	Facial
I	-	Incisal

ONE LETTER PER SURFACE - Easy for the front office to understand -

Additional Abbreviations:

EX	-	Examination
EMEX	-	Emergency Examination
P	-	Prophylaxis
FL	-	Fluoride Treatment
BSS	-	Black Silk Suture
PFS	-	Pit and Fissure Sealant
CMC	-	Cast Metal Crown
PFM	-	Porcelain Fused to Metal Crown
SSC	-	Stainless Steel Crown
PULP	-	Pulpotomy
RCT	-	Root Canal Treatment
TR	-	Tooth Removal
RL	-	Reamer Length
DL	-	Diagnostic Length (Capital "D")
_		A dash at the bottom of the line represents a pontic 6_8. _ means #7 is a pontic.
•		One dot means a restoration was deep.

••   Two dots means a restoration was
                          deep, and a base was placed.

•••   Three dots means a restoration
                          was deep, a base was placed and
                          there was a pulpal exposure.

ROOT CANAL ABBREVIATIONS
FOR TRADITIONAL
3-STEP APPOINTMENT PROCEDURE

The first number represents the number of canals in the tooth being treated.

The second number represents the number of the appointment on this tooth.

RCT 1-1	-	Root Canal Treatment - 1 canal, 1st appointment
RCT 1-2	-	Root Canal Treatment - 1 canal, 2nd appointment
RCT 1-3	-	Root Canal Treatment - 1 canal - 3rd Appointment (Obturate)
RCT 3-1	-	Root Canal Treatment - 3 canals - 1st Appointment
RCT 3-2	-	Root Canal Treatment - 3 canals - 2nd Appointment
RCT 3-3	-	Root Canal Treatment - 3

**canals - 3rd Appointment
(Obturate)**

TOOTH #	CANALS	APPOINTMENT
14	3	1

From the above abbreviations the front office knows to bill the patient for a 3-canal root canal treatment and to set the patient up for an appointment in 5 to 7 days.

During this first appointment we may record the reamer lengths under RL as we remove reamers after taking the x-ray with the reamers in place.

	RL
m	18
d	20
L	21

Once the developed film is returned we may add the diagnostic lengths:

	RL	DL
m	18	20
d	20	20
L	21	21

When the reamer lengths are close enough (within 2-3mm) to the desired diagnostic lengths we establish our diagnostic lengths, circle them on the chart, and use these circled lengths for our desired obturation lengths.

Then our chart looks like:

		RL	DL
Tooth # 14	m	18	(20)
	d	20	(20)
	L	21	(21)

For the next appointment your dental assistant will have your reamer stops set at 21mm, the longest circled length.

Efficiency in root canal treatment is increasing rapidly. A larger percentage of dentists are obturating on the second appointment, increasing the efficiency by eliminating an appointment.

Electronic apex locators as well as warm gutta percha techniques are growing in popularity.

Further, a current wave of practitioners are reporting success with single appointment root canal treatments. This will indeed be a boon to the efficiency technique if it proves to be an accepted and reliable treatment.

We are taking a guardedly optimistic position onto these changes at the time of this writing.

THIS IS THE WAY IT READS ON OUR CHARTS WITH THE ABBREVIATIONS IN USE:

EX	-	**Examination**
P	-	**Prophylaxis**
11-dL	-	**A 2-surface restoration was placed on tooth #11.**
13-o.	-	**A 1-surface restoration was placed on tooth #13. The restoration was deep.**
12-do..	-	**A 2-surface restoration was placed on tooth #12. The restoration was deep and a medicated base was placed.**
19 mod...	-	**A 3-surface restoration was placed on tooth #19, the restoration was deep with pulpal exposure and a base was placed.**
30-mo...	-	**A 2-surface restoration was placed on tooth #30, the restoration was deep to the extent of a pulpal exposure - a medicated base was placed.**
A-SSC	-	**A stainless steel crown was placed on Tooth A**

32-TR	-	**32 was extracted**
4-mod	-	**A 3-surface restoration was placed on tooth #4**
5-do	-	**A 2-surface restoration was placed on tooth #5**
13-o.	-	**A 1-surface restoration was placed on tooth #13. The restoration was deep.**
12-do..	-	**A 2-surface restoration was placed on tooth #12. This was deep and a medicated base was placed.**
8-RCT 1-3	-	**One canal root canal treatment was finished on tooth #8. The 3 means the tooth was obturated.**
6 _ _ 9 PFM	-	**Four unit porcelain fused to metal bridge. 6 and 9 are the abutments, 7 and 8 are the pontics.**
8 PFM	-	**A porcelain fused to metal crown was placed on tooth #8**
31 CMC	-	**A cast metal crown was placed on tooth #31**
A-PULP	-	**A pulpotomy was performed on tooth A**

A-SSC - **A stainless steel crown was placed on tooth #A**

YOUR DENTAL ASSISTANTS' PARTICIPATION IN EFFICIENCY

<u>PLEASE BE FULLY AWARE OF YOUR LOCAL REGULATIONS ON DENTAL ASSISTANTS! WE WILL PRESENT VARIOUS IDEAS WHICH MAY OR MAY NOT BE APPLICABLE IN YOUR LOCATION!</u>

Dental assistants are wonderful! We could not produce big numbers without them. Some of us could not produce any numbers without them.

We must keep constantly aware of their position ... boredom is often their biggest challenge. Our best strategy for combatting their boredom may be to include them as important members of the dental team (which they are) in our daily conversation.

- We can say, "Boy we sure did have a struggle with that lower third molar yesterday, didn't we?" rather than saying "That lower third molar nearly wore me out yesterday."

- We can say, "We really whistled through those 4 quadrants of operative on Amber. We're really quite a team, aren't we!"

- We can say, "We sure can get a lot more done when you have everything so organized! We did a crown preparation on Jack and Jill in adja-

cent operatories all in about 40 minutes with you getting x-rays, taking
opposing models, holding the
impression trays, helping the patient
choose a shade and getting tempo-
raries fit. About all I had to do was
anesthetize, cut the preparations,
pack the retention cord and place the
impressions."

The more the dental assistant participates and feels valuable the less
likely she is to be bored.

Our assistants -- during preparation procedures -- have the aspirator
in one hand and the air/water syringe in the other. Even though a little unorthodox, the air/water syringe is often used also to retract the
lip, cheek or tongue when we are using the high speed turbine.

When removing caries with the slow speed the dental assistant blows
air into the preparation while aspirating and keeps a constant clear
and clean field. This saves countless moves from our previous routine of hanging up the handpiece and picking up the air/water syringe,
cleaning the preparation only to see we were not through with caries
removal yet, picking up the handpiece and on and on ad infinitum.
Love that learning curve!

Our assistants routinely remove wedges while the dentist is busy
carving proximal amalgam restorations.

The fewer the number of hand transfers (passing of instruments) the
more efficient. The more the assistant participates, the less bored she
becomes.

Therefore, rather than passing articulating paper, using it and passing
it back 3 or more times, the assistant places the articulating paper on
the occlusal surfaces. We have the patient tap or grind her teeth
together and the assistant pulls the paper out. The dentist becomes
the spectator. Especially on a shiny gold crown the dentist will often

ask the dental assistant what she sees because these articulating paper spots can be very difficult to see and her angle of vision may have less glare. Besides, four eyes are better than two -- and she gets to participate and feels more valuable and more involved, and we get finished with the procedure more efficiently and more effectively.

MULTIPLE ASSISTANTS
FURTHER INCREASE EFFICIENCY

Let's take a peek at a particular Monday afternoon scenario. We see the dentist preparing tooth number 3 for a build-up as a second dental assistant is mixing Miracle Mix® while the chairside dental assistant is aspirating and blowing air into the preparation, a third dental assistant is bringing another patient into an adjacent operatory and going through her health history and other questions she has heard the dentist ask many times -- "Has this tooth been hurting you long? Keeping you up nights? Sensitive to hot? Cold? Sweets? Pressure? Does it start aching without stimulation?" She can give the patient a Q-tip to bite on to tell which tooth hurts.

She further questions the patient, "Would you like to save this tooth, if possible?"

This assistant takes an x-ray, has it developed and takes it to the dentist for a quick review. If it looks like a root canal treatment and crown, she can then set up for the root canal treatment and be ready when the dentist is available. In our state she can even have the topical anesthetic in place.

Do you think these dental assistants are getting bored? No way! They say they can't believe "how times flies...!

The more a good dental assistant gets to think and do the happier she is.

Our assistants stay with the patient until the dentist arrives. The same assistant also stays with the patient when the dentist is finished, monitors how well they are feeling if they have had nitrous oxide/oxygen analgesia, cleans their face, gives them instructions, and escorts the patient to the front desk for their next appointment.

Also in our office the dental assistants place the amalgam with an amalgam carrier, which is allowed in our location. The dentist points to the desired location for amalgam placement with the Condensaire Pneumatic Amalgam Plugger tip, the assistant places the amalgam and refills the carrier while the dentist is packing. The dental assistant then places the restorative material from the full carrier to the next desired location. This system saves many hand transfers per restoration from the previous conventional method of the dentist placing the amalgam and also gives the assistant a feeling of greater participation.

(See Figure 4-4, Chapter 4, Page 45.)

Another aid to efficiency is having the rubber dam punched, available and ready, the dental assistant can have the rubber dam clamp in the dam and the rubber dam forceps in the clamp so that after anesthetizing it is just one smooth move to have the rubber dam on and we are ready to go!

Again, the more the dental assistant is allowed to participate, the more involved she becomes, and the more pride she takes in the end result. The more pride the assistant takes the more potential we have for serving more patients.

For maintaining a strong positive rapport with the patients, it is essential to escort the patient into the operatory at her scheduled appointment time. If we are running a little late, the patient must be informed at her scheduled appointment time that a delay has occurred along with the anticipated amount of delay. When one recognizes that each patient may have gone through a series of heroic challenges in order to be at her appointment on time, the dentist also should be prompt.

Therefore, the policy of taking the patient into the operatory at her scheduled appointment time -- let's say 2:30 -- is imperative. This means 2:30 - not 2:31 or 2:40 because each minute may be an incredible stress creator to the anxious patient who has made every effort to get to the dental office on time. Once the patient is in the operatory, the dental assistants are instructed to step in and engage the patient in conversation until the dentist can get to them or to offer them a headset to listen to their favorite radio station while they wait.

If all else fails the dental assistants are then instructed to go to the F-O-R-M system and ask about:

FAMILY   -   (this is as far as they usually get)

How many brothers and sisters, or

How many children, or

How many grandchildren?

OCCUPATION -   What type of work do you do?

RECREATION -   What do you enjoy for recreation?

MOTIVATION -   What motivates you? -- (They never seem to get this far.)

Any patient's interests are noted on the top right hand corner of the back of the patient's chart -- for example, nickname "Buzz", "raises sled dogs", "winters in Texas", "likes golfing, sailing, etc."

When the dentist arrives the conversation can begin with anything other than teeth -- like "I hear you winter over in Brownsville" or "How old is that cock-a-poo?" The dentist glances at the patient's chart for clues; neighboring town, Emily, Outing, Palisade, or years at present address - 56; or "referred by Buck Reem," for example.

This helps put the patient at ease and tends to guard against the rushed feeling which patients can experience when the dentist is running behind.

FURTHER MAXIMIZING
THE DENTAL ASSISTANTS' PARTICIPATION

Have you noticed that the busier you are the more you feel that you have accomplished, the faster the time appears to pass, and the more content you tend to become with your staff and your role in life. The same is true for your dental assistants. Keep them very busy!

This is a two-edged sword:

1.   Generally, a dental assistant's chief complaint is boredom. The more the assistant participates the less bored she becomes. Maximum participation = minimum boredom.

2.   The more the assistant participates the greater the efficiency of the dentist.

   Illustrations of how this is achieved:

   A.   Amalgam placement:

           How many transfers can be avoided per restoration by letting the dental assistant place the amalgam?

ANSWER: approximately 12.

   B.   Articulating Paper:

           It is a simple task - one week maximum - to train a dental assistant to

80

position the articulating paper for an occlusion check. All she really has to know is that the mandible moves and the maxilla is fixed.

C. Removal of Wedges:
The assistant removes the wedges while you carve the amalgam.

D. Topical Anesthetic Application:
Five minutes prior to injection, when possible, for maximum benefit.

E. Blow a constant stream of air into the preparation with one hand while aspirating with the other while the dentist is removing caries with the slow speed round bur or excavator.

F. Getting to know the patient better until the dentist arrives creates a time buffer for the dentist.

Obviously, from a monetary standpoint, your time is much more valuable than an assistant's. Keep extra assistants on board. Train them to do whatever will make the dental machine function more smoothly.

Have assistants do post-operative instructions, answer patients' questions and escort patients to the front desk when treatment has been completed.

Every new patient (unless contraindicated) receives four bite wing x-rays, a panoramic film, and periapical x-rays of any teeth which are bothering. These are completed prior to the dentist's arrival in the operatory.

Dental assistants in our office are trained to talk with the patient until the dentist arrives -- then let the dentist take over and establish rapport.

The first dental assistant is trained by the dentist. All assistants after the first are trained by an assistant who knows the procedures.

Watch for a teacher-type dental assistant with a lot of patience. Have her train the new recruits. The new dental assistants learn by doing. Have them set up an operatory for a procedure then have the teacher dental assistant check it prior to the dentist's arriving in the operatory. This doing, checking, doing, checking may go on for several weeks until the checking by the experienced dental assistant is no longer necessary.

The same system works with the tray set-ups. The new assistant is allowed to set up trays right away, and is required to sign them (every tray set up is signed by the dental assistant who set it up). However, the set-up tray does not go into the cabinet until it has been checked by the teacher assistant or another veteran. When they are placed in the operatory they are all identical to the most minute detail.

The new dental assistant is further trained in the six-handed position where the veteran assistant talks her through the procedures. Only after a period of this observation/participation is she ready to assist chairside. When the new assistant is ready, we again do six-handed with a veteran supporting her by having everything ready a step ahead and just talking her through the procedure. This is when the new recruit really learns....by doing!!

PRETEND YOU ARE A TIME/MOTION ANALYST

Let's pretend that you are a time/motion specialist brought in to analyze the dental team (you and your assistants) and how they work. You observe every move the dental team makes. You assign as many of the dentist's moves to the dental assistant as the assistant can legally perform.

Some of your assignments to her might include:

- Adjusting the light when the patient moves.

- Air/Water syringe for keeping the preparation clean and dry during excavation.

- Articulation paper insertion.

- Any additional tasks that work for you.

Eventually you would get the assistant so busy that she needs an assistant ...wonderful...congratulations---you have now progressed to the six-handed approach and your efficiency goes up substantially.

Down the road you may look back and shudder to think of your previous technique when, during a restoration procedure, the number of instrument transfers probably approached triple figures. Now you have them down to a small fraction of what they once were.

The dental assistants now feel they are participating much more. They may even feel that you could not function without them. They are more content and generally feel much better about themselves.

Any procedure the dentist does not legally need to do can probably be delegated.

Play this game often. You may even choose to pretend you are in a space capsule up near the ceiling where you can observe this dental team and coach them to high efficiency.

DENTAL AUXILIARY UTILIZATION AS IT RELATES TO DENTAL HYGIENE:

There are many dental hygienists across the nation routinely taking x-rays and polishing teeth. Routinely, dental assistants are qualified and competent and can certainly do a satisfactory and even an excellent job of taking x-rays and polishing teeth while being much more cost effective. If you are to reach maximum efficiency in your dental office you will want to take a look at "Double Hygiene" which means the dental hygienist/dental assistant team. With the team concept they treat two patients simultaneously. The hygienist performs those duties only the dental hygienist is legally able to do. The dental assistant does all the rest. For instance, the hygienist does the scaling and measuring of pocket depths. The dental assistant does the x-rays, the flossing, the polishing, the charting and whatever ASSISTS the hygienist to high efficiency. This dental assistant is responsible to the dental hygienist and performs all functions her state legally allows her to perform.

In a recent clinical exercise we created a scenario where a hygienist and her dental assistant accomplished more production per month than many dentists are currently producing.

Dental auxiliary utilization applies to hygiene as much as to dentistry.

A dental assistant can very much help a hygienist become more productive by --

    --   preparing the operatory and seating patients.

    --   charting pocket depths as the hygienist calls
              them out.

    --   aspirating and retracting during ultrasonic scaling.

--   placing sealants - the hygiene assistant gets another dental assistant to help her with this procedure.

--   taking and developing x-rays.

--   giving oral hygiene instructions.

--   polishing patient's teeth.

--   giving fluoride treatments.

--   flossing the patient after polishing.

Whatever the dental assistant is qualified to do in your state the hygienist may choose to delegate to her. Like all teams -- the more efficient they become the more fun they have! The more fun they are having the smoother the dental machine is functioning.

And when the dental machine is functioning smoothly it is a consideration to:

MAXIM

COMPLETE THE PATIENT'S DENTISTRY IN A SINGLE APPOINTMENT, WHEN POSSIBLE

Your flexibility to complete restorations at the time of the examination is paramount. It is extremely efficient when the patient is seated, the operatory is therefore already "contaminated", to do their restorations the same day.

This is true especially when the patient has come a long distance to your dental facility - 40, 50 or even 60 miles. Also, for third party payment patients, where the patient's financial obligation is minimal or non-existent there is little or no financial obstacle to finishing their restorations in one visit. This also applies to a patient who is on a tight schedule, or a patient who travels on business and is not home often. Also, this strategy is advantageous when you have a cancellation on your schedule.

Furthermore, this scenario often works well for those third party payment patients who dislike going to the dentist and who have put off getting their teeth checked for a long time (measured in years). If you ask, after seeing your schedule and their mouth and x-rays, "How would you like to get all your teeth fixed today and not have to come back?", they usually respond positively and gratefully. This patient would almost always prefer to stay today and not have to worry about coming back. This is the best solution for this particular patient as they get their restorations completed. If, instead, you restore the tooth which is bothering her today and reschedule she may not return until another problem arises. A large percentage of this group of patients will fail their follow-up appointments, creating a lose-lose scenario for both patient and dentist.

Explain that you will give them rest periods and bathroom breaks because you will need to attend to other patients, but you will make every effort to complete their work today.

This creates a patient who is happy to be completed in one day (instead of the many appointments she expected because of the condition of her teeth) and you have a very productive day. Another win-win situation.

Now that we have a background in efficiency and efficiency in action we are ready to take a quantum leap into Flexibility!

CHAPTER 6

FLEXIBILITY

Efficiency is to flexibility what the high speed turbine is to the cavity preparation.

As the dental team becomes much more efficient as in Chapters 4 and 5, the potential for increased flexibility grows exponentially. If a crown preparation is now taking 15 or 20 minutes of the doctor's time as opposed to an hour and the other procedures are likewise becoming more efficient, we are seeing incredible possibilities of working more and more patients into the schedule.

EMERGENCIES AND FLEXIBILITY

PATIENTS IN PAIN --

The question often arises - "How can you possibly work half a dozen or more emergency patients into an already packed schedule?"

The answer is through **EFFICIENCY AND FLEXIBILITY**.

This policy of seeing patients who are in pain the same day is so important to the rapid growth of a dental practice that it is imperative we find a way.

Of all your marketing practices, this may be the most powerful!

MAXIM

THE ABILITY TO REMAIN FLEXIBLE
MAY WELL BE YOUR GREATEST ASSET

The auxiliary personnel do most of the work!

A receptionist reviews the patient's insurance or lack of it and discusses how payment will be made.

A dental assistant takes x-rays, often a Panorex, and bite wings as well as periapical films of all painful areas.

She discusses with the patient his motivation for saving his teeth.

A dental assistant may even have the patient bite on a Q-tip to discover which tooth is tender.

At the appropriate time, the assistant places a Q-tip with topical anesthetic on it in the patient's mouth to prepare for an injection of local anesthetic.

When all x-rays are developed and mounted the assistant takes them to the dentist for review.

One quick glance usually will suffice for a tentative estimate as to the diagnosis and the instruction is, "TR" (white tray and forceps) or "root canal treatment" (blue tray and green tray).

A receptionist discusses with the patient the financial aspects of the anticipated procedure.

Now the assistant can begin to set up for the procedure.

The dentist lets his current patient "rest her jaw a minute," disposes of his contaminated gloves, washes up, re-gloves and moves over to confirm the diagnosis and inform the emergency patient of the proposed treatment. The dentist then anesthetizes the patient. The emergency patient's dental assistant stays with her and chats until the doctor is able to return chairside.

The dentist finishes up on the current interrupted patient, then, after washing up and re-gloving, returns to treat the emergency patient.

This emergency patient was told over the phone "we are going to work you in." This allows some flexibility because the scheduled patient gets the bulk of our time and attention. The emergency patient can be getting numb for three or four minutes or thirty minutes, depending upon what else is going on at the moment. Nearly all emergency patients will accept this as they were told that there may be some delay because they were unscheduled emergency patients.

FLEXIBILITY IN ACTION

There are several aspects to flexibility --

When it appears an emergency patient may have to wait some time before we can treat him, we may use Marcaine® -- a long acting local anesthetic. This gets him out of pain and lets him relax until our return.

When starting a root canal treatment, it may be preferable to instrument all canals and obtain working lengths during the first appointment. However, when time is limited you can take a film with the reamers in the canals, record the reamer lengths when you remove the reamers, use a barbed broach to extricate the pulp, rinse, dry, medicate, seal with Cavit® and you have it! You can usually have the patient out of pain in five minutes.

When the film comes out of the processor perhaps you are with another patient and the root canal patient has already left your office. An assistant brings the mounted periapical film to you with the chart. She may have written the following:

		RL	DL
Mesial	m	20	
Distal	d	21	
Lingual	L	19	

You may say add 3mm to lingual, 1mm to mesial and the distal looks fine.

She then records on the chart the diagnostic lengths and circles them.

		RL	DL
Mesial	m	20	(21)
Distal	d	21	(21)
Lingual	L	19	(22)

This can all be done by predistinguished hand signals and body language so that no confidential information on any patient is divulged in front of another patient.

The next time you see this patient all reamer stops have been set at 22mm (the longest circled diagnostic length). For the mesial and distal canals the doctor estimates the 1mm less.

Flexibility also comes into play with the original patient in this scenario. You may opt to do a little less on her than originally intended. Or, on the other hand, things may be going better than anticipated because of your increased efficiency and you may finish her up and still have 5 minutes to spare for our root canal treatment patient.

When this emergency proves to be an extraction with the patient being profoundly anesthetized, the tooth can usually be elevated out in a minimal amount of time.

Some emergency patients present with pain from a severe periodontal condition or an apical abscess. When these teeth are beyond repair and need to be extracted, it can usually be accomplished without complications.

With the periapical abscess there may be considerable bone loss around the root tip and also pressure "going in your direction." With the periodontally involved tooth the bone loss is usually sufficient to facilitate removal.

Once you have observed some movement of the tooth, and if it is not coming loose, let the patient "rest his jaw a few minutes," go to another patient and return in five to thirty minutes. You will often be delighted at how the rest period has allowed the tooth to loosen. **(YOU MUST HAVE MOVEMENT OF THE TOOTH PRIOR TO TAKING THE REST FOR THIS TECHNIQUE TO BE BENEFICIAL.)**

If it is still tough going, inject some Marcaine® if you haven't already done so, elevate some more and give the patient another rest.

Easy does it...what you do not need is to have to raise a flap in the middle of a hectic schedule.

This is the extreme. Most of these extractions roll right out, but the point is, go about your regular schedule and stop back to your emergency patient in between regularly scheduled patients. The emergency patient is usually grateful and understanding that he is being "worked in" and very pleased to get treatment the day of his crisis.

KEEP ALL OPTIONS OPEN:

We often do crown preparations on emergency patients with little or no time allocation in our schedule.

While we anesthetize, a second, or sometimes a third assistant puts the burs in place, brings the crown and bridge tray, cuts the retraction cord, brings the temporary crowns, loads the Astrigident® syringe, prepares impression syringes, gets impression putty out and ready to mix.

By working as a team the crown preparation impression and temporary crown are completed in minimal time.

When the patient presents with a missing restoration or for routine restorative procedures and the possibility exists that we may have extra time in the schedule we usually ask (especially when third party payment is the case) "Would you like us to do as much as possible today?" or "While you're numb on that side would you like us to finish that area if possible or would you prefer to do just one tooth at a time and come back several more times?"

Note that all questions are structured to get "the green light" as one of our assistants calls it. The assistants are trained to hear these cues and gather around when it is a "green light."

Once the go-ahead is attained we proceed full speed ahead - monitoring the patient's comfort periodically with phrases such as "Are we having fun yet?" When we use the nitrous oxide/oxygen analgesia the answer is surprisingly often "Yes."

Depending upon the situation we often anesthetize the upper right and upper left quadrants, do the upper right quadrant and as we remove the rubber dam from the upper right if "the patient is having fun" we will anesthetize the lower left quadrant, do the upper left and if time looks possible, anesthetize the lower right, do lower left then finish up the lower right.

Often a third party payment patient will finally get up the courage to come to the dentist with a particular tooth bothering him and is thrilled to leave with a total examination, a prophylaxis and all restorations completed the same day.

Suppose we started our marathon at 1:00 p.m., and it is approaching the 2:00 p.m. hour. We do not ever slow down. When 2:00 p.m. comes the 2:00 patient is taken into the operatory, an assistant gets the patient comfortable, places topical anesthetic, if indicated, chats with the patient or gets the patient a magazine or headphones if the patient doesn't want to "chat," and this is our cue to wind down. In a few minutes we move over and anesthetize the 2:00 patient and come back to our marathoner until we come to a stopping point...occasionally offering to finish up yet today if she wants to rest her jaw awhile and we'll be back.

We use a lot of rubber gloves in our office but the cost of the rubber gloves is minimal compared to the benefit of having happy patients!

On the other hand, if we see that our 2:00 p.m. patient has not been seated by an assistant (no-show, for instance) we know it is *ALL SYSTEMS GO* on the current patient -- either way we win! We are programmed to stay busy all day long.

This go ahead, "green light" phenomenon can be pursued when any of the following situations exist:

1. Third party is responsible for payment and the patient desires to have dentistry finished the same day, if at all possible.

2. Patient has received an estimate and says something to the effect "It has to be done...the sooner the better." "How many times will I have to come back?" or "How many appointments will it take?"

3. Patient has traveled a long distance and

desires to have the needed dental work completed in as few appointments as possible.

4.   Patient gives any clue as to not liking being in the dental office...and financial obligation is not a problem, and he wants his teeth fixed **as soon as possible!**

5.   Patient just desires to be finished in one visit, if possible.

6.   Patient has a very busy schedule and prefers a minimal number of business days interrupted for dental appointments.

TAKE ADVANTAGE OF OPPORTUNITIES

This section is devoted to the combination of flexibility, efficiency and best utilization of time. **It is essential that you act in the best interest of the patient and the best interest of the patient is your highest priority at all times.**

SITUATION: Mrs. Wilcox presents with good oral hygiene, is a regular recall patient, has good insurance coverage, her chief complaint is that the lingual cusp of number 21 is fractured. A periapical film of the bicuspids 20 and 21 reveal good bone support and no abnormalities. Clinical examination reveals number 20 has a very large MOD amalgam - much larger than 21.

PROPOSAL: It is in the patient's best interest to suggest doing porcelain fused to metal crowns on both bicuspids while she is numb.

This can be done in approximately the same amount of time as one preparation. She only gets numb once. It saves her time and discomfort.

Whenever it is in the patient's best interest, get the patient's approval and finish up the quadrant while she is numb.

SITUATION: Patient is in pain from number 19 decayed into the bone...numbers 17 and 18 are in equally disasterous condition...the patient has third party payment.

PROPOSAL: Explain the situation to the patient, get the patient's approval...remove the remains of all three teeth while the patient is numb.

You are acting in the patient's best interest and it makes good sense to finish the quadrant while the patient is numb.

SITUATION: A 4-year-old child presents crying with a toothache. The dental assistant is fortunate enough to obtain bite wing x-rays -- you get the patient on the "tunes" (with the stereo headset) and nitrous oxide/oxygen analgesia and convince her "we are having fun". You complete the pulpotomy and place a stainless steel crown on tooth "B". The patient also has rampant decay in two other quadrants.

PROPOSAL: Ask your receptionist to report to the parents that their child is doing great, that the offending tooth has been restored. Would they like the dentist to continue and attempt to restore the rest of her teeth before they start bothering her?

This is in the patient's and parent's best interest to complete as much of the child's dentistry and divert further discomfort from decay for the child.

SITUATION: Patient has driven a long distance to his dental appointment or is out of town on business regularly, being home for only a few days. This patient needs a lot of restorative dentistry. The next patient scheduled has just cancelled.

PROPOSAL: Offer to do as much as we have time for today.* By stating it this way we are staying flexible. We have not committed to finish, however, the opportunity exists if time permits.

95

* Our normal procedure is for an assistant to bring the 2:00 patient back at 2:00 p.m. This is our cue to finish up in 5 or 10 minutes. If it is after 2:00 p.m., and no patient is back we begin to question what is happening. This is often when we discover further opportunity to serve the needs of the patient we have seated.

SITUATION: Mom is in for restorations. You finish her restorations on time. Her daughter, Sue, has had an examination and is scheduled for Friday of next week to begin her restorations. Her daughter happens to be with her today. Your next patient has cancelled.

PROPOSAL: You offer to seat Sue, do her restorations and save Mom a trip next Friday. Mom is very happy with your proposal and Sue is glad it's over with. You have a whole week now to fill Sue's appointment for next Friday. A win-win situation!

FLEXIBILITY: A STRATEGY
FOR CATCHING UP WITH THE CLOCK.

Some days when the clock is running faster than the chronology of your procedures, remember flexibility has a flip side also.

We run a very busy schedule. We do a lot of surgery and usually only refer severely medically compromised patients to the oral surgeon. If there is anything that can really disrupt your schedule, it is surgery.

Flexibility can be a way to catch up. Some of the things we do to catch up are:

OPERATIVE: "Oh, I think we are going to take it easy on you today. How does that sound? The usual response is "Great." We do 3-o today and reschedule for 12-do, 13-mo, 19-o, 20-do, next visit. Patients are usual-

96

ly all right with this even though at times you may need to commit to finish them up at their next visit.

ROOT CANAL
TREATMENT: First appointment - open the tooth, take a film with reamer(s) in place; extricate pulp, rinse, dry, and medicate today, and instrument the next time. You may have been able to complete and fill today had time permitted.

ROOT CANAL
TREATMENT: Second appointment - open the tooth, rinse, dry, medicate and reschedule to obturate. Frequently we can fill on the second appointment when time permits.

SURGERY
IN PAIN: Patient needs to have a tooth extracted. Patient is slightly swollen - we would usually extract the tooth. If indicated, we can exercise an option and put the patient on antibiotics due to swelling and reschedule for three to five days later.

BROKEN CUSP: We would usually do a porcelain fused to metal crown - may fill or smooth off sharp edges for today and reschedule next week for the crown preparation.

VIEW CANCELLATIONS
AS AN OPPORTUNITY

Regardless of how heavily you are scheduled, occasionally you are going to have a gap in your schedule.

View this as an opportunity to spend time with your staff. It will be rewarding and the time will pass quickly. This time spent developing more efficient ways to serve patients, may well be the most important time you spend in your office.

By keeping a note pad on your desk where you keep a running list of "ways for the team to become more efficient and flexible" you will have a ready list of topics to go to the board with at any time. A chalk board (or marker board) is a must. We play school often!

By discussing how efficiency might be improved upon in situations which have occurred since your last meeting (which will be reflected on your yellow pad) you can instruct your staff, hear their views and mutually agree on a strategy for more efficient operation.

MAXIM

THINGS WILL NEVER BE PERFECT
AND THAT IS WONDERFUL --
FOR WE CAN ALWAYS SEEK IMPROVEMENT

Although we strive for perfection, rest assured we will never attain perfection.

Our goal is to get as close to perfection as we can, while realizing we must accept our achievements as realistic rather than perfect.

Much useful input is routinely received by seeking the staff's observations and comments on how efficiency might be increased.

The staff's entirely different perspective is often very valuable.

MAXIM

THE BETTER WE LISTEN THE MORE WE LEARN

By working as a team and benefiting from everyone's input we can climb the efficiency curve much more rapidly.

Welcome and encourage all suggestions even if empirical evidence has proven the suggestion may not work. Only by exercising our minds do we come up with great ideas.

Sometimes, on a limited basis, it may be useful to let the staff implement ideas which have previously proven unsuccessful, in order to encourage their input. The more they keep thinking the more likely they will come up with a great idea!

When your list of discussion topics gets thin invite the staff to ask questions concerning procedures which they were unable to ask in the presence of the patient.

This time spent with staff can be invaluable. Having the staff feel the team spirit and recognize that their input is important will make the whole office function much more smoothly.

Now that we are efficient and flexible let's see how this affects the scheduling possibilities as we move on to Chapter 7.

CHAPTER 7

SCHEDULING

"Shoot for the moon. Even if you miss it you will land among the stars."
Les Brown

SCHEDULING is so important that an entire volume could well be dedicated to it.

As a starting point, the dentist needs to provide the receptionist(s) with a list of all the intended procedures and the customary time allocations for each appointment.

For example, the young dentist may wish to make a list something like this:

Examination	30 minutes
Crown Preparation	1 hour
Restorations	4 surfaces per hour
Root Canal Treatment	45 minutes
Extraction	30 minutes
Prophylaxis	30 minutes

This is to give the receptionist(s) a feel for the approximate time desired. This will automatically be adjusted by how the dentist performs and his general attitude and disposition. Constant monitoring and coaching are necessary to train your receptionist(s) to get the maximum production out of "her" dentist.

BEWARE - the scheduler can rule the practice and can seriously limit production.

Scheduling can be responsible for:

- Eliminating lunch

- Turning the practice upside down

- Causing lots of confusion

- Setting up situations where patients get upset from having to wait too long

- Helping you create the million dollar practice and far beyond

The way your receptionist responds depends on many factors:

- Her confidence in the dentist to be flexible, competent, timely and friendly when she squeezes in suffering patients.

- The amount of coaching and support she

gets from the dentist.

- The guidelines established by the dentist.

- How the dentist responds when there is a gap in the schedule - (this one goes a little crazy): "Where is everyone?" "What's the deal?" "What's going on?" "Who didn't show up?" "Where's our back-up patient?" "Who was confirming patients yesterday?"

  By contrast, some dentists will welcome an hour or two to read or catch up on errands.

- How the dentist responds when all operatories are full, the waiting room is full and patients are standing in the entryway also affects how future scheduling is performed.

  Some dentists will panic; therefore, the receptionists will avoid letting this situation ever occur again.

  My usual response when all operatories are full and the receptionist reports the number of the patients in the waiting room is excessive is one of relative calm. When she inquires if she is keeping me busy enough, I might reply..."Just Right!" as the sweat runs down my brow.

Our receptionists know that if anyone is hurting she should get them in the chair AS SOON AS POSSIBLE.. This flexibility of being able to get the emergency patient in right away may be our best marketing tool.

When the dentist consistently, graciously works in the emergency patient, it is a gigantic influence on what guides the receptionist's behavior in the future. If the dentist were to totally flip out from "overload" and panic at the fact that he is buried and can see no escape, the receptionist would tend to avoid the overload situation at all costs.

On the other hand if she receives the most "static" when there is a two minute gap in the schedule she will tend to avoid any gaps.

This script is written with the assumption that you have read and are following through on Chapter 21, the Marketing section, and have sufficient patient flow and the phones are buzzing.

The receptionist(s) type the next day's schedules the night before and place them on the scheduling book on the front desk. (We make six copies on carbonless paper.) The schedules are not taped up in their respective final destinations throughout the office because they are awaiting the early morning write-ins which consistently occur.

The dentist arrives between 7:30 to 7:45 a.m.; we often add two or three names by our starting time of 8:00 a.m.

Those patients who were up all night with a toothache say that they start about 7:00 a.m. looking for the first dentist open. The early dentist who can get the patient in right away gets the patient.

When taking calls early in the morning, we tell the patients in pain to come in and we will work them in as soon as possible -- we also tell them to bring a book along in case we cannot get to them immediately. They appreciate the honesty and the fact that they will get relief soon. Our write-ins are added to the schedule.

At about 8:00 a.m., a receptionist places one schedule in each operatory where the dentist and dental assistant can see them from a working position, one in the laboratory/sterilization room, and one in the hall by the dentist's office. As patients are added after 8:00 a.m., a receptionist must make the rounds to update the schedule periodically.

On the schedule an asterisk behind the name signifies a "new" patient

(Ex. Jo Mill*). Each asterisk prior to the name means the patient has failed previously (EX. ***Jill Mill has failed three times). This gives the staff some feel for the potential of a failure which may be just what is needed to make the day flow smoothly.

If *** Jill Mill is scheduled for 2:30 p.m. you can be assured other patients are scheduled at the same time because the receptionists constantly watch for a possible failure time to add in emergency patients. If they all show up we get ambushed. So what! We've been there before!

THE PATIENT WHO IS IN PAIN:

The patient who is in pain presents a unique opportunity.

Having heard time after time from patients who have been up all night agonizing in pain and the earliest appointment they have been able to secure is a week or more in the future, it becomes apparent the tremendous window of opportunity available to the dentist who is willing and able to treat these patients spontaneously. This patient most likely tells at least a dozen people where he got relief. Getting patients who are in pain into the office immediately is a great marketing tool!

AMBUSH SCHEDULING

We do what we call ambush scheduling - scheduling two or three or four patients at the same time.

This often occurs at 1:00 p.m., although it can happen any time during the day (or evening). The reason we do ambush scheduling is that this gives us an opportunity to see the patients and determine exactly what they need. A chipped tooth over the telephone may really mean anything from smoothing off a minute chip which the tongue will not leave alone to surgically removing a retained root and everything in between. If we were to schedule a chipped tooth for an hour and it turned out to be nothing but a tooth in need of disking off we have an hour open. Therefore, by ambush scheduling we keep busy on the group who ambushed us. This ambush scheduling often challenges our flexibility tactics, which is good because this stretching makes us grow.

Experiencing repeated challenges stimulates our growth.

Let's say we get ambushed at 1:00 p.m., by:

CHAIR #1   -   a toothache

CHAIR #2   -   a broken tooth

CHAIR #3   -   a chipped tooth

CHAIR #4   -   a denture adjustment

THIS IS HOW IT GOES IN OUR OFFICE:

The dentist usually is back from lunch (has his teeth brushed, has washed up, and is ready to go) by 12:55.

The dental assistants send him to #4 Operatory to do a denture adjustment as all the rest of the patients require pre-diagnosing before he arrives.

> NOTE: The assistants send the dentist to Operatory #4. This is a clue. Let the assistants run the show! Let them worry about the schedule! Insist that they keep you approximately on time but let them attend to the details. Then the dentist can concentrate on treating patients.

While the dentist is having a delightful chat with Mrs. Jones about her upcoming trip to Seattle and adjusting her denture, an assistant is taking a panoramic film, a periapical film and bitewing x-rays in the #1 Operatory. As she quizzes the patient she finds the tooth was quite sore last week and is gradually getting better. Nothing shows on the x-rays, nothing seems clinically apparent.

A second assistant makes an experienced, educated guess (for purposes of setting up the operatory) that the patient in Operatory #2 may need a porcelain fused to metal crown on tooth #12 as the entire lingual cusp has fractured and the tooth otherwise is asymptomatic. She has taken an x-ray, given the patient a written estimate (even though the patient has had other crowns done recently) has taken the opposing model, has placed topical anesthetic and is busily chatting with the patient about the patient's new grandchildren.

As the dentist exits his conversation with Mrs. Jones, he is directed to #2 Operatory to make a diagnosis which just happens to be congruent with the assistant's pre-diagnosis. So he is able to anesthetize and then move on to Operatory #3 to replace a fractured restoration in tooth #14. This is an occlusal lingual which has been in for what looks like 50 years. This assistant has EVERYTHING set. The dentist opts to proceed without anesthetic as the patient is in the post-retirement age group and the dentist assumes secondary dentin gives sufficient insulation. The dentist pops the rubber dam on and is in and out in record time.

The dentist was correct about not needing anesthetic. The patient is very much surprised to be finished in perhaps less than three minutes. The dentist loves to discuss the marvels of our modern dental equipment and the vast improvements in the speed and efficacy of dentistry. The dentist tells our patient of the extreme speeds of the state-of-the-art air turbines and even shows him the "headlights" on the highspeed turbine. The patient comments on how wonderful it is to not have to be numb. The patient leaves our office delighted with the care he has received.

Next, off to #1 Operatory with an assistant's pre-diagnosis of a periodontal ligament bruise. After doing the examination and confirming that this is, in fact, the case, the dentist checks the films and the tooth and suggests to the patient (if the pain is too bad) we can do a root canal treatment or if the pain is getting a bit better we can just keep it under observation. She predictably opts for the latter so she is advised to keep in touch (and our receptionist will monitor her by telephone, too). If her tooth gets worse she can come in any time.

The dentist moves on to Operatory #2 where he does the crown preparation (the rubber dam is already on and anchored on tooth #14. This was done as the dentist was getting ready to exit Operatory #1.)

After the tooth has been prepared, the retraction cord, which was cut and has been soaking in Astrigident®, has been packed and the occlusal clearance for our laboratory friends verified, the dentist then places the impression material in the mouth and turns it over to the dental assistant.

When the timer rings the dental assistant removes the impression tray with a SNAP and adapts a temporary crown. Another assistant quietly delivers the final impression to the dentist in an adjacent operatory for approval of the impression. The patient is temporized and rescheduled for two weeks later when his permanent crown is back from the dental laboratory.

This is just one of an infinite number of possible ambush scenarios.

What happens when you get ambushed by four crown preparations? This can happen. Not too likely, but possible, of course. We would do two and perhaps even three crown preparations finding at least one that can be either smoothed off or filled with Miracle Mix® and rescheduled for the very near future.

With the assistants doing most of the work -- everything set up to the most minute detail, sharp burs in place, and so forth, assistants chatting with the patients until the dentist arrives, you can pull it off! What a team!

MORE ON SCHEDULING

The scheduling possibilities with any one dentist, with any one receptionist or receptionists, with any group of dental assistants, is a kinetic, not a static situation.

As the dentist gains efficiency and flexibility and his dental assistants become better and better trained, the scheduling possibilities grow exponentially.

The scheduling potential changes as each new assistant is put in place and trained. Therefore, scheduling as well as working in emergencies is an ever-changing process.

Scheduling is immensely important. Keep an eye on it! Coach the schedulers. When a day goes particularly well (you know when things just seem to flow smoothly) keep the schedule and take a look at it. Have the receptionist use this schedule as a pattern to go by. Have the staff analyze it, particularly the receptionists. Discuss this pattern at the staff meetings. Attempt to duplicate it daily.

For instance, we try to schedule crown and bridge (especially big cases) early in the morning. With the open operatory concept the dentist can overhear one of the receptionists saying "How about coming in early next Friday morning and getting that bridge preparation over with early so you have the rest of the day to go fishing?" Our schedule is satisfied and the patient feels accommodated.

By having the current schedule posted in view of every operatory, with the asterisks in front of the name (indicating a possible failure), and our learned flexibility we are usually able to keep steadily busy all day long.

When a gap in the schedule looks possible, we often select a third party payment patient and offer the possibility of doing as much as possible today if she would like to spend some time with us.

While we were building the practice we even offered patients who required a horrendous amount of restorative dentistry, to be able to finish in one day if they were willing to spend the day with us. The response was nearly always to get finished that day, if at all possible.

This patient was then worked in and around scheduled patients and given a chance to "rest his jaw periodically" while the dentist cared for other scheduled patients.

The patient may have anticipated ten to fifteen visits and might have traveled 50 or 60 miles one way to our facility. Patients are delighted with the "one-stop shopping" and tell their friends about their wonderful experience of getting all their dental work completed in one day, the examination day. This is incredible after ignoring one's dentition for several to many years. We continue to see many patients who had not previously been to a dentist for perhaps 10 or more years.

This ability to "flex" your schedule for your needy patients creates the following four-fold results:

1. It fills the schedule - a full schedule keeps the staff alert, busy and happy. The assistants as well as the dentist have a real sense of accomplishment at the end of a busy day. Conversely, a void in the schedule can lead staff to lethargy if it is not handled properly by the dentist. (An opportunity for further training.) A full schedule is a much better environment which creates a better impression for other patients. A full schedule handled efficiently equals profitability.

2. It saves the patient much time and travel expense - in getting all of his dentistry completed in one day, the examination day.

3. It creates a happy patient - "It's great to be finished."

4.   It creates great marketing - "word of mouth"
        - your *best* advertisement.

Even though this technique of finishing a patient in one day is not always applicable to our practice today (unless possibly in a severe weather situation when the less hardy don't make it to their appointments) IT IS GREAT FOR A START-UP PRACTICE -- you benefit your patients and you help your practice too. Our office uses this concept to fill small gaps in our schedule and we probably always will. The production possible with long appointments tends to explode in a geometric fashion rather than an arithmetic one with each additional unit of time available.

The fewer patients the better is a contradictory sounding statement often uttered. The meaning is that a busy schedule with few patients is most productive. When we have two or three big bridge cases in the morning and a couple of full mouth restorative cases in the afternoon we could have a very, very productive day with few patients.

The key is getting a lot of necessary restorative dental work done at a single sitting and having the patient thank you for it!

Beware of scheduling long appointments and have the patient not show! OUCH!

Our office likes one or two back-up patients for a long appointment - a new examination or two.

The counter situation to the long appointment is the patient needing one or two fillings and/or maybe a couple of sealants. Routinely, especially with kids, we tend to offer to do the restorations at the examination appointment.

We just ask the assistant to check with the mom and see if she would prefer to get Susan finished today, if possible. The answer is nearly always "yes." We have saved the patient a trip, taken very little of the dentist's time and we do not have to deal with short non-productive appointments which would be created by rescheduling for one or two fillings.

Depending on the schedule -- maybe even three or four restorations can be done at examination time, if your patient is anxious to get the work completed. Obviously, if we are behind in our schedule we would reschedule the patient. Being flexible is so very important!

The concept of avoiding short operative appointments is that it takes perhaps three times as long to do 2 fillings per patient on 10 patients as it does to do 20 fillings on one patient --- OUCH AGAIN! We would only do 20 fillings per sitting after the patient was given the option of coming back 6 or 8 times or finishing today. Further, the patient would be given the option of stopping after each quadrant was completed. Every time the rubber dam was removed. As well, each of our patients is instructed to raise a hand if for any reason they need something.

It is a great practice builder to be able to work your emergencies in on a daily basis...go ahead and schedule it tight and then, due to your flexibility, work your emergencies in also.

In our office, patients in pain can always be worked in somehow.

APPOINTMENT BOOK HINTS

In our appointment book we schedule using several columns:

1ST COLUMN: is the dentist's column (neat and uncluttered) - solid work, i.e., crown preparations, operative, extractions, etc.

2ND COLUMN: is 1 or 2 fillings - short appointments which can be worked into the schedule.

3RD COLUMN: is denture adjustments, try-ins, adjustments to crowns, and so on.

4TH COLUMN: hygienist schedule

5TH COLUMN: hygienist schedule

6TH COLUMN: lab (denture repair) schedule

This is the theory with the columns, but, unfortunately, this is not always the way it works. When we do get behind on the schedule, everyone pitches in -- the assistants chat with the patients and explain that we are running a little behind schedule; the receptionist informs the patients when they arrive (occasionally they will want to know if they can run a fifteen minute errand and come back). All working together, we work through it. It takes cooperation of all staff members.

If you never get behind you are not scheduling tight enough for maximum production.

If you get behind too often, you can benefit from becoming better organized and more efficient. Good luck - schedule up a storm!

Each evening the next-day patients are called to confirm their appointment for the following day. It is noted in our scheduling book if and when each patient has been reached, if they have confirmed, or if there was no answer. Not only do patients appreciate our calling to confirm their dental appointment, but it is easier for us to determine what will be happening the following day in our schedule.

So far we have discussed scheduling as if homogeneity were a factor in our patient base. Since this is not the case, the next Chapter is devoted to the Patient Factor!

CHAPTER 8

THE PATIENT FACTOR

"When your patient is ideal it is indeed your lucky day. However, we know that this is rarely the case."

C. Ferdinand Benzie, D.D.S.

The patient factor is ever present and must be taken into consideration in any discussion of scheduling or efficiency.

In this chapter we discuss the patient factor and how it affects scheduling, production, frustration levels and general longevity of the dental team.

We all have some patients, however sweet, whom we would prefer to have someone else treat. Learning to cope with these challenges is a major step toward our success.

Following are some patient factors which we need to consider:

1.   **THE WIGGLER** – Love those little ones!   Some children are not capable of sitting still for very long and some are not capable of sitting still at all.

POSSIBLE SOLUTIONS:

A.   Headphones are often effective as a diversion tactic. A dental assistant can tell the patient if he holds very still he will be allowed to listen to the headphones.

B.   And as long as he holds still he can turn the volume up as **LOUD** as he likes.

C.   Nitrous Oxide/Oxygen Analgesia (see Chapter 10) – Let the children play the "space ship" game as long as they hold still – analgesia is a great help and when the children think of the dental office as a place where they have a good time it greatly facilitates treatment.

D.   Rubber Dam – (see Chapter 11) increases efficiency and helps protect the patient's tongue and cheek; helps keep debris out of the patient's mouth and makes the procedure much easier on the dental team. The stretching of the rubber dam helps the patient hold open and the combined effect of the nitrous oxide/oxygen analgesia and rubber dam tends to separate the patient from the treatment being performed.

E.   Six-handed – the Team Approach – is most beneficial to getting the procedure completed quickly and effectively.

F.   Premedicate - pre-medication is indicated for those patients who cannot otherwise hold still for treatment.

2.   **HYPERGLOSSIA** -   The large, strong tongue can be a horrendous handicap to an efficient procedure.

POSSIBLE SOLUTIONS:

A.   Rubber Dam - (See Chapter 11).   Rubber Dam can often save the day when the tongue wants to dominate the entire oral cavity.

B.   Nitrous oxide/oxygen analgesia may help relax the tongue beneath the rubber dam.

C.   Muscle Relaxants - prescribing muscle relaxants will often help.

3.   **EXTREME GAG REFLEX** -   An extreme gag reflex can create a real challenge.   We experience all degrees of this problem -- from slight to moderate to extreme.

POSSIBLE SOLUTIONS:

A.   Topical spray is often very effective.

B.   Rubber dam often helps. Apply after topical spray - - you may have to talk the patient through the application as the rubber dam placement may cause gagging until the frame is in place and the rubber dam is stretched tightly over the frame. Have the patient breathe deeply through his nose while applying the rubber dam. If additional distraction is necessary, have the patient raise his left leg off the chair or anything else to distract him for the critical moment you are applying the rubber dam.

C.   Nitrous oxide/oxygen analgesia is an important adjunct.

D.   Headphones may help in diverting the patient's attention.

E.   Distraction technique: during the impression, x-ray or rubber dam placement procedures, if additional distraction is necessary, have the patient hold his left arm out parallel to the floor or anything else to refocus his mind for long enough to complete the procedure, confirming in a loud voice (further distraction) that they are "doing great" while the critical time is elapsing.

4.   **ANESTHESIA CHALLENGES** - The patient is either not profoundly anesthetized or perceives himself as not being profoundly anesthetized.

POSSIBLE SOLUTIONS:

A.   Nitrous oxide/oxygen analgesia to help raise the pain threshold. Turning the concentration up for a short critical period is often indicated. In combination with any or all of the following solutions your success is almost certain.

B.   Re-anesthetize - go through the entire sequence again - for instance: lingual, inferior alveolar and long buccal; then infiltrate on the lower. On the upper a palatal block is sometimes necessary - even for routine operative procedures.

C.   Periodontal ligament injection - is very effective and can usually be successful with a regular aspirating syringe. The need for getting out the intraligamental syringe is overemphasized.

118

D. Upper bicuspids may require a palatal block.

E. Upper first bicuspid may require a nasopalatine as well as a posterior palatine block.

F. **Perceived pain syndrome.** If the patient exhibits a perception phenomenon, it is usually pressure or noise which stimulates the perceived pain.

When this is the case stop and explain the pressure phenomenon by pressing on the patient's shoulder, "but this is only pressure and doesn't really bother anything." "You will feel **PRESSURE** as we wiggle this tooth out of the socket for you."

When it's noise, having your patient turn up the volume on the headset may help.

Nitrous oxide/oxygen analgesia helps in nearly any case and turning the nitrous oxide concentration up for a short critical period is often indicated.

G. If you feel that lack of anesthesia is possibly due to an infection, put the patient on an antibiotic and reschedule the patient in 5 to 7 days.

5. **OBESITY** - Excessive adipose tissue interfering with treatment can be a great challenge.

POSSIBLE SOLUTIONS:

A. Rubber Dam is wonderful and often saves the day. See Chapter 11 and learn The Modified Technique.

B. When restoring the facial surface of the upper molars have the patient close the jaw part way and move his mandible to the side you are working on.

6. **EXTREMELY APPREHENSIVE PATIENT -** The patient is in pain, and often has been in pain for an extended period of time, but is so afraid of going to the dentist that he avoids presenting until the pain is overwhelming. This is the patient who becomes very anxious even at the thought of going to the dental office and is nearly non-functional once inside your office.

POSSIBLE SOLUTIONS:

A. It is often imperative that you spend a few minutes chatting with this patient from a SAFE distance - 5 or 6 feet away, prior to donning your mask and gloves. Sometimes it is very valuable to ask the patient what it is that frightens him about being in the dental office. Many times a patient will tell horror stories about how he had a tooth extracted in the past and how the dentist "stood on the patient's chest" to get that tooth out. As soon as the patient relates his "horror story" or reason for his anxiety you are in a much better position to treat the patient.

For example, if he relates his experiences from childhood, you can explain how you also were petrified of the dentist when you were a child, if this is the case, or how many patients who have not been to a dental office for a long time feel this way, but how much the technology has changed, or whatever is applicable to communicate how treatment is entirely different now. Generally, a patient who is told what to expect is greatly relieved. Because many patients feel they are not in control of the situation in a dental office, simply telling them that as soon as they raise their hand the dentist will stop may help them through the procedure.

B.   Nitrous oxide/oxygen analgesia - these patients must be very closely monitored and the dentist must continually suggest and confirm the fact that "the laughing gas" is helping them relax and they are doing better now. As long as you are able to stimulate positive feedback from the patient, the nitrous oxide/oxygen is working in your favor.

C.   Headphones - let the patient know he can select his favorite radio station and turn the volume on the headphones up as loud as he likes.

D.   Rubber dam - inform the patient this rubber shield will separate you from the procedure -- "we will be working outside of this shield and you will be on the inside."

E.   Premedicate as indicated - consulting with the patient's pharmacist or physician often will reveal what the patient has taken previously for pre-medication.

F.   When the patient reports that "Novocaine never works on me," assure him that we have a new anesthetic called Xylocaine, or Carbocaine, or Marcaine -- or whatever you will be using -- which will work and that we do not use Novocaine any more.

G.   Assure the patient that you are accustomed to working with apprehensive patients and that we always work our way through it. And each time it becomes a little easier for the patient. Your confident reassurance is often a most important factor.

7.   **HYPERSALIVATION** - Excessive saliva flow can create a challenge.

POSSIBLE SOLUTIONS:

A.   Rubber Dam (Chapter 11)

B.   Saliva ejector behind the rubber dam.

C.   Premedicate as indicated.

D.   Hypnotic suggestion - with proper training this can be very successful. The dentist must remember to turn the flow back on when the procedure is completed.

8.   **INABILITY TO OPEN WIDE OR STAY OPEN -** A very difficult and frustrating scene for the dentist, the dental assistants, and the patient.

POSSIBLE SOLUTIONS:

A.   Rubber Dam - (Chapter 11) rubber dam helps the patient hold open as well as keeping the field of vision clear.

B.   Mouth Prop - ratchet type - must be presented properly to the patient and explained in detail. "If you open real wide, we will slip this prop in to hold your mouth open so you can just relax and let the prop hold your mouth open. See, that's pretty neat, isn't it?"

Both the rubber dam and the mouth gag can be used simultaneously if you follow this sequence:

1.   Insert the rubber dam clamp into the rubber dam.

2.   Place the rubber dam clamp over the anchor tooth.

3.   Watch the patient's lips so they stay clear of the space between the mouth prop and the occlusal or incisal edges of the teeth as you insert the mouth prop.

4.   Activate the mouth prop by squeezing.

5.   Stretch rubber dam over the rubber dam frame.

With any one or a combination of the above factors, a given procedure may take three to four times longer than average. If you are getting behind schedule while wrestling with the patient, it is frustrating and a strain on everyone involved. Communicate with the front office to allow more time than usual when this patient returns for additional appointments.

At the risk of being duplicitious, on most of the above patients the rubber dam is often the most beneficial tool you have in your armamentarium. Use it to your advantage and explain the benefits to the patient before placing it. "This rubber shield will help keep the spray out of your mouth and make it much easier for you." or "This rubber shield will protect your tongue so it doesn't come into the working field."

MAXIM

**WHEN PATIENTS KNOW <u>WHY</u> YOU ARE PLACING
A RUBBER DAM -- THAT IT IS FOR THEIR
BENEFIT -- THEY TEND TO BE
MUCH MORE COOPERATIVE**

In Chapter 9 we will coach the dental team to set up the operatory for maximum efficiency prior to the dentist's arrival.

CHAPTER 9

TRAY AND OPERATORY SET-UPS

The time and effort invested in standardization of equipment and operatory preparation pays big dividends!

PREPARATION PRIOR
TO THE DENTIST'S ARRIVAL
IN THE OPERATORY

The degree to which the consistent standardization of procedure trays and operatory set-ups enhances efficiency is astounding! When every possible detail has consistently been addressed prior to the dentist's arrival in the operatory, the completion of the procedure is significantly smoother, more efficient, and less stressful for the patient, the staff, and the dentist.

Prior to taking the patient into the operatory, standard operatory sterilization procedures are ALWAYS followed.

The proper instrument tray is set in position on the mobile cart with the mirror and explorer toward the dentist. The tray is then unwrapped. The mouth mirror is coated with Ultradent No-Fog®.

Sterilized handpieces are attached and placed in all handpiece holders. Burs are placed in the handpieces to the dentist's consistent predetermined specifications. All high speed handpieces are primed to assure water is to the bur when the dentist steps on the rheostat.

The chart is placed on the mobile cart and situated such that the dentist can read the chart upon his arrival. Current x-rays are set out for viewing.

The rubber dam clamp is placed in the rubber dam and the rubber dam forceps are placed in the clamp.

The **WARM** anesthetic carpule is placed in the anesthetic syringe.

The appropriate amalgam capsule is loaded in the amalgamator when indicated.

The patient's bib is placed over the instrument tray to cover the instruments for the patient's arrival. Since some patients are less than fond of dental instruments, it is a good policy to have the instrument tray covered during the patient's entry into the operatory.

The aspirator tips are placed on the terminal ends of the aspirator hoses.

The entire operatory is checked for cleanliness, including the dental light, which is right in front of the patient's eyes. The floor is checked for cleanliness. Everything! When all is neat and clean the assistant takes the patient into the operatory, seats the patient and places the bib on the patient.

If this is one of a series of visits, the dental assistant confirms that the patient is doing well with their restorations placed during the last visit. If the patient reports symptoms which sound like the possibility of a high filling, the dental assistant checks the occlusion with articulating paper. If she anticipates that an occlusal adjustment may be necessary she places the appropriate bur in one of the handpieces. She further explains, when indicated, that a large filling close to the nerve may be sensitive to cold for several weeks to a few months. This saves the dentist time because the dental assistant may be more patient and emphatic than her dentist and her vocabulary may be more consistent with the patient's vocabulary.

If the assistant does find a possible high spot she tells the dentist when he arrives and, with the mark on the tooth from the articulating paper and the dentist's favorite bur in the handpiece, ready to go, it is a trivial procedure for the dentist to adjust the filling.

Next, the dental assistant confirms the procedures scheduled for today with the patient. Depending upon our schedule, the assistant inquires about the patient's desire to complete as much dentistry as possible today. The assistant then makes a tentative plan.

The assistant helps the patient make a shade selection if prosthetics are involved. If composite restorations are anticipated the dental assistant selects the desired shade or shades. She often selects two shades and sometimes three for a single restoration to get the desired effect.

When the dentist arrives the dental assistant states to the dentist that, "Carmela has a lot of restorations to do and she would REALLY like it if there is any way possible to finish her up today."

BEAUTIFUL!!!! The stage is set, we have the "go ahead" to finish her restorations today. Yet we have not committed that we do have time (the back door is still open) if the dental assistant was over zealous. The dental assistant has already made the decision that we may be able to finish her restorations today. When the assistants become very good at watching the time and the schedule the dentist can relax about those considerations. As long as everything is moving along

127

at a satisfactory pace, let the dental assistant assume the stress of the ticking clock. Furthermore, when it is her idea that we can finish all of the restorations today, she is much more enthusiastic than she would be if it were the dentist's idea!

OPERATIVE DENTISTRY

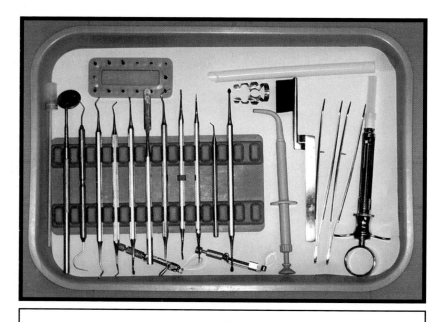

FIGURE 9-1
Operative Dentistry Tray Set-up
Details -- See Figure 9-21

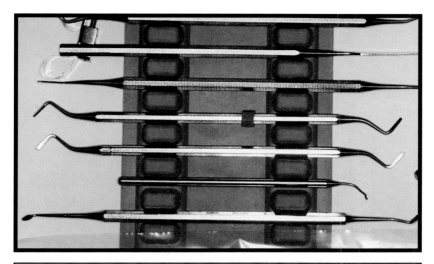

FIGURE 9-2
Distal off-angle hatchet banded for easy identification

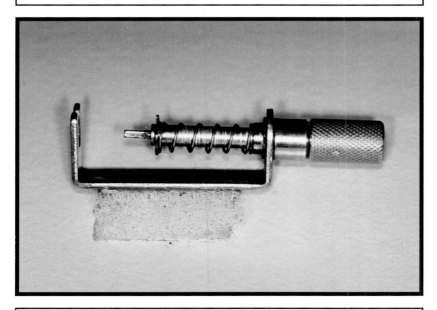

FIGURE 9-3
Bur changing tool with strip of velcro attached

FIGURE 9-4
Bur changing tool with velcro attached to top of unit

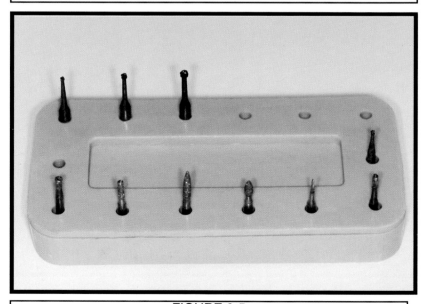

FIGURE 9-5
Standard bur block - See Figure 9-20 for more detail

SET UP FOR <u>OPERATIVE</u> PROCEDURE:

BURS IN PLACE

SLOW	HI	HI	HI
#4	1558	Pointed	35
		Diamond	

Operative tray is on mobile cart and unwrapped.

All handpieces are primed to assure water is to the burs.

Aspirator tips are in both high volume evacuation hoses.

Saliva ejector is in place.

Patient's chart and current x-rays are out to view.

Rubber dam clamp is in the rubber dam.

Rubber dam forceps are in the rubber dam clamp ready to place in the mouth.

Amalgam capsule is in the amalgamator when indicated.

Mouth mirror is coated with Ultradent No-Fog®

Shade is selected if composite restorations are scheduled.

Patient is seated and the chair is adjusted to operating position.

Patient bib is placed on the patient.

Last visit's favorable results are confirmed, if applicable.

Today's anticipated treatment is confirmed with the patient.

Composite shades selected when indicated.

Topical anesthetic is in place.

READY for the dentist to appear.

ROOT CANAL TREATMENT

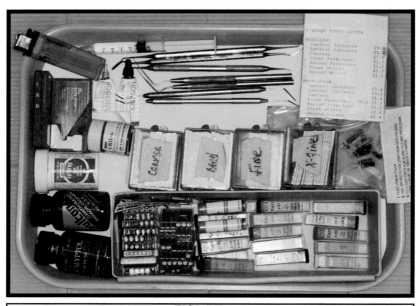

FIGURE 9-6
Root Canal Treatment Procedure Tray Set-up

SET UP FOR <u>ROOT CANAL TREATMENT PROCEDURE:</u>

BURS IN PLACE			
SLOW	**HI**	**HI**	**HI**
#4	**Hourglass**	**1558**	**35**

Operative tray (Figure 9-1) is on the mobile cart, unwrapped AND

Root Canal Treatment tray is in place and checked to confirm its completeness.

All handpieces primed to assure water is to the burs.

Aspirator tips in both high volume evacuation hoses.

Saliva ejector is in place

Confirm that we have a satisfactory periapical film of the tooth or teeth on which the root canal treatment is anticipated. Take and develop any necessary films. Place all such x-rays out for the dentist's re-inspection prior to starting the procedure.

Patient's chart is out for viewing.

Rubber Dam clamp is in the rubber dam.

Rubber dam forceps are in the rubber dam clamp ready to place in the mouth.

Gutta percha point heater is plugged in.

Sonic apex locator is ready.

Hypochlorite syringe is filled and ready.

Mouth mirror is coated with Ultradent No-Fog®

Patient is seated and the chair is adjusted to operating position.

Bib is placed on the patient.

Today's anticipated treatment is confirmed with the patient.

Topical anesthetic is placed.

If this is the first appointment, the dental assistant confirms with the patient which tooth is to be treated. If this is the first appointment she sets the reamer stops to predetermined lengths (of average lengths) - from the chart (Figure 9-6 below). If this is not the first appointment she sets the reamer stops to the length determined on the patient's last visit.

READY for the dentist.

AVERAGE TOOTH LENGTH

MAXILLARY

Central Incisors	**24.0**
Lateral Incisors	**22.5**
Canines	**27.0**
First Premolars	**21.7**
Second Premolars	**21.5**
First Molars	**21.3**
Second Molars	**21.1**

MANDIBULAR

Central Incisors	**21.4**
Lateral Incisors	**23.2**
Canines	**25.4**
First Premolars	**18.5 - 27.0**
Second Premolars	**23.2**
First Molars	**22.8**
Second Molars	**22.8**

FIGURE 9-7
Average Tooth Length Chart
This is of appropriate size to be photocopied and attached to
a 3 x 5 card, laminated and placed on your root canal tray

CROWN AND BRIDGE

FIGURE 9-8
Crown and Bridge Tray Set-up

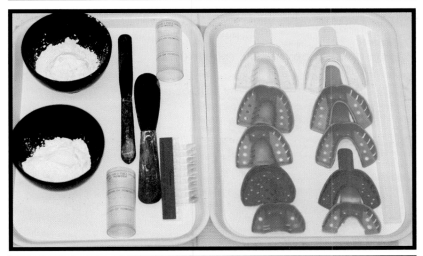

FIGURE 9-9
Alginate Set-up for Opposing Impression

SET-UP FOR <u>CROWN AND BRIDGE</u> PROCEDURE:

BURS IN PLACE			
SLOW	**HI**	**HI**	**HI**
#4	End Cutting 1.4mm	Pointed Diamond	1558

Operative tray is on mobile cart, unwrapped AND

Crown and Bridge tray is in place and checked to confirm its completeness.

All handpieces primed to assure water is to the burs.

Aspirator tips in both high volume evacuation hoses.

Saliva ejector is in place.

Patient chart is out to view.

Rubber dam clamp is in the rubber dam.

Rubber dam forceps are in the rubber dam clamp ready to place in the mouth.

Pre-measured alginate in bowls.

Pre-measured water in tubes.

Spatulas for mixing alginate.

Mouth mirror is coated with Ultradent No-Fog®.

Confirmed that patient is doing fine after last visit, if this is a series of visits.

Confirm today's scheduled treatment with the patient.

Confirm the presence of a satisfactory current periapical film of ALL TEETH to be crowned. Take and develop any needed films. Place all such x-rays out for the dentist's re-inspection prior to starting the procedure.

Cut the retraction cord for teeth to be prepared and place in Astringident® to soak.

Astringident® syringe is loaded and ready for use.

Patient is seated.

Bib is placed on the patient.

Today's anticipated treatment is confirmed with the patient.

Take an alginate impression of the opposing arch.

Select the impression tray to be used for crown and bridge impression.

Help patient select the shade for esthetic crown and/or bridge.

Prepare the syringe with tip to inject Polysiloxane impression material around the preparations. (We use Polysiloxane Imprint™ - 3M Wash and Schein VPS (Vinyl Polysiloxane) Putty.

Topical anesthetic is placed.

Lab slip is on the mobile cart filled out as far as it can be completed prior to treatment.

READY for the dentist.

REMOVABLE PARTIAL DENTURES
(1st Appointment)

SET-UP FOR REMOVABLE PARTIAL DENTURES (1ST APPOINTMENT):

(See Figure 9-5 Standard Bur Block; See Figure 9-9 - Alginate Impression Tray Set-up.)

BURS IN PLACE			
SLOW	**HI**	**HI**	**HI**
	Hourglass	35	Cylinder

Mirror and explorer are on the mobile cart.

Bur block is on the mobile cart.

All handpieces are primed to assure water is to the burs.

Aspirator tips are in both high volume evacuation hoses.

Saliva ejector is in place.

Mouth mirror is coated with Ultradent No-Fog®

Patient's chart and current x-rays are out to view.

Premeasured alginate is in bowls on the mobile cart.

Premeasured water is in the measuring tubes.

Impression trays and bead wax are on the mobile cart.

Impression trays are selected and the bead wax molded around the peripheries.

Spatulas are on the mobile cart.

Shade guide is available on the mobile cart.

Patient is seated.

Bib is placed on the patient.

Today's anticipated treatment is confirmed with the patient.

Patient is shown the shade guide and with the dental assistant's help has selected a desired shade.

Chair is adjusted to operating position.

Base plate wax is in hot tap water and will be delivered at the appropriate time by another assistant upon the number one assistant's request, if the dentist desires it today.

Topical anesthetic is placed.

Lab slip is on the mobile cart filled out as far as it can be completed prior to treatment.

READY for the dentist.

REMOVABLE PARTIAL DENTURES - 2nd Appt

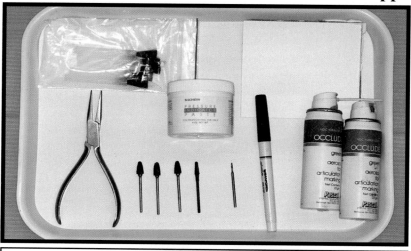

FIGURE 9-10
Removable Partial Denture (2nd Appointment)
Try-In Framework - Take Bite Set-Up Tray
(or insertion if patient has occlusion such that a positive
bite was possible on the first appointment. If this is the case,
move on to insertion set-up)

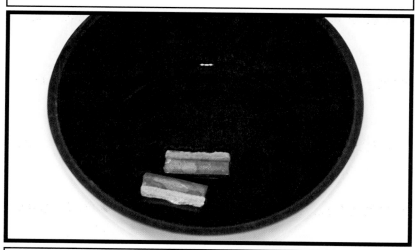

FIGURE 9-11
Dental Assistants have pre-cut pieces of Alu wax in hot water

SET UP FOR REMOVABLE PARTIAL DENTURES (2nd APPOINTMENT - TRY-IN FRAMEWORK - TAKE BITE (or insertion if patient has occlusion such that a positive bite was possible on the first appointment. If this is the case, move on to insertion set-up):

BURS IN PLACE

SLOW	HI	HI	HI
Vulcanite	-	-	-

Mirror and explorer are on the mobile cart.

Mouth mirror is coated with Ultradent No-Fog®.

Blow torch and marble slab are on the mobile cart.

Alu wax is in hot water on the mobile cart.

Fox guide is on the mobile cart.

Laboratory pan with patient's models and framework and wax pads are on the mobile.

Spatulas (flat and #7 wax) are on the mobile cart.

Patient is seated in the operatory.

Chair is adjusted for treatment.

Bib is placed on the patient.

Today's anticipated treatment is confirmed with the patient.
Lab slip is on mobile cart filled out as far as it can be completed
prior to treatment.

READY for the dentist.

REMOVABLE PARTIAL DENTURES
(3rd Appointment)

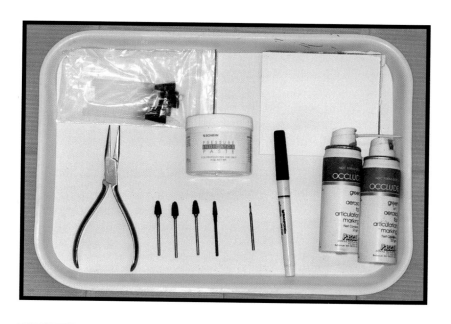

FIGURE 9-12
Removable Partial Denture (3rd Appointment)
Tray Set-Up

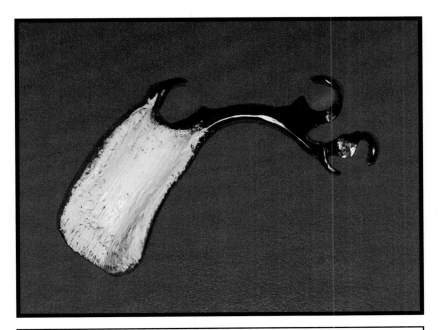

FIGURE 9-13
Dental Assistant has partial denture coated with
PIP paste ready for insertion

SET UP FOR <u>REMOVABLE PARTIAL DENTURES</u> (3rd Appointment - Insertion):

BURS IN PLACE

SLOW	**HI**	**HI**	**HI**
Vulcanite	-	-	-

Mirror and explorer are on the mobile cart.

Mouth mirror is coated with Ultradent No-Fog®.

Articulating paper in articulating paper holder out and ready.

143

Pressure indicator paste ready.

Disposable brush is ready.

Mixing pad on which to place pressure indicator paste.

Partial denture removed from sealed plastic bag and checked CAREFULLY for any potentially lacerating protrusions or rough spots on the tissue surface left behind in the processing.

Any such protrusions are relieved.

Patient is seated in the operatory.

Bib is placed on the patient.

Chair is adjusted to operating position.

Today's anticipated procedure is confirmed with the patient.

Partial denture is dried thoroughly and coated with pressure indicator paste. At this point the dental assistant can inform the dentist of the status of the progress. The dentist may opt to have the patient try in the appliance or may give the patient and the assistant an opportunity to chat until he can get there.

READY for the dentist.

REMOVABLE FULL DENTURES
(1ST APPOINTMENT)

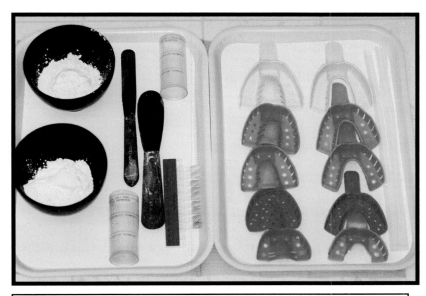

FIGURE 9-14
Set-Up for Removable Full Dentures
(1st Appointment)

SET UP FOR <u>REMOVABLE FULL DENTURES</u>: (1st Appointment):

BURS IN PLACE			
SLOW	**HI**	**HI**	**HI**
Vulcanite	-	-	-

145

Mirror and explorer are on the mobile cart.

Mouth mirror is coated with Ultradent No-Fog®.

Premeasured alginate is in the mixing bowls.

Premeasured water is in the measuring tubes.

Spatulas are ready for use.

Impression trays and bead wax are ready.

Shade guide is available.

Patient is seated in the operatory.

Bib is placed on the patient.

Chair is adjusted to operating position.

Today's anticipated treatment is confirmed with the patient.

Dental assistant assists the patient in selecting the shade for her dentures.

Bead wax is placed around the periphery of the appropriate size trays.

Lab slip is on the mobile cart and filled out as far as it can be completed prior to treatment.

Dental assistant inspects the patient's mouth and confirms that no denture adhesive has been used. If denture adhesive is present, dental assistant and patient remove denture adhesive thoroughly.

READY for the dentist.

REMOVABLE FULL DENTURES
(2nd APPOINTMENT)

SET UP FOR <u>REMOVABLE FULL DENTURES</u> (2nd Appointment) **Vertical Dimension and Bite (usually 1 hour after first appointment):**

	BURS IN PLACE		
SLOW	**HI**	**HI**	**HI**
Vulcanite	-	-	-

Mirror and explorer are on the mobile cart.

Mouth mirror is coated with Ultradent No-Fog®.

Denture wax tray with spatulas are on the mobile and checked for completeness.

Marking pen for spot on chin and upper lip.

Millimeter ruler is on the mobile cart.

Blow torch is on the mobile cart.

Marble slab for wax drippings is on the mobile cart.

Fox guide is on the mobile cart.

Patient mirror is on the mobile cart.

Alu wax is in hot water in mixing bowl.

The patient is seated in the operatory.

Bib is placed on the patient.

Today's anticipated treatment is confirmed with the patient.

Lab slip is on the mobile cart and filled out as far as it can be completed prior to treatment.

READY for the dentist.

REMOVABLE FULL DENTURES
(3rd APPOINTMENT)

SET UP FOR <u>REMOVABLE FULL DENTURES</u> (3rd Appointment - Try-in):

BURS IN PLACE			
SLOW	**HI**	**HI**	**HI**
Vulcanite	-	-	-

Mirror and explorer are on the mobile cart.

Mouth mirror is coated with Ultradent No-Fog®.
Blow Torch is on the mobile cart.

Marble slab for wax drippings is on the mobile cart.

148

Patient mirror is on the mobile cart.

Additional assistant is available throughout the procedure.

Patient is seated in the operatory.

Bib is placed on the patient.

Today's anticipated procedure is confirmed with the patient.

Lab slip is on the mobile cart and filled out as far as it can be completed prior to treatment.

READY for the dentist.

Bring bowl of hot tap water after the dentist arrives.

REMOVABLE FULL DENTURES
(4th APPOINTMENT)

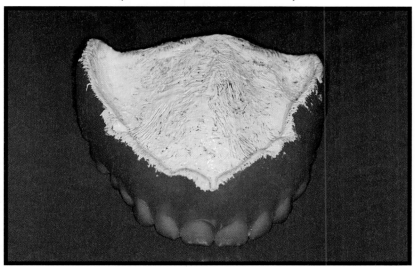

FIGURE 9-15
Dental Assistant has placed PIP paste in upper full
denture - ready for insertion

SET-UP FOR REMOVABLE FULL DENTURES (4th Appointment - INSERTION):

BURS IN PLACE			
SLOW	**HI**	**HI**	**HI**
Vulcanite	-	-	-

Mirror and explorer are on the mobile cart.

Mouth mirror is coated with Ultradent No-Fog®.

Dentures are taken out of the bubble pack.

Dentures are dried off, checked thoroughly for any rough spots on tissue surfaces - any sharp protrusions are smoothed off.

Denture is coated with pressure indicator paste.

Articulating paper is in articulator paper forceps available on the mobile cart.

Patient mirror is on the mobile cart.

Patient is seated in the operatory.

Bib is placed on the patient.

Today's anticipated procedure is confirmed with the patient.

READY for the dentist.

ORAL SURGERY/EXTRACTION PROCEDURE

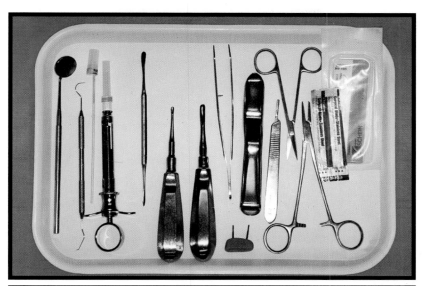

FIGURE 9-16
Oral Surgery Tray Set-up

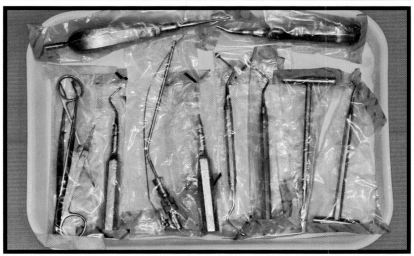

FIGURE 9-17
Special root tip picks, elevators, bone files, etc., for surgery

FIGURE 9-18
Extraction forceps in drawer

FIGURE 9-19
New assistants can easily find correct forceps as set up here

SET UP FOR EXTRACTION/ORAL SURGERY PROCEDURE:

BURS IN PLACE			
SLOW	HI	HI	HI
-	-	Surgical 1557	Surgical 1557

Extraction/Oral Surgery tray is on the mobile cart and checked for completeness.

Mouth mirror is coated with Ultradent No-Fog®

Special surgical tray with special elevators, picks, and bone file is in place within assistant's reach.

Scalpel blade is inserted into scalpel handle when indicated.

Suture pack is at fingertips.

Patient is seated and the chair is adjusted to operating position.

Bib is placed on the patient.

Today's anticipated procedure is confirmed with the patient.

Pertinent x-rays are taken and developed or retrieved from the patient's chart and set out for the dentist's review prior to beginning the procedure.

Extra gauze pack ready for patient to take with her.

Topical anesthetic is placed.

An additional assistant is available throughout the procedure.

READY for the dentist.

STANDARD BUR BLOCK

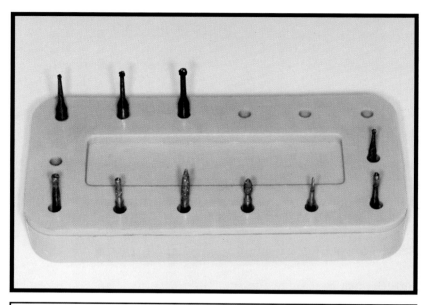

FIGURE 9-20
BUR IDENTIFICATION

<u>UPPER LEFT TO RIGHT</u>

#2 Round (100-6411)
#4 Round (100-1847)
#6 Round (100-8765)

35 CARBIDE
(100-2484)

<u>LOWER LEFT TO RIGHT</u>

HOURGLASS (100-5034)
CYLINDER (100-7127)
POINTED (100-4140)
FOOTBALL (100-7944)
169 CARBIDE (100-1864)
1558 CARBIDE (100-4372)

SCHEIN ORDER NUMBERS

OPERATIVE TRAY INSTRUMENTS

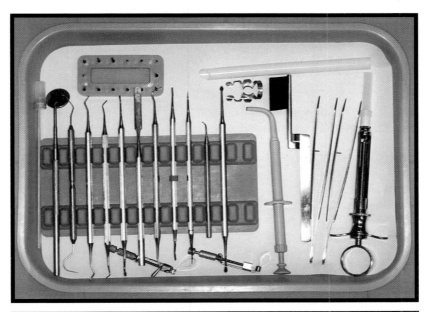

FIGURE 9-21
Operative Tray Instrument Identification

READING LEFT TO RIGHT:

Henry Schein Cotton Tipped Applicators (Topical) 100-9175
HuFriedy Mirror (600-0781) and Handle (600-9906)
HuFriedy Explorer #508
HuFriedy 2/3 Jacquette Scaler #30/33 600-1032
Schein Spoon Excavator #17 100-0704
Schein Amalgam Plugger/Packer 1/2 Black 100-0892
Schein #5 Cement Spatula 100-9387
Schein PFI (Plastic Filling Instrument) #PF4 100-2712
American Dental Hatchet (banded) (All distal surfaces) EG2210
   15-8-14 10-10
American Dental Hatchet (mesial surfaces) EG2005
   15-8-14 10-11
Dycal Applicator/Dycal Placer 222-9518

FIGURE 9-21
Operative Tray Instrument Identification
(Cont'd. Left to Right)

Schein #3/6 Carver 100-8494

(2) Premier College Cotton Pliers 378-3758

Miltex 90⁰ Amalgam Carrier 100-3022
Schein Aspirating Syringe 100-9808

UPPER PORTION OF TRAY:

Standard bur block
Monoject Suction tip 194-7717
Ivory #21 cotton roll holder
Articulating paper holder

LOWER PORTION OF TRAY:

Tofflemeier Matrix Retainers (2) - Universal 100-9547
Matrix Band #1 .0015 ga - 100-3556
Wizard Wedges (2) Slim Jim 112-9259

EXTRACTION/ORAL SURGERY INSTRUMENTS

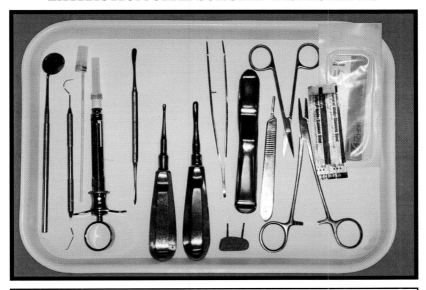

FIGURE 9-22
Extraction/Oral Surgery
Instrument Identification

LEFT TO RIGHT:

Hu-Friedy Mirror (600-0781) and Handle (600-9906)
Hu-Friedy Explorer #5 DE 600-4475
Henry Schein Cotton Tipped Applicator 100-9175 (Topical)
Schein Aspirating Syringe 100-9808
Henry Schein #7 wax spatula 100-3035 (Periosteal Elevator)
Schein #34 S Elevator 100-6436 (301)
Schein #34 Elevator 100-2019 (34 Elevator)
Premier College Cotton Pliers 378-3758
U of MN Retractor - Hu-Friedy 600-5811
Henry Schein Surgical Handle #3 100-7520
Surgical Scissors
Needle Holder 100-2492
Monoject Vented Aspirator Tip 194-7717
Burs: Schein Carbide 100-0282 Surgical Burs #556
Scalpel Handle (Bard-Parker)
Schein Silk Sutures 4-0 3/8 Circle 100-6830
Schein Stainless Steel Surgical Blade #15 100-0249

In the next chapter we will explore the benefits of using nitrous oxide/oxygen analgesia.

CHAPTER 10

NITROUS OXIDE/OXYGEN ANALGESIA

Certainly a good time is preferable to a bad time.

NITROUS OXIDE/OXYGEN ANALGESIA is an adjunct which can increase the rapid growth of your dental practice and should most certainly be used whenever indicated.

We find that about 50% of our patients love it, 30% are indifferent toward it and about 20% do not want it.

Those patients who love it would not be without it. They have a good time "on the gas" and are likely to tell their friends about "how much fun they had at their dental office." This kind of advertising is more valuable than any advertising you can purchase, and word of mouth is free!

For this reason alone nitrous oxide/oxygen analgesia is a valuable asset. In addition, it greatly assists the patient who is apprehensive of being in the dental chair. Also, local anesthesia can more readily be administered without the awareness of the patient who is under nitrous oxide/oxygen analgesia. You have a powerful accessory in nitrous oxide/oxygen analgesia.

Anything you can do to make your patient's visit more enjoyable or less stressful is worthwhile.

Always ask your patient if he or she has used nitrous oxide/oxygen on prior dental visits. If he acts puzzled, call it "the gas" or "laughing gas". If he responds in the affirmative, ask if he would like it again today. If he says he has to drive explain that we will "flush your system with oxygen before you leave the office, and we won't let you leave until you feel completely normal." You may want to tell him that nitrous oxide/oxygen tends to relax him and may make the time go a little faster while in the dental chair. If he seems uncertain, suggest that he may like to try it once and if he does not like it you will discontinue its use any time he raises his hand.

With the patient who has not been previously exposed to nitrous oxide/oxygen analgesia, you may choose to start out at a very low level and tell him what to expect. "You may feel a little 'floatie' or 'dreamy' or maybe like you have had a beer or two; but no hangover." This level may be at about 25% to 30% and monitored verbally as well as physiologically CONSTANTLY! Ask the patient every minute or two if he feels anything yet. He will often say he feels nothing different and you may choose to turn him up slightly. We want to guard against a panicky feeling which can develop instantly. One moment he reports no unusual sensation and the next instant he feels out of control.

So turn the concentration of nitrous oxide up very slowly and monitor the patient CONSTANTLY. It is much better to complete the procedure without the patient ever feeling the effects of the nitrous oxide than to have him be uncomfortable from its effects in any way.

Tell the patient that the first time you keep the concentration quite low and the next time you will be able to increase it a little as he gets more accustomed to the nitrous oxide/oxygen.

Whenever the patient is feeling the gas and perceiving it as a good time you are okay. Ask often: "are we having fun yet?" or "if it's fun on the gas?" If they stay positive the experience is positive.

It cannot be stressed enough here the importance of close monitoring of the patient who is on nitrous oxide/oxygen. It is imperative that someone is with the patient AT ALL TIMES when the patient is on nitrous oxide/oxygen. If you ever observe the hands placed over the stomach -- turn the concentration down immediately and talk him through the procedure. This is an early consistent warning sign that something may be coming up, and that is literal. You can usually talk him out of any nausea with your calming voice.

THE PRIMARY DENTITION
AND NITROUS OXIDE/OXYGEN ANALGESIA

Virtually all routine operative procedures on the primary dentition can be completed with nitrous oxide/oxygen analgesia without any local anesthetic.

> Our office changed our approach to children's dental care as a result of reading the article by Dr. John Wilde in Dentistry Today (August, 1993). He reported that most deciduous teeth including proximals with Toffelmeier bands can be successfully treated using only nitrous oxide/oxygen analgesia and no local anesthetic.
>
> Now, we offer all children the AM-FM headphones (we use SONY - Walkman®), show them the controls, let them tune in their favorite station and turn the volume up as high as they like - - - - WOW!
>
> Then we put the nitrous oxide/oxygen analgesia on and adjust it as necessary - it does not usually take too much.

We do six-handed dentistry on children and often, if the child is doing well and we have the parent's approval, we finish all four quadrants reminding them how much fun we're having all along the way.

The article in <u>Dentistry Today</u>, August of 1993, talks about 44% (4 parts nitrous and 5 parts oxygen) for treating deciduous teeth and up to 50% for injections. Others claim that some oral surgeons use nitrous oxide up to 80% (and that we should have no problem using nitrous oxide up to 60%). We find that if the patient is breathing through his nose (the rubber dam helps this happen) then around 40 to 45% usually suffices. Watch closely and if the patient puts his hands over his stomach or if the eyelids start to get heavy, turn the nitrous oxide concentration down.

You will only have the patient at this level for a very brief time; as soon as the last matrix bands are removed he can go to 100% oxygen and get flushed out thoroughly.

He may experience some slight tiredness afterward, but once we mention that it is time to head for the toy box he comes right out of it and is raring to go.

Children are open to suggestion and by telling them "We surely have a good time when you come to see us." or "It's sure fun flying up among the clouds, isn't it?" they are usually convinced of the good time (at least relatively pain-free time) and are eager to return.

Children looking forward to their next dental visits are great promoters for a dental practice.

The next chapter, on the merits of Rubber Dam and the Modified Rubber Dam Technique, may be the one which will be the most beneficial. Hope you enjoy it!

CHAPTER 11

RUBBER DAM

Rubber Dam is wonderful, and, with the Modified Rubber Dam Technique, where close to zero time is spent in its placement, it is the best efficiency bargain in dentistry.

RUBBER DAM - One of the best kept "secrets" in Dentistry.

If you could get 90% of the benefits of the rubber dam with "zero time" invested in the placement, would you be interested? My guess is your answer is at least "perhaps."

The rubber dam usage presented here has evolved during twenty years of practice. By routinely using this Modified Rubber Dam Technique for all operative and crown and bridge as well as endodontic procedures, one can become so proficient that placement is no obstacle whatsoever.

The advantages of rubber dam use are so widely touted that it is obvious that a system of use which affords the majority of the benefits without the frustration of placement is a Godsend.

163

Those dentists who routinely use the rubber dam effectively will be found to be happier and much less stressed out.

Imagine what your response would be if you were asked "Would you rather work in a room with the tongue and cheek present or would you prefer to work in a room without the tongue and cheek?"

MAXIM

WORK IN A ROOM WITHOUT
THE TONGUE AND CHEEK
-- USE RUBBER DAM

Even though the Modified Rubber Dam Technique may seem crude by Ivory Tower standards, it is functional and very valuable while the techniques taught in many dental schools have fallen by the wayside for many practicing dentists.

The reward vs. time spent in application slope is dramatically more favorable for the Modified Technique:

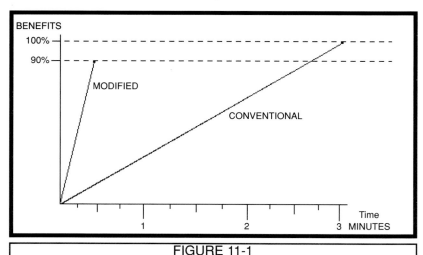

FIGURE 11-1
Note Steep Slope of Reward vs. Time Graph for the
Modified Rubber Dam Technique

164

When you can attain 90% of the benefits for 6% to 8% of the time expenditure you have a great deal!

Train your assistants to prepunch the rubber dam. With only a small amount of your time your assistants can learn to prepunch rubber dams using only the largest punch hole in the following pattern:

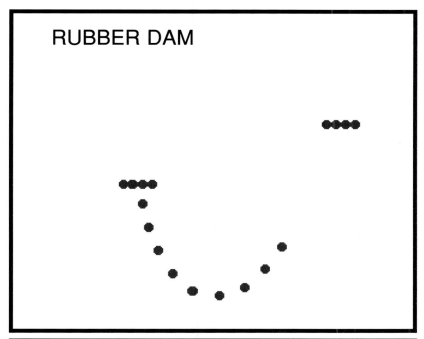

FIGURE 11-2
4 Connected Large Holes
The Remainder Being Single Large Holes

The series of holes are designed to go from the first molar to the opposite cuspid in any quadrant but who is counting? You can often skip teeth or put two teeth through one hole -- how ever, it all falls into place.

Just keep in mind that the object is to keep the cheek and tongue out of the operating field and to allow visibility of the tooth or teeth being operated upon. As a bonus, it will keep debris out of the patient's mouth.

MAXIM

**THE MORE YOU USE THE RUBBER DAM
THE HAPPIER YOUR "DENTAL LIFE" WILL BE!**

RUBBER DAM CLAMPS:

This section reminds me of a patient talking about his motorcycling trip. When asked what kind of bike he had he looked at me a little askance, was silent for a while, then blurted out, "There is only <u>one</u> manufacturer of motorcycles."

This, needless to say, was a Harley Davidson owner! We all had a good laugh and I learned my lesson -- there is only one rubber dam clamp and it isn't even a rubber dam clamp at all! It is an Ivory #21 cotton roll holder - and it is not manufactured any more due to "lack of demand." A rubber dam clamp solution is currently being sought.

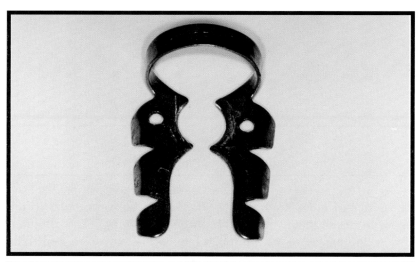

FIGURE 11-3
#21 Ivory Cotton Roll Holder

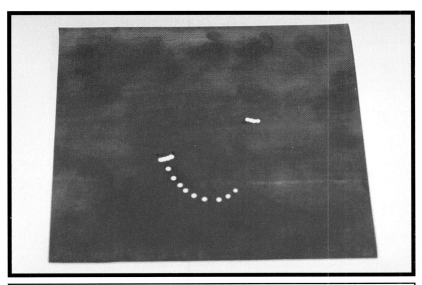

FIGURE 11-4
The single hole in the upper right can be used
to isolate any single tooth in any quadrant.

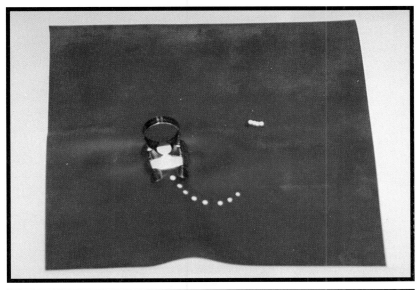

FIGURE 11-5
Modified Rubber Dam Technique

167

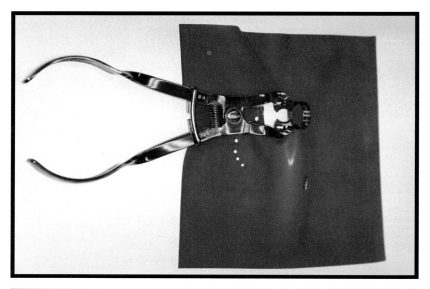

FIGURE 11-6
Modified Rubber Dam Technique

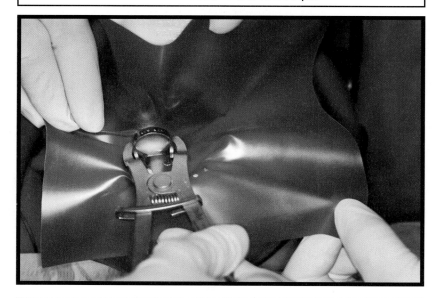

FIGURE 11-7
Modified Rubber Dam Technique

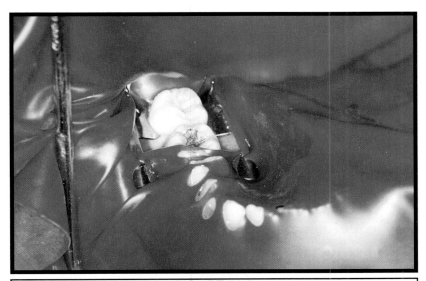

FIGURE 11-8
For occlusal restoration on #31 -
Modified Rubber Dam Technique

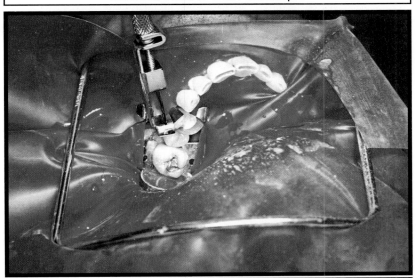

FIGURE 11-9
Rubber Dam in place for occlusal on #3; do on #5; m on 8;
and m on 9 - Modified Rubber Dam Technique

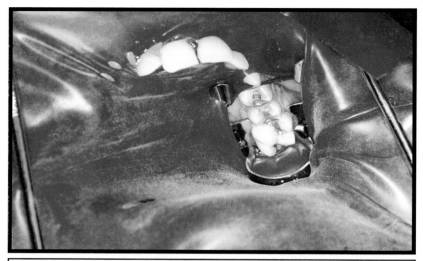

FIGURE 11-10
Rubber Dam in place for d on 9; m on 10; mod on 13;
mo on 14 - Modified Rubber Dam Technique

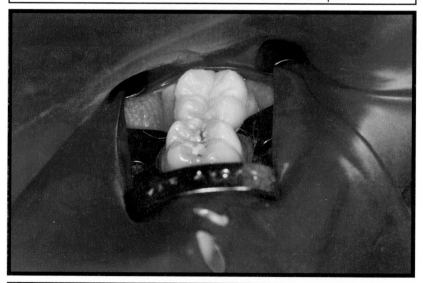

FIGURE 11-11
Height of contour is still below the tissue on #18, #21 cotton
roll holder was placed backwards on #19 to expose #18 and #19
for occlusal restorations - Modified Rubber Dam Technique

The #21 Cotton Roll Holder works on all permanent 1st and 2nd Molars as well as deciduous 2nd Molars.

The only possible exception is we very occasionally use an Ivory 2A on a bicuspid if there is not a molar in the quadrant of operation.

Operative procedures require having a system, possibly starting with the upper right quadrant and following to upper left quadrant then lower left and finally lower right just as the numbering system goes 1 through 32. Our assistants know that we start with the smallest number or letter and work our way up the numbers or through the alphabet. Therefore, when the dentist arrives at the patient's side, all burs are in place, all hand pieces have been checked to assure water is to the burs, tray and materials are ready, topical is placed, anticipated medicaments are ready, napkin is on the patient, the patient is comfortable and reclined to working position and engaged in conversation. The #21 clamp is in place in the rubber dam and positioned for the quadrant the assistant knows we will be starting with. The rubber dam forceps are locked onto the clamp and it is only one smooth move away from the target tooth.

Once the quadrant is anesthetized, you can place the rubber dam and go to work, informing the patient to raise their hand at any time if we are not having fun.

MAXIM

YOU CANNOT DO WELL
WHAT YOU CANNOT SEE WELL!

The rubber dam, by keeping the tongue and cheek out of the way and applying a constant opening tension, which gradually fatigues the closing muscles of the mouth, gives you a continually wider access in which to operate. This wider access and dry field greatly facilitate the smooth and efficient completion of your procedure. The wider opening alone is well worth the slight effort of placing the rubber dam.

These rubber dam placements are different from flossing through all of the contacts and inverting the dam around every cervical area of every tooth taught in many dental schools. The fact that such a high percentage of dentists are not currently using rubber dams suggests that the traditional method of rubber dam placement has been voted down by many.

Depending on the procedure you can often just pop the #21 clamp over a second molar and do occlusal fillings on 1st and 2nd molars without flossing through any contacts. If the first molar is not fully visible, pull the dam forward and pull a web of the rubber dam through any contact. The contact distal to the cuspid is often an easy contact to get the rubber dam through.

If you have occlusal fillings on 18, 19, 20 and 21, then you often can pull a rubber dam web through 19-20 contact and the next web through 21-22 contacts.

MAXIM

RUBBER DAM IS TO DENTISTRY
WHAT FLOSSING IS TO HOME DENTAL CARE

Using the Modified Technique the rubber dam affords so much benefit for so little effort!

MORE ON RUBBER DAM - - - OR IS IT RUBBER DAMN?

Most dentists are aware of the benefits of rubber dam. However, for many the time and frustration of placement outweigh the benefits.

Placing the rubber dam in nearly "zero time" is possible with the following approach:

Use 6 x 6 heavy rubber dam and only the largest punch hole. The dental assistants prepunch the dam using 3 or 4 connected largest holes for the molar and single largest holes for the other teeth. (They prefer the Miltex rubber dam punch with the terminal hinge.)

Our dental assistants have the dams universally punched with the clamp in position on the rubber dam when the dentist arrives at the patient's side.

We use the Young rubber dam frame with our rubber dam technique.

Now that we have the Modified Rubber Dam Technique in our armamentarium we can easily and confidently move on to Pedodontics in the next Chapter.

CHAPTER 12

PEDODONTICS

"Kids say the darnedest things"!

Art Linkletter

A few moments spent with the small patients in a practice can be like a breath of fresh air in a hectic schedule.

I am reminded of Art Linkletter's radio and television programs in which he had conversations with children. If you can find some tapes of these old programs, they would be fun to watch and may help you get the hang of dealing with children.

Our office sees a lot of children. One of our favorite child patient/dentist conversations goes like this:

Dentist: "How old are you?"

The patient responds, "Six."

Dentist: "How old would you like to be if you could be any age?"

Patient: "Eight."

Dentist: "What could you do if you were eight?"

Patient: "I'd get to stay up until 8:30 at night like my brother."

And the patient who is five would like to be six so he could ride the school bus.

And the patient who is eleven would like to be twelve so he could take firearm safety classes.

And on and on....

Take a break, have a chat, have fun, but BEWARE you will sometimes end up on the short end of the conversation.

Recently, while having a long 'round-a-bout' chat with a very fluent 7-year-old girl, when asked how old she would like to be she replied she would like to be 18 years old. Somewhat in shock, I muttered, "What could ... well ... um ....ah .... let's take a look at your teeth." The staff roared with laughter at my expense. Doesn't your staff just love it when you get in over your head?!!

So, children in your practice can be a great blessing and a lot of fun -- enjoy the little ones. They are precious commodities as they are the patients, dentists, and leaders of tomorrow.

Since the assistants have the operatory set up and the patient is ready to begin, let's take a look around the operatory --

SET-UP FOP PEDODONTICS PROCEDURE:

		BURS IN PLACE	
SLOW	**HI**	**HI**	**HI**
#4	**Hourglass**	**Pointed**	**35**
		Diamond	

Operative tray is on the mobile cart and unwrapped.

Mirror is coated with Ultradent No-Fog®.

Water is up to the burs.

Rubber dam with clamp and forceps are in place and ready to insert. The #21 clamp fits the deciduous molars as well as the permanent molars.

Young rubber dam frame is ready.

High volume evacuator tips are in place.

Saliva ejector is ready.

Nitrous Oxide/Oxygen is ready with the pedodontic mask.

Chart and x-rays are in place.

Bib has been placed on the patient.

The patient is ready to begin.

177

Topical anesthetic has been placed around deciduous molar where the rubber dam will button on.

The patient is placed in operating position.

READY for the dentist.

PEDODONTICS can be a large part of a growing practice and may well be your niche if you have a gift of getting along well with children.

A practice can expand rapidly if it is located in an area where there is a generous supply of children and/or where a Pedodontist is not conveniently available.

If you feel this is your forte', inform other dentists in the area. Probably they all have a few children they would gladly send to you. Once you have completed a few challenging children, the regular ones are so easy it is almost fun!

There are countless promotional items for children in the dental catalogues. Take their pictures and make buttons out of their photographs, give away big teddy bears, sponsor drawings for bicycles, have coloring contests and so forth. Children represent a large market segment; many parents place a higher priority on their children's dentition than they do on their own.

Many of us get plenty of kids without promoting them, but it is a legitimate group to market to and may be a very good way to get started.

Our office treats all pedodontic patients six-handed so that the patient can be completed while he still is having fun. Kids are very susceptible to suggestion and something like "We sure have a good time when you come to see us." or "...nothing to it for the boys." or "Sometimes I think the girls do better than the boys." or "**WOW**, you can open **WIDE** -- you surely did surprise me!" will tend to increase

178

their cooperation even more.

We use nitrous oxide/oxygen analgesia only and no local anesthetic on all routine operative procedures on the primary dentition. For pulpotomies and extractions we do add local anesthetic after the nitrous oxide/oxygen has them feeling good. We even occasionally do a facial restoration on a lower 1st or 2nd permanent molar with just nitrous oxide/oxygen and no local anesthetic. Avoiding the mandibular block is a great help in convincing these kids that "We are having a good time."

Because kids are so susceptible to suggestion, especially from an authority figure, we let them play "The Spaceship Game" and "Fly along like an astronaut." We tell them "I can't wait until you come to see us again." "We're sure having fun now!" We also often tell them, "You're the best patient we've had yet today."

We use rubber dam for virtually all pedodontic procedures. We usually rub a little topical anesthetic where the rubber dam clamp "buttons onto the tooth." See Chapter 11 for full details on the Modified Rubber Dam Technique.

Everyone gets a portable radio headset to listen to and the kids can crank the volume up as much as they like!!! We use the SONY Walkman® with rechargeable batteries and have no complaints with the way they hold up. They even seem to bounce when they are dropped to the floor periodically.

As long as the patient is doing well, one of our receptionists asks the parents if they would "like us to get as much completed as we can today." We will often do all four quadrants and explain to the parent that Johnny was such a good patient and having so much fun we were able to finish his restorations today!!

The parents are happy, the patient is happy and proud, the assistants are happy and most of all, the dentist is happy!

Recently, as I approached an eight year old male patient he reported "My classmate said I should come here to his dentist because he is silly and looks like the absent-minded professor. He wears ties that have cartoons on them. Sometimes he wears a tie that looks just like a Walleye -- Yup, this is the guy."

Patients referring patients -- the key to your success.

In the next Chapter we will explore the world of Root Canal Therapy!

CHAPTER 13

Root Canal Therapy

If this tooth were in my mouth I would want a root canal treatment and a crown on it.

The root canal candidate is one who may well become one of your BEST marketers. The patient in severe pain remembers a long time and often tells many about his or her quick relief.

Our goal is to get the emergency patients out of pain promptly, with a minimal of disturbance to our busy schedule.

In our office if a patient is in pain we get them in right away. For the routine root canal treatment, the dental assistant has the patient comfortably seated in the operatory, and the offending tooth is located -- usually by the patient and the dental assistant first -- then it can be confirmed by the dentist. After profound anesthesia has been established by the dentist, when necessary, the tooth can usually be opened quickly. On the first appointment it is nice to get an x-ray with reamers in place, extricate the nerve tissue, rinse with sodium hypochlorite, dry, medicate with camphorated parachlorophenol and seal with Cavit® in a minimal amount of time. The receptionist will reschedule the patient in 5 to 7 days for the next treatment.

OPERATORY SET UP FOR
ROOT CANAL TREATMENT PROCEDURE:

BURS IN PLACE			
SLOW	**HI**	**HI**	**HI**
#4	**Hourglass**	**1558**	**35**

THE EFFICIENT DENTAL ASSISTANTS HAVE:

The operative tray out on the mobile cart, unwrapped AND

The Root Canal Treatment tray in place and checked to confirm its completeness.

The dentist's favorite burs in the handpieces as shown above.

All handpieces primed to assure water is to the burs.

Aspirator tips in both high volume evacuation hoses.

Saliva ejector in place.

Confirmed that we have a satisfactory periapical film of the tooth or teeth on which the root canal treatment is anticipated. If not, they have taken and developed any necessary films and have placed all such x-rays out for the dentist's re-inspection prior to starting the procedure.

The patient's chart out to view.

The rubber dam clamp in the rubber dam.

The rubber dam forceps in the rubber dam clamp ready to place in the mouth.

The gutta percha point heater plugged in.

The sonic apex locator ready.

The hypochlorite syringe filled and ready.

The mouth mirror coated with Ultradent No-Fog®.

The patient seated, the patient bib placed, and the chair is adjusted to operating position.

Today's anticipated treatment confirmed with the patient.

Topical anesthesia placed.

If the offending tooth is known, stops are set on all reamers either to the average length from the chart (Figure 9-7) or if this tooth has been treated previously to the length determined from a previous appointment.

Recorded the tooth the patient reports as being the one giving the trouble (when the patient is able to tell) and confirmed that the patient has the right tooth. Or, if the patient is unable to tell which tooth it is, the dental assistant has some clues such as when the patient closes on a Q-tip on #s 14 and 19 he jumps but is unable to determine which one is causing the problem -- we have periapical films of both teeth.

Either way, it is the dentist's responsibility to confirm the dental assistant's estimate or to determine which tooth is causing the discomfort.

THE DENTAL DETECTIVE

Determining which tooth is causing your patient's pain can be a most interesting challenge.

While many offending teeth can be located readily, some can be more evasive.

Following is a hierarchy of tests most relied upon, - THE MOST RELIED UPON FIRST:

I.   <u>Symptoms and Patient History</u>

Listen most carefully to your patient. They will very often lead you right to the tooth which is causing the pain. No other human being has the intimate perspective that the patient is privy to.

When the patient reports "The whole side of my head hurts" ask them to think back a day or two, or a week or a month to when the pain began...and which tooth did they first notice bothering. When they are able to recall which tooth it started with it often is a good clue.

Verify to your satisfaction and then proceed.

II.   <u>Pain to Percussion</u>

Prior to tapping on the tooth with your mirror handle simply touch possible offenders with your finger. This is often all that is necessary.

184

The tooth most tender to percussion is <u>almost</u> always the one causing the problem.

III.   <u>Ice or Heat</u>

IV.   <u>Response to Pressure - Patient biting on a Q-tip</u>

V.   <u>Ausculatory Percussion</u>

VI.   <u>Electronic Pulp Tester</u>

Long before this list is exhausted you will (usually) have your tooth located. However, if you end up more perplexed than you started -- beware of the possibility of the ***OTHER TOOTH SYNDROME - (OTS).***

OTHER TOOTH SYNDROME - (OTS)

Several years ago I saw a patient who reported severe pain of sufficient magnitude to repeatedly wake her up at night. She reported this pain in tooth number 20.

Upon examination, evidence to be comfortable with initiating root canal treatment could not be gathered.

During the next several weeks this patient presented at least a dozen times.

The staff was very much amused by my being total-ly perplexed to the point of "walking down the hall talking to himself" as one of the staff reports.

As I was walking out the back door of the office one night after a particularly tough day, one of the assis-tants reported, "'Flossie's coming in to see you again tomorrow."

At 3:00 a.m. the following morning I awoke abruptly with the thought "I'm going to tap every tooth in her head today."

She responded severely to percussion on <u>tooth number 10</u>. Root canal therapy was initiated and the symptoms on tooth number 20 disappeared immediately and permanently!

The patient was happy and the dentist was relieved.

Since there was no logical explanation for this, I would be interested to hear from others who have had similar experiences.

The point of the OTHER TOOTH SYNDROME (OTS) is that you must be careful in diagnosing root canal candidates; teeth can and will give you some very bizarre symptoms over the years. Be aware of sinus problems which can manifest in the dentition. This will often involve several adjacent teeth.

Watch for the hyperextended (super erupted) tooth in one arch, say #3 which is abscessed but not hurting; however the occlusion is traumatizing #30, which is bothering today.

Be aware that more than one tooth may be involved -- investigate -- get a detailed history of the problem. Trauma? Pain weeks or months earlier? Recent restorations? With sufficient questioning the patient often will lead you to the clue you are looking for.

Occasionally adjacent teeth will appear to be the co-culprits.

If you suspect that more than one tooth may be involved, inform the patient and begin with your favorite candidate tooth - keeping the back door open to initiate another root canal later on the same day, if necessary.

Percussion seems to be the most consistently reliable test. Be aware of the ausculatory element of percussion as well as getting the patient's feedback from their vantage point -- this will usually be sufficient to confirm your suspicions.

The next best test available seems to be thermal. The dental assistants wrap a small ice cube in a 2 X 2 gauze and smash it with the amalgam well. (They really like that smashing process for some reason. Maybe it's a vent! Purchasing an ice crusher has been considered, but it might spoil the assistants' fun.)

With a little chip of ice in the cotton pliers begin checking the suspect teeth with the one closest to the center of the earth because the cold water from the melting ice is pulled by gravity and will drip on untested teeth if you start away from the center of the earth. Have the patient let you know as soon as he feels the cool. When he feels it without severe pain and the cool sensation subsides soon, the tooth usually is fine. Always have the topical anesthetic in place and the anesthetic syringe loaded and ready to inject when you bring out the ice because the problem tooth may cause the patient excruciating pain. Apologize (from the heart) and inject immediately.

If you suspect a gangrenous pulp, heat will readily confirm this!!

After establishing profound anesthesia, if indicated, making your access opening, and locating the canal(s) place a reamer in each canal with a rubber stopper marking the length of each.

After the x-ray has been taken with the reamers in place the assistant records the reamer lengths as we remove the reamers; later she records them in a grid on the chart as follows:

		RL	DL
RL= Reamer Length	m	19	
DL= Diagnostic Length	d	14	
m= Mesial	L	21	

L= Lingual

d= Distal

When the x-ray is returned after developing we decide on a diagnostic length of 20 for the mesial canal, 21 for the lingual canal and take a swag estimate of 20 for the distal canal.

At this point the dental assistant fills in the diagnostic lengths and circles those we are comfortable with on the mesial and lingual canals.

For the distal canal the 6mm estimation is much too much for comfort so it is not circled. It is to be checked and confirmed at the next appointment.

		RL	DL
RL= Reamer Length	m	19	(20)
DL= Diagnostic Length	d	14	20
m= Mesial	L	21	(21)

At the next appointment we will begin by placing a reamer in the distal canal to 19 or 20 mm and taking an x-ray in an attempt to confirm our 20mm estimate. The assistant will have the stops on all the reamers set at 21mm (the length of the longest circled diagnostic measurement) prior to the dentist's seeing the patient.

On the second appointment, if the tooth is asymptomatic and we are able to get it dry, we usually fill with gutta percha. This elimination of an appointment reduces chairtime and therefore increases efficiency. When symptomatic or if we are unable to get dry we schedule the traditional third appointment.

We currently are putting more and more patients on antibiotics during treatment and this regimen appears to facilitate the procedure.

Perhaps 1% or 2% of our endodontic cases are sent to a specialist, but only after a valiant attempt has been made to complete them first.

You learn by doing -- conquer the tougher ones and the rest look easy!

"REPETITION IS THE MOTHER OF SKILL!"

"We grow by stretching. It is all right to feel stretched by the end of the day -- you are growing!"

Throughout this chapter we have stayed pretty close to the traditional root canal methods. This is safe, this is accepted, and you will not go too far wrong going down this path. However, it is conservative.

We are currently performing selected root canal cases, where no swelling is involved, in a single appointment. This technique saves two appointments from the conventional method and is a boon to efficiency.

We are also experimenting with electronic apex locators, and warm gutta percha obturation. We are taking a guardedly optimistic approach on both of these and believe that a significant breakthrough may be on the horizon.

Just in case the tooth cannot be saved, let's take a look at Removable Partial Dentures in Chapter 14.

CHAPTER 14

REMOVABLE PROSTHETICS

"The arrangement of artificial teeth to make them appear natural requires study and training to differentiate between that which is natural and in good taste and that which is unnatural and in poor taste."

Textbook of Complete Dentures, Fifth Edition, p.330, 1993
Arthur O. Rahn and Charles M. Hartwell, Jr.

REMOVABLE PARTIAL DENTURES:

Removable partial dentures are often the best solution for your patient's dental needs. Do not overlook this as a viable option for your patient.

In situations where you have good bone support, but fixed bridges are contraindicated for any of several reasons, removable partial dentures may be the answer.

MAXIM

ALWAYS CONSIDER PLACING SURVEY CROWNS WITH RESTS ON ABUTMENT TEETH PRIOR TO PARTIAL DENTURE CONSTRUCTION

Always assess the possibility of placing survey crowns with rests on the patient's abutment teeth. This will ensure an excellent end result and a happy patient. Also, with reasonable home care and regular dental checkups and prophylaxis the patient will be happy five, ten, and fifteen years from insertion. When you do it right you usually only have to do it once and it is better for the patient. Even though there is more of an investment up front, it is less expensive for the patient in the long run.

Be sure to remove all questionable teeth prior to partial denture construction so the patient can expect to be trouble-free for an extended period of time.

On lower arches when you have good solid cuspids you may consider sacrificing the bicuspids if they are at all questionable. Then place survey crowns on the cuspids.

Carefully evaluate the lower incisors and make a decision whether to keep them or remove them prior to lower partial denture construction. This decision can be made based upon radiographs, mobility, oral hygiene and patient motivation or enthusiasm about taking care of their remaining teeth. If you have an in-house laboratory, as we suggest, any or all lower incisors can be added in an hour or so if you do have to sacrifice them at a later date.

192

Please remember, it is up to you to make the decision and present it to the patient. The patient cannot be asked to decide what is best for himself as he does not have enough information on which to base an educated decision. He will probably opt for a complete lower denture if given a chance. We all know this is most likely not in his best interest. **IMPORTANT POINT -- SHOW THE PATIENT HIS OPTIONS, EXPLAIN WHY YOUR CHOICE IS HIS BEST OPTION AND HAVE IT PRESENTED TO THE PATIENT, OR PRESENT IT YOURSELF; LET'S SAY, TWO SURVEY CROWNS ON 22 AND 27 AND A LOWER PARTIAL. IF THE PATIENT IS UNCOMFORTABLE WITH THIS TREATMENT, YOU SHOULD LOOK AT OTHER ALTERNATIVES; FOR INSTANCE, A LOWER PARTIAL WITHOUT CROWNS. JUST LOOK AT ONE OPTION AT A TIME UNTIL YOU GET A FIT WITH THE PATIENT'S FINANCIAL AND EMOTIONAL SITUATION.**

ALWAYS present the patient with samples of removable partial dentures so he is aware of the type of appliance you are talking about.

In summary, make the treatment decision and inform the patient that proper home care and regular office visits will allow him to keep his remaining precious teeth for the rest of his life. Then if the patient does lose a tooth five years down the road to periodontal disease, and has missed ten consecutive recall appointments, he is aware it is his fault and not your responsibility.

PARTIAL DENTURE TECHNIQUE: We use alginate in a stock tray with a bead of wax around the entire periphery -- see photo. Modern Materials utility wax 3/16" x 11" - Order #569-1329 - Henry Schein.

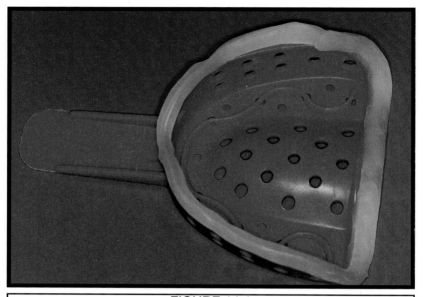

FIGURE 14-1
Dental Assistants select trays and place
bead wax around the periphery

THE DENTAL ASSISTANT CAN:

1.   Check for tori.

2.   Confirm that we have x-rays and take and
        develop any which are needed.

3.   Select the impression trays.

4.   Take the opposing alginate impression.

5.   Place the bead of utility wax around the periphery
        of the tray and have our favorite occlusal rest
        preparation bur in the high speed handpiece.

6.   Have baseplate wax in hot water for bite registration.

7. Help the patient select a shade.

8. Fill out the laboratory prescription to the extent she can prior to the dentist's dictation.

9. Show the patient samples of removable prosthetics.

10. Have mirror and explorer out and mirror coated with Ultradent No-Fog®.

The dentist can check the need for occlusal rests, prepare the same if indicated, make the alginate impression, take the bite, dictate laboratory instructions; and go on to the next patient. The assistant then pours the models, packs the models, along with the bite and prescription, and sends the package to the dental laboratory for processing.

When we have a tooth-born occlusion which the laboratory can articulate we usually take a wax bite (Base Plate Wax folded over into 3 thicknesses and placed in hot top water) which the patient bites into in centric occlusion. (See photo) (Modern Materials Baseplate Wax - Pink Regular -- Order # 569-4545.) Henry Schein.

FIGURE 14-2
Base Plate Wax folded into 3 thicknesses in hot water

In this case we instruct the laboratory to "Go to Finish."

The second time we see the patient we insert the partial denture, adjust if necessary, check the occlusion, and we are finished.

Often total chair time is fifteen minutes or less and the dentist's time may be as little as five minutes. This is a clear example of efficiency in action.

When we do not have sufficient occlusion, such as a posterior extension case abutting on the lower cuspids, we instruct the laboratory to construct the framework and return with wax pads for the bite registration. We take this bite with alu wax and then go to finish.

(See Alu wax in bowl of hot water - Chapter 9 - Figure 9-11.)

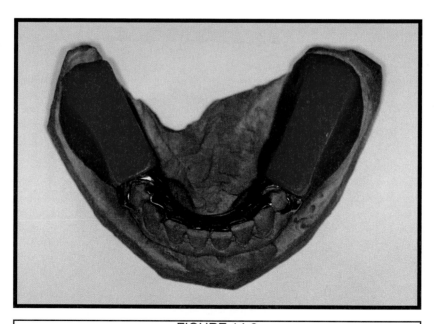

FIGURE 14-3
Bite rim with wax blocks as returned from the laboratory.
Reduce wax free of occlusion then add alu wax.

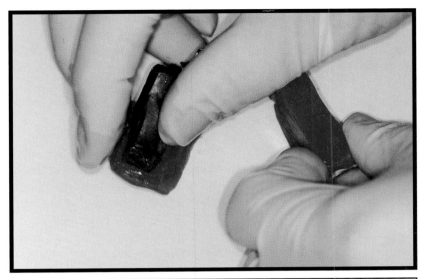

FIGURE 14-4
Mold warm alu wax to bite block.

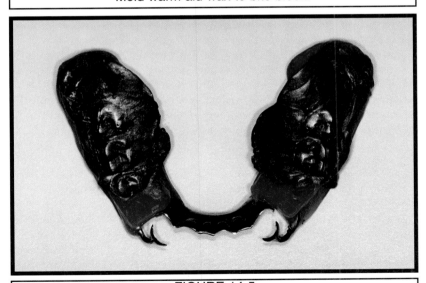

FIGURE 14-5
Results of patient's closing in centric. Entire
bite process in a couple of minutes when the
assistants have everything ready.

Removable Prosthetics can be fun, easy and rewarding!

Always have the patient pick the shade with the assistant's help and when the finished product gets back compliment the patient on a fine job of picking a great shade (this reminds him that it was his selection in case he does not particularly care for it.) He will tend to defend his decision on shade selection.

If the removable prosthetic appliance is a bit tight going in (possibly some drifting during construction time), explain to the patient that it is normal for it to be "snug" for a few days. Emphasize the importance of keeping it in and the teeth will adjust, becoming a little more comfortable each day until eventually it becomes completely comfortable. The key here, of course, is that he keep the appliance in his mouth. It will not fit better if it stays on his bureau or bathroom lavatory for a month.

FULL DENTURE TECHNIQUE:

Full dentures may well present one of our greatest challenges!

Perhaps the most important appointment is the first appointment. This is the time to make the decision whether or not to take on the task of making your patient a denture. It is most important to establish good rapport prior to agreeing to accept the challenge. No rapport - no denture - it's that simple! Just tell the patient, "I really do not think I will be able to do you any good, Mrs. Jones. I can see from these five sets of dentures you have shown me that your former dentists have tried everything I would try....sorry."

MAXIM

WHEN YOU REALLY DON'T FEEL YOU CAN HELP THE PATIENT TELL THEM YOU REALLY DON'T FEEL YOU CAN HELP THEM.

The patient is likely to respect you for your straightforward honesty and refer her friends to you!

FIGURE 14-6
Initial consultation establishing rapport prior to
agreeing to make the patient a denture.

At this first appointment we inform the patient of a University of Minnesota School of Dentistry study which found the best denture they could find displayed a 15% chewing efficiency as compared with the natural dentition. Next point out their minimal ridge or any other obstacles to success. Finally, if you do decide to proceed, agree only with their promise "to not expect too much." "We'll do everything we can to make this work - just don't expect too much."

Once the go-ahead is agreed upon the quicker you can finish the patient's denture the better. We take alginate impressions in stock trays border trimmed with utility wax. As soon as the impressions are taken a dental assistant swoops into the operatory, picks them up and while the original assistant is helping the patient select a shade the models are poured with slurry water for immediate bite rim construction in our in-house laboratory. The patient returns in an hour for establishing the vertical dimension and bite. At this time the patient selects his midline ("Since you are the only one with one eye on each side of your nose, you tell me where your midline is.") The next visit is the try-in. If all is well with the try-in, which is usually the case when the vertical dimension and bite were accurate, the next appointment is for Insertion.

Dentures can be fun and rewarding once you have completed a sufficient number of cases to catapult yourself up the learning curve to where the view of the denture scene is much more enjoyable.

In summary, our full denture technique consists of:

1.   1st Appointment - establish rapport prior to agreeing to make a denture. Make an alginate impression.

2.   2nd Appointment - establish the vertical dimension and get bite with alu wax.

3.   3rd Appointment - try in - we have the option of a Zoe® wash after a satisfactory try in.

4.   4th Appointment - Insertion.

Now that you are comfortable with Removable Prosthetics let's move on to Fixed Prosthetics in Chapter 15!

CHAPTER 15

FIXED PROSTHETICS

Do it right the first time -- don't patch it -- Crown it!

Crowns and bridges are probably our finest gifts to our patients. When we restore their teeth and/or arches in this manner, we usually think of it as lasting a lifetime, with reasonable home care and regular dental check-ups.

Once one recognizes that it is in the patient's best interest to crown his broken down teeth as soon as possible and replace his missing teeth with bridges, one is on the right track toward a successful practice and toward doing what is best for his patients.

We owe it to our patients to propose the best treatment available to them. Very often the best treatment is crown and bridge.

MAXIM

WE OWE IT TO OUR PATIENTS TO RECOMMEND CROWN AND BRIDGE TREATMENT WHENEVER IT IS INDICATED

Use lines such as "If that tooth was in my mouth, I would want a crown on it," if you would.

"A bridge surely would look nice in there," and for the guys add "and would make for a much stronger bite" ...while the guys are just as interested in esthetics as women the "strong bite" gives them something masculine as an excuse to proceed.

"Well, I suppose, Doc, if it will make the bite stronger. Let's do it!"

Use whatever it takes for the patient to be comfortable with the dentistry which NEEDS to be accomplished.

If you are not 100% convinced that doing good crown and bridge for your patients is in the patient's best interest then do not read on...go back to the beginning of this chapter and start over. Only proceed once you have yourself totally convinced.

Each of us has to establish a way of "breaking it to the patient" which we can be comfortable with. Following are a few examples of ways of informing the patient that a crown or a bridge is indicated.

Whatever feels most comfortable to you; pick one, try them all, or create your own -- but establish a means of communicating with your patients their need for crowns and bridges:

1. "If that tooth were in my mouth I would want a crown on it!"

2. "If you were my Mom (Dad, Son, Daughter, Brother, Sister) I would want a crown placed

on that tooth."

3.   "My teeth were a lot like yours and I had mine crowned."

4.   "The least expensive and the BEST in the long run is to trim this tooth down and put a crown on it to make it strong again!"

5.   "A porcelain veneer crown to match your other teeth would certainly make a pretty smile."

6.   "A porcelain veneer crown to match your other teeth would last a lifetime with reasonable home care and regular dental check-ups!"

7.   "A porcelain veneer crown would surely look nice."

8.   "Rather than the added expense of patching that tooth up now and having to do a crown soon anyway, we would be farther ahead doing the crown right now."

9.   "I'm just wasting your money and my time by patching any more -- this tooth needs a crown."

10.   "Before you bite down on that tooth and split it up the root we'd better get a crown on it."

By taking a strong positive stance and expecting your patient to go along with your recommendations you can do an amazing amount of crown and bridge work -- a win-win situation.

The desirability of crown and bridge over other options can be exemplified by sharing an experience from the distant past:

In empathy with an insistent patient, we unwittingly tackled a totally broken down molar in an attempt to "just patch it up and get the patient by for a while." After a seemingly endless battle in which we encountered most of the patient factors discussed earlier we had accomplished a restoration which we could only hope the patient would get out of the office before it collapsed -- so we could rest up from our fatigued condition before we had to face that tooth again.

Much to our surprise we didn't see the patient again that day or the next and eventually the fiasco began to fade slightly from our minds.

Then, over three years later, one bright spring day the patient returned and greeted us with, "Hey, Doc, your filling fell out!"

He said, "Do you remember that tooth?"

I responded, "How could I ever forget?"

THE POINT IS:

MAXIM

IF YOU TRY SOMETHING WHICH IS A COMPROMISE IN AN ATTEMPT TO SAVE THE PATIENT SOME MONEY OR BUY THE PATIENT SOME TIME, YOU OWN IT!!!! IT BECOMES YOUR RESTORATION AND IT WILL EVENTUALLY COME BACK TO HAUNT YOU!!! -- DO IT RIGHT THE FIRST TIME. CROWN IT!!!

If the patient totally resists having the tooth crowned, then totally disown it when you do it. Tell the patient outright "This is not the right way to restore this tooth." "You are going to have to have a crown sooner or later -- we can't patch it again and we shouldn't have done it this time. " Get the monkey totally off your back. Now, if he has trouble with that tooth -- you warned him -- it's his fault -- if it lasts a while you are a hero.

The faster you learn to do more crown and bridge work the better you will serve your patients and the more successful you will be.

Good crown and bridge treatment equals happy patients and happy patients equal great referrals.

Don't let a patient talk you out of doing it right!

In our office we do so many unscheduled crowns and bridges it has nearly become routine for the assistants to set up for crown and bridge whenever they see: BROKEN TOOTH, CHIPPED TOOTH, FILLING OUT, POSSIBLE CROWN or BROKEN FILLING on our schedule.

After you have completed a crown or two and your patients see how great they feel and especially how nice they LOOK they start calling the receptionist and saying, "I broke another tooth and I need a crown. When can Doc do it?"

CLINICAL PROCEDURES:

BURS IN PLACE			
SLOW	HI	HI	HI
#4	End Cutting*	Pointed Diamond	1558

* 1.4mm end cutting bur is kept on the Crown and Bridge tray.

THE EFFICIENT DENTAL ASSISTANTS HAVE DONE THE FOLLOWING:

Operative tray is on the mobile cart, unwrapped AND

Crown and bridge tray is in place and checked to confirm its completeness.

All handpieces are primed to assure water is to the burs.

Aspirator tips are in both high volume evacuation hoses.

Saliva ejector is in place.

Patient chart is out for viewing.

Rubber dam clamp is in the rubber dam.

Rubber dam forceps are in the rubber dam clamp ready to place in the mouth.

Mouth mirror is coated with Ultradent No-Fog®.

All the equipment and operatory is checked again for cleanliness.

Brought the patient back into the operatory and seated the patient.

Confirmed that patient is doing fine after last visit if this is a series of visits.

Confirmed today's scheduled treatment with the patient.

Confirmed the presence of a satisfactory current periapical films of ALL TEETH to be crowned. Has taken and developed any needed films. Placed all such x-rays out for the dentist's re-inspection prior to starting the procedure.

Cut the retraction cords for teeth to be prepared and placed them in Astringident® to soak.

Astringident® syringe loaded and ready for use.

Taken an alginate impression of the opposing arch (we use all full arch impressions for our crown and bridge procedures).

Selected the impression trays to be used for crown and bridge impression.

Helped the patient select the shade for esthetic crown and/or bridge.

Prepared the syringe with tip to inject Polysiloxane impression material around the preparations. (We use 3-M Imprint™ Vinyl Polysiloxane and Schein VPS - Vinyl Polysiloxane Putty.)

Topical anesthetic is placed.

Lab slip is on the mobile cart filled out as far as it can be completed prior to treatment.

Loaded the anesthetic syringe.

READY for the dentist.

The dentist arrives and greets the patient, anesthetizes, places the rubber dam, cuts the preparation, packs the retraction cord.

The dental assistant removes the rubber dam, checks to make sure it is all intact, selects and pre-fits temporary crowns free of gingival margins and takes opposing impression, if not taken prior to the dentist's arrival.

The dentist returns, checks the dental assistant's selection and trimming of the temporary crowns, and adjusts them, if necessary, places syringe material into the sulcus while the dental assistant aspirates, keeping the area dry, and pulls the retraction cord. A second assistant mixes the putty.

The dentist places the impression tray; the dental assistant holds the tray as the second assistant sets the timer.

The dentist is free to go to another operatory.

When the timer rings the assistant removes the impression tray with a SNAP. If the dentist is available he stops by after the timer has rung to approve the impression. If the dentist is busy, the assistant runs the impression by him. Upon his approval of the impression the dental assistant places the temporary crown(s) and dismisses the patient to the front office to be scheduled for cementation of the crowns.

It took a while to realize that if a crown is cemented a little out of occlusion it will soon erupt and take its place in the arch just as all the originally erupting teeth do.

MAXIM

ON ALL POSTERIOR CROWNS INSTRUCT THE DENTAL LABORATORY TO TAKE THE CROWN OUT OF OCCLUSION

Have you ever cemented a posterior crown and had it high -- especially the most distal tooth? What happens - you grind and grind and grind and polish and maybe see them the next week and grind and polish some more.

What happens if it's a little out of occlusion?

You cement it and it erupts into occlusion just as every other tooth in both arches did -- naturally.

You choose which method you like best.

TEMPORARY CROWNS

Dental Assistants and Temporary Crowns -- MOVE SLOWLY: This takes much training. Temporary crowns are CRITICALLY IMPORTANT, as you know, and even though this sounds easy, it is not!

Use the following steps in this regard:

Step 1:   The first step in this all-important training process is to have your dental assistant select the temporary crowns for you. (We use Ion® Pre-formed Temporary Crowns and only occasionally construct a custom temporary crown.

Step 2:   Eventually allow your dental assistant to try the temporary crowns in the mouth for you. At this point they must learn to be SUPER CAREFUL of the gingival tissue and not let the patient close down on a too-long crown (occluso-gingivally) and destroy the tissue to the extent you may never see it again.

During this phase the dental assistant is trimming the temporary crowns, you are examining them, showing her the adjustments you make and cementing them.

Step 3:   Only after a dental assistant has successfully trimmed several temporary crowns short of the tissue should you let her place one. After she places the crown and removes excess cement you inspect the product and give her feedback about cement still under the margins or, "looks good," or whatever is applicable.

It is imperative that you check very carefully each temporary which is placed by your dental assistant until she can place the temporary with the exacting results you insist upon. You have to delegate, but it is critical that you monitor the performance and proceed very slowly.

Step 4:   Only after you have checked a sufficient number of her temporary crowns to be totally comfortable is she allowed to finish up from the point of your inserting the impression, as discussed in the preceding text. Even then, periodically spot check a temporary to confirm she is taking her responsibility very seriously.

NOTE: You must be aware of whether or not your dental assistants are able to perform this expanded function in your location.

MORE HINTS FOR CROWN AND BRIDGE:

MATERIALS USED IN CROWN AND BRIDGE: Astringident® from Ultradent; retraction cord from Ultradent; Imprint™ Syringe Material from 3M; Vinyl Polysiloxane VPS Putty from Henry Schein; Zone® Temporary Cement; Ion® Iso-Form® temporary crown forms.

BUR ROTATION: Be aware of bur rotation...looking down through the top of the handpiece your bur is spinning in a clockwise rotation...therefore by moving your bur counterclockwise around the preparation it is cutting more efficiently...try it and you'll see. Observe the difference!

CEMENTING PERMANENT CROWNS: While the assistant is mixing the cement and fills the crown with cement, have her place the crown with cement on the prepared tooth, rather than have her transfer it to you and then you put it in the mouth. This saves a messy transfer, saves the possibility of recovering the tooth from the floor, and keeps the sticky cement off the dentist's gloves. It is also quicker and lets her participate and think, "Which is the lingual?", that is,

"Which way does it go?" The more the assistant gets to THINK AND PARTICIPATE the happier she will be.

PICKING THE SHADE FOR CROWN AND BRIDGE:

Picking the proper shade or shades from the shade guide is a critical matter.

Much effort was expended in dental school to train us in shade selection:

- We studied hues as determined by the dominant wavelength of the light.

- We studied shades and the interception of the rays.

- We studied tints and how adding white lessens the saturation.

- We studied lights.

- We studied incandescence light sources.

- We studied fluorescent light sources.

- We studied natural lighting.

- We were instructed to take the patient to a north facing window to get the true natural light.

- We were *experts* in shade selection by graduation day.

Why, then, is shade selection so difficult?

Of all of the learning curves one might encounter in dentistry this may well be the one which offered the most resistance.

> Once in practice, of course, being the expert, I selected the shades the first few years out of dental school (to my chagrin) that is until one day when I tried in a lady's upper central incisor porcelain fused to metal crown and MY VERY OUTSPOKEN ASSISTANT said (in front of the patient) "That looks terrible. You can't use that!"

> Once the steam quit rolling out of my ears, with the patient's mind obviously having been made up for her, we put the temporary back on the tooth and sent the crown back to the laboratory; this time ordering a shade picked by the very outspoken assistant.

For some reason this shocking experience was a real eye-opener and marked a another milestone in my career -- ENTER DENTAL ASSISTANTS --

The next several years were devoted to having our dental assistants pick the shade... This was definitely an improvement. The next slow advancement was to involve the patient. The assistant would give the patient a mirror and the two of them would pick a shade. This went even better and continues to be an excellent choice

Finally, after years of experimenting, we have evolved the technique of having the patient pick the perfect shade. Since everyone's eyes interpret color a little differently, and since it is the patient we strive to please, it makes good sense to have the patient's input in the shade selection.

IT WORKS BEAUTIFULLY!

If the patient is clearly off base, the assistant is instructed to suggest other alternatives for consideration but to strive to get the patient to make the final selection. (Some older men will not participate -- they say they do not care and then the assistant picks a shade and we have NEVER had a problem with this.) Once the patient has selected a shade the assistant agrees with, the assistant compliments the patient on **HIS** selection.

Upon the dentist's return to the operatory he can confirm that **the patient** has made a great choice. Now it is confirmed and reconfirmed that **the patient** has selected the shade.

Once the crown or partial denture or denture is inserted it is reconfirmed by the assistant, the dentist, other assistants and the receptionists that **the patient** has made a great selection.

Did you ever notice how much more protective and complimentary you are of your own decisions than anyone else's?

Let this fact work for you.

No one rushes to admit to a mistake. The patient doesn't either. Besides, our patients really appreciate being involved in decisions that involve THEIR mouth.

In crown and bridge we will often instruct the laboratory to use A-3.5 cervical 1/3rd and blend to C-1 for the incisal 2/3rds or fake a proximal restoration on the distal of #10 or place vertical striations of tan coffee stain or mix A-1+B-1 for the entire tooth.

TREATMENT ALTERNATIVES

MAXIM

SHOW YOUR PATIENTS THE ALTERNATIVES
THEN HELP THEM MAKE THE DECISION

We owe it to the patient to give him alternatives. However, we also owe it to the patient to make a decision for him which is comfortable or at least palatable to his situation.

Unless the dentist is capable of educating the patient sufficiently to make the decision --- and this education would necessarily take at least the four years spent in dental school -- the treatment decision rests solidly on the dentist's shoulders.

Let's take a look at a possible scenario which might go on in some well-meaning dentist's office:

The patient is given four estimates, let's say:

1.   12 _ _ 15 bridge...................................... $1,600.00

2.   12 + 15 survey crowns and
        upper partial denture $1,430.00

3.   Upper partial denture without crowns.....$ 630.00

4.   Upper full denture and ten extractions....$1,000.00

The patient is shown samples of each of these alternatives. Then the patient is to go home and make a decision.

This would be like having a 3-year-old child make the decision to go out in the street to play. They do not have the background or the experience to make a satisfactory decision.

The patient may well opt for the least expensive or the full denture and be "through with it" (they think).

This is why the dentist must take responsibility for the treatment decision.

The dentist's perspective is a legitimate starting point for the discussion with the patient. However, the reaction of the patient to your proposal must be closely monitored.

MAXIM

IT IS THE DENTIST'S RESPONSIBILITY TO PRESENT THE BEST POSSIBLE SOLUTION FIRST

The best possible solution is often crown and bridge. This is how you would want it restored if it were your mouth or your parent's mouth or your sibling's or children's mouths. You must not prejudge that the patient will want the least expensive solution. If you do you are doing your patient and yourself a disservice.

Offer the best possible solution first. Only if the patient objects do you need to go into treatment alternatives.

When you have good bone support, reasonable oral hygiene, and can work out the financial arrangements, you are serving your patients best with crown and bridge.

Be aware, however, that different value systems, different priorities, and different socio-economic conditions all play a tremendous role in the treatment decision. For the dentist to understand this and see the patient's dilemma through the patient's eyes is to really connect with that patient.

The goal is for the dentist to be coming from the position of being totally absorbed in determining what is the best treatment from the patient's perspective! While this may sound trivial at first glance it is far from trivial and in fact, is of utmost importance in your success. The catch is understanding the scenario from the patient's perspective.

In summary, it is the dentist's responsibility to help the patient or the patient and his family make the decision. Once the dentist understands the patient's situation, a decision can be made and treatment begun.

In order to do beautiful crown and bridge work you must have a laboratory that you can work very closely with and which will do exactly as you wish so you join together in synchronicity to make a product as close to perfection as possible.

In our next chapter, Love thy Lab, we will show the importance of using a lab you love!

CHAPTER 16

LOVE THY LAB

Develop a synergistic relationship.

S trive to find a dental laboratory or laboratories with which you can develop good rapport. This makes life in the dental office much more enjoyable for everyone because a compatible relationship will promote better patient care.

How does this happen? By taking responsibility for any complications which occur and working together with the dental laboratory to learn what you can do to make their life easier.

THE DENTIST/DENTAL LABORATORY
RELATIONSHIP PHENOMENON

After having studied this closely for many years I am convinced that at least 90 to 95% of the dental laboratory product problems we encounter have their etiology in the dental office and not in the dental laboratory. Sorry about that fellow dentists -- but that is the way it appears.

This is not unreasonable when you take into consideration that the dentist's working environment is at least 100 times more difficult than the laboratory technician's environment.

Having not done a crown preparation on the bench since the sophomore year in dental school it is tough to imagine how uncomplicated that might be.

We as dentists are in a position to see both sides of the story, we have waxed and cast crowns and set up dentures in dental school and we have worked in the oral cavity with limited visibility, limited space, saliva, tongue, cheeks and moving heads, as well.

The laboratory technician has only seen the bench view perspective in most cases.

I can't help but think if I were a laboratory technician and would see some of the preparations coming in I could be very critical when evaluating the dentist's lack of sufficient occlusal reduction or lack of parallelism or undercuts in the preparations.

Therefore, by offering to take full responsibility when something goes wrong the dental laboratory seems to not allow me to be considered "the responsible party."

The key is probably just don't let problems occur too often.

Communicate with and coach your dental laboratories constantly about how they might make your life a little easier. If the proximal contacts on your crowns and bridges are too tight, let them know you would like them to lighten up on the proximal contacts. If they overdo it, let them know the contacts are now open. They eventually, with your constructive coaching, will zero in on what you want and you will be cementing the crowns "untouched" in most cases.

If you are not happy with your laboratory technician, look around until you click with one, then concentrate on building great rapport. You can easily send cases to several different dental laboratories, examine their work and settle on the one which is most compatible with your priorities.

Our policy is that every patient must be not only satisfied but happy with every aspect of our services. This includes full dentures, partial dentures, crowns and bridges as well as restorations. Any service we provide. If we get just a "hint" a patient is not totally 100% happy with any of the work we have done, we will, without hesitation, replace, remake or redo whatever the patient is not completely happy with.

The dental laboratories we use always absorb their costs in these situations. Because of the rapport we have established and the fact that such remakes are so rare, we're not viewed as the "guilty party," even though we may be the cause of the challenge.

> I recently contacted our crown and bridge laboratory and told them I wanted to get some feedback on my crown preparations such that a year from now I wanted my preparations to be exactly the way they like them. They replied, "the preparations are fine, no problem." I said I wanted my preparations to be the best in their laboratory and told them I would appreciate their coaching to get me to that point so their work would be easier.
>
> I am currently getting some occasional feedback, and I very much appreciate it. Rather than putting up with some of my challenges on a permanent basis, they are now letting me know what I can do to make life easier for them and we are improving the working relationship and the rapport, which was excellent to start with.
>
> It is quite infrequently that we converse on the telephone. However, when we do I routinely leave the conversation a little watery-eyed from emotion with

their sincere expressions of gratitude from the massive workload we are providing and as well, their sincere appreciation for our desire to make their work easier.

This type of rapport is not something which can be measured monetarily.

In the next Chapter we will discuss Operative Dentistry!

CHAPTER 17

Operative Dentistry

"Every man's work, whether it be literature, or music, or pictures, or architecture, or anything else, is always a portrait of himself."

Samuel Butler

OPERATIVE DENTISTRY has been said to be the bread and butter of the general practice. This is definitely true. Therefore, it is very important that we get maximally organized for it. Your efficiency pays great dividends.

Eventually, as the practice grows, the dentist must realize that he has only two hands and a limited number of hours in each day. At this point he must take a closer look at dental auxiliary utilization. The dentist should examine everything he is doing right down to the most minute details and then start delegating anything that anyone else is allowed to do in his location. This contributes to developing a very responsible staff who take a lot of pride in their work.

You can strive toward this goal by continually training and monitoring your dental assistants. The dental assistants can seat the patient, take x-rays, learn of the patient's desires, pre-diagnose for and set up anticipated procedures, place topical anesthetic, load the anesthetic syringe, place the rubber dam clamp in the rubber dam, secure the rubber dam forceps in the clamp while the dentist is still with the preceding patient.

As you get busier and busier you want to do ONLY what no one else is allowed to do.

This is how we get the maximum accomplished in the minimum amount of time -- by utilizing our dental assistants to do all they are legally allowed to do.

Six-handed dentistry works very well for operative dentistry. This way the chairside dental assistant has her own dental assistant to plan a step or two ahead, to mix cements and prepare medicaments, spin the amalgam, get the Copalite ready to pass to the dentist, change burs, if necessary, pack amalgam in the amalgam carrier, and generally free up the chairside dental assistant to aspirate and do whatever else is helpful inside the oral cavity.

This way the primary assistant can keep the aspirator in place and keep the work flow going constantly. With a sufficient number of well-trained auxiliaries, the dentist's focus can be on the tooth or teeth for the entire procedure.

Local anesthesia is often *at least* uncomfortable at injection, takes time to become effective, and may be uncomfortable for an hour or two afterwards.

With the use of nitrous oxide/oxygen analgesia, as discussed in Chapter 10, we are doing operative procedures on all deciduous teeth without local anesthetic. This includes posterior proximal restorations with matrix bands.

Many older patients can have routine operative procedures completed without analgesia, without anesthetic, and without discomfort. This is at least partially due to the secondary dentin having filled in and the pulp having receded sufficiently. Encourage them to try the procedure without anesthetic. Take it a little easy at first, observe their reaction closely, and give them anesthetic if they prefer it. Many are grateful to leave the office with a mouth that is not numb.

We do virtually all of our operative dentistry with the rubber dam in place. As one of my mentors often chided, "I'd sooner give up my high speed handpiece than the rubber dam." Though that may be stretching it a bit, you might say it is at least a toss-up.

Our Modified Rubber Dam Technique (See Chapter 11) keeps the tongue out of the way, the cheek out of the way, and it helps hold the mouth open. It is a barrier between our operating field and the throat. Other than that there are very few similarities to the Dental School rubber dam technique. We never spend more than ten to fifteen seconds "placing" the rubber dam.

EFFICIENCY IN OPERATIVE DENTISTRY IS INCREASED AS THE NUMBER OF HAND TRANSFERS IS REDUCED.

First of all, **NEVER** give up your mouth mirror. University of Minnesota DAU (Dental Auxiliary Utilization) Clinic, Dr. Panky stressed this technique. As you become proficient at working with the mouth mirror tucked in your non-dominant hand, your efficiency will increase markedly.

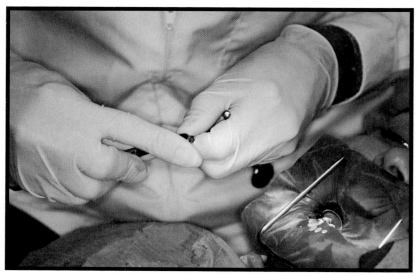

FIGURE 17-1
Dentist working with mouth mirror tucked
in palm of non-dominant hand

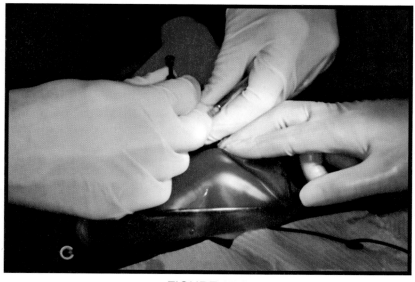

FIGURE 17-2
Dentist working with mouth mirror tucked
in palm of non-dominant hand

SET-UP FOR OPERATIVE PROCEDURE:

BURS IN PLACE			
SLOW	**HI**	**HI**	**HI**
#4	Hourglass	Pointed Diamond	35

The operatory is set up as we learned in Chapter 9:

Operative tray is on mobile cart and unwrapped.

All handpieces are primed to assure water is to the burs.

Aspirator tips are in both high volume evacuation hoses.

Saliva ejector is in place.

Patient's chart and current x-rays are out to view.

Rubber dam clamp is in the rubber dam.

Rubber dam forceps are in the rubber dam clamp ready to place in the mouth.

Amalgam capsule is in the amalgamator when indicated.

Mouth mirror is coated with Ultradent No-Fog®

Shade is selected if composite restorations are scheduled.

Patient is seated and the chair is adjusted to operating position.

Patient bib is placed on the patient.

Last visit's favorable results are confirmed, if applicable.

Today's anticipated treatment is confirmed with the patient.

Composite shades are selected when indicated.

Topical anesthetic is in place.

Anesthetic syringe is loaded.

READY for the dentist.

During cavity preparation procedures the dental assistant holds the aspirator in one hand and her air/water syringe in the other. She is retracting with the air water syringe (unconventional, yes, but effective) or spraying your mirror, if necessary, during the high speed phase, and keeping the field clean.

She is blowing a constant stream of air into one side of the cavity preparation with the evacuator tip on the opposite side when the slow speed is removing decay. You may shudder to think of all the thousands of times you hung up your slow speed to pick up the air water syringe to clear the field to see the extent of the remaining decay or the closeness of the emerging pulp.

Now all you have to do is pause a moment and look to get a clear/clean view. Occasionally you may suggest a little spray and then some air, but you make no more instrument transfers to see where you are with your decay removal project (saving hundreds of transfers a day).

Upon completion of the cavity preparation, the matrix band for the proper quadrant is passed and placed and cavity varnish and wedge follow. Never having to look up as each successive instrument is slapped into your hand like clockwork is truly a beautiful scene. While the band is being placed the Amalgamator is spinning. With the Condensaire Pneumatic Amalgam Packer (See Footnote at the end of this chapter) just point to the desired spot for amalgam placement and the assistant places the amalgam from the carrier. While you pack, she reloads the carrier and then you point again. Each placement deletes two hand transfers. This adds up to 20, 30 or more transfers in a quadrant of amalgams and your dental assistants are more involved and, therefore, less bored.

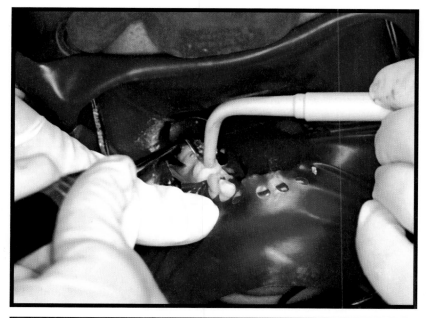

FIGURE 17-3
Dentist is packing amalgam in "T": while dental assistant is placing amalgam in "S". Patient is "floating along" on nitrous oxide/oxygen while listening to the "tunes."

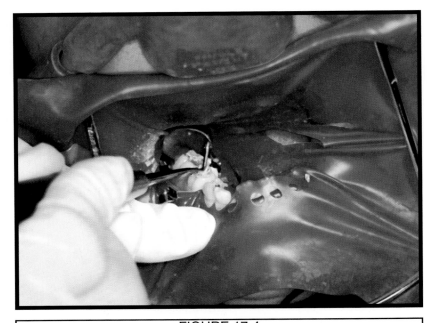

FIGURE 17-4
Dentist using elbow of Condensaire Pneumatic Packer
as an overpacker
(See more on Condensaire, this Chapter.)

While you carve you receive the explorer, carver, explorer, carver and so on. (We have only one carver on each tray and always use the same end). Your dental assistant removes the wedge. She holds it up in your view for a second for an inspecting glance, to confirm it is intact. This saves two more transfers.

After you finish the carving you remove the rubber dam. The dental assistant clips the interproximal rubber dam with the scissors, if necessary, and carefully inspects the rubber dam to make sure it is intact and there is no rubber stuck in the interproximal contacts.

You flush the mouth and dry. The dental assistant places the articulating paper instructing the patient to "close and then open." Examine and adjust the occlusion -- the dental assistant places the

228

articulating paper again (she never put it down - just as the dentist never puts the carver down during this phase of the procedure), instructs the patient to close and grind back and forth. The dentist carves, the dental assistant slips the articulating paper in again, the patient closes and grinds, the dentist inspects the occlusion until he is comfortable with the end product and moves on to the next quadrant or, if completed with the patient, on to the next patient.

Efficiency is not having to wait for:

1. the patient to be seated in the operatory - the patient has been escorted to the operatory and the dental assistant is busily chatting with the patient prior to the dentist's arrival in the operatory.

2. the confirmation of today's treatment - the dental assistant tells the dentist that Jill would like to start with the upper right quadrant because this area has been sensitive or Jack would like to have all of his restorations completed today, if possible.

3. the topical anesthetic - the dental assistant already has placed it.

4. the local anesthetic - the syringe is loaded and ready for the dentist.

5. The rubber dam - the clamp is in the prepunched rubber dam. The rubber dam forceps are in the clamp, one move away from placement, or already placed if the assistant sees you approaching and the patient is anesthetized or prefers not to be anesthetized.

6. Aspirator

7. Cavity varnish

8. Air or water or spray

9.   Medicaments

10.   Amalgam

11.   Wedges

12.   Matrix band

13.   Articulating paper

14.   Bur replacement - the second assistant replaces burs when necessary between restorations or between quadrants or whenever the handpiece is returned to the holder by the dentist.

The fifth and sixth hands of the six-handed team see to it that no delays occur. The dental assistants always make sure your mirror is coated with Ultradent No-Fog®. If you "paint it" with cavity varnish accidentally, simply request a new mirror and the chairside dental assistant's assistant prepares a new mirror and snaps it into your hand.

The third team member can be selecting shades for anterior restorations while the other dental assistant and dentist are doing the preparations. For composite restorations try swirling two or more shades, putting them together but not mixing thoroughly. When a large anterior restoration is all one uniform color, it attracts more attention than one which is a mixture of different shades close to the tooth color -- shades swirled together.

Even though this may sound strange, it works! -- give it a try and see what you think!

We have found six-handed dentistry to be much more efficient than four-handed. It may seem a little slow for the second dental assistant until she understands that she does nearly everything and the first dental assistant primarily aspirates - and blows air, water and spray.

If you are currently practicing four-handed dentistry, begin to become aware of the way a second dental assistant could increase efficiency. Take a close look at any time when you are waiting for your dental assistant to perform a function. Then fantasize how a second dental assistant planning a step or two ahead could have avoided the delay. At this point let your main focus be on spending less of the dentist's time in the completion of a procedure.

Let your imagination run wild and see yourself working, never waiting for anything. That's great -- you have the concept. Now implement it!

Your regular dental assistant will often fight the change. She may see herself as super efficient with no room for improvement.

Presenting it as a way to let a new dental assistant help a little just to learn how we do things has worked successfully for us. This way the regular dental assistant is doing the new girl a favor and does not feel threatened. Eventually when they realize how much more efficient they are together, they become a team and take great pride in how good *they are together."* When you observe this you have arrived at the six-handed dental team plateau. Congratulate yourself! You are becoming much more efficient, and the more efficient you become the more patients you can serve.

FOOTNOTE: - (Condensaire Pneumatic Amalgam Packer"

This is a relatively "slow speed" pneumatic plugger (150 to 250 cycles per second) which has been on the market for many years and has been used by your author for 20 years. THIS IS NOT TO BE CONFUSED WITH THE ULTRASONIC AMALGAM PACKERS which received negative publicity.

"ABOUT THE CONDENSAIRE PNEUMATIC AMALGAM PACKER:

"Following are excerpts from an article titled "Pneumatic versus hand condensation of amalgam: effect on microleakage, by Kenneth W. Chapman (Associate Professor, Department of Primary Patient Care, University of Louisville, School of Dentistry, Louisville, Kentucky 40292) and Gary A. Crim (Professor, Department of Primary

Patient Care, University of Louisville).   QUINTESSENCE INTERNATIONAL
Volume 23, Number 7/1992.

"This study compared two techniques of amalgam condensation
for effect on early microleakage. Class V preparations were
restored with a high-copper amalgam using pneumatic condensation or conventional hand condensation. Significantly less
microleakage was observed when pneumatic condensation was
used. Further, pneumatic condensation proved equally effective
in reducing early microleakage whether or not a dentinal sealant
was used as an intermediary." (Quintessence Int 1992; 23:495-
498.)

Discussion

"Pneumatic condensers are commercially available, but their use
has been discouraged because of their potential to damage the
enamel margins of cavity preparations.[28] Considering that most
cavity preparations designed to receive amalgam call for enamel
cavosurface angles as close to 90 degrees as possible, the argu-
ment to preclude using pneumatic condensers on this basis is not
a strong one.

"One of the advantages of pneumatic condensation is the capacity it gives the operator to apply consistent forces of condensation to freshly triturated amalgam. Such forces help prevent lam-
ination of the amalgam as successive increments are condensed
by bringing any superfluous mercury to the surface. The possibility exists that use of these condensers could result in improved
margination and concurrent reduction in microleakage at the
enamel-amalgam interface.

"The leakage pattern that was observed in the hand-condensed
samples that had no dentinal sealant was interesting. Except for
one specimen, no leakage was detected at the occlusal margin.
However, severe leakage (degree 3) occurred at all gingival margins. Two groups of researchers have reported similar findings.[29,30] It may be possible that more cracking and chipping
occurred along the gingival margin where the enamel was relatively thin. Good adaptation of hand-condensed amalgam to this
margin evidently did not occur.

"A recent scanning electron microscopic study described an
enamel-amalgam interface gap present along the periphery of
freshly placed amalgam restorations that were condensed by

hand.[31] It could be possible that the favorable early microleakage results obtained with pneumatic condensation in the present study could be attributed to the partial or total elimination of such a cavosurface-amalgam gap.

"The results of this study should encourage the use of pneumatic condensers. Their ease of use and low cost and the consistent condensing forces they produce with minimal operator fatigue are benefits that the practitioner can utilize to maximal advantage." (Emphasis added.)

In our next chapter, let's take a look at communicating with the patient and "your dental personality."

CHAPTER 18

PERSONALITY
AND COMMUNICATION

"I rate enthusiasm even above professional skill."
                                        Sir Edward Appleton

As Dale Carnegie stated: "....an engineer's success is only 15% due to their engineering skills and 85% due to their personality." This probably applies to dentistry as well. Studies have shown that there is very little correlation between success in dental school and success in private practice!! Of course clinical knowledge is required for each, but they are two entirely different games requiring some entirely different skills.

Success in attracting and keeping patients is much more closely correlated to personality than to clinical skills. What a blow after spending what seemed like forever gaining clinical skills. Even though this may be a hard pill to swallow it is an opportunity for one to look at one's own personality and benefit greatly from such knowledge.

This information ties in closely with every phase of your practice.

Two ways you can benefit from this information:

1.   You can work on developing a winning personality by:

        -- taking classes and courses
        -- personality clinics
        -- a myriad of audio and/or video cassettes available
        -- private counseling
        -- countless seminars

2.   You can be cognizant of the importance of:

      A.   employing staff members who supplement and complement our personality.

          i.   if you are not a great communicator or do not enjoy communicating, you can employ staff members who are.

          ii.   Personality profile tests can be enlightening and informative for present staff and new employees coming on board.

             a.   For instance, you want an outgoing, smiling, friendly, bubbly, talkative personality at the front desk.

             b.   You want more of an anticipatory, organized and methodical individual as a dental assistant.

      c.   Integrating certain personality types into your practice can play a gigantic role in your success as a dentist.

Having had opportunity to practice with numerous dentists over the years, there are many personality types that patients are comfortable with all the way from shy to boisterous.

Once you know more about your own personality you can look intelligently for a niche to expand into. Many patients appreciate a warm, caring, sincere, trustworthy personality while an outrageous-type personality may adapt well to Pedodontics. Kids may well be entertained by and respond well to an outrageous personality.

Exploit your personal strengths in your marketing. If you are very outgoing and fluent perhaps radio or television talk shows will get you great exposure, and be enjoyable for you. If you are analytical - invent something to get your name in the public eye: The Inventor Dentist!

Let your imagination be your guide. Picture yourself playing a myriad of roles and determine where you are most happy and most natural, then take "massive action" as Tony Robbins says, and head in that direction.

As Nike says, "Just do it!"

Great care must be exercised when working with staff to explain that there is nothing good or bad, superior or inferior about the way we rank on a personality test, but that we are using the personality scale only to explore how we might best all work together to serve the patient and to better understand ourselves and each other -- how we might best complement each other and where each of us would fit in and be the most comfortable, happy and effective.

Many personality tests are readily available. They can be taken in only a few minutes and are incredibly accurate.

> The one we use is one developed by Dr. Geir in the early 1970s at the University of Minnesota available from The Carlson Companies, Phone 800/777-9897, or Q.T. Smith at (612) 489-8552.

If your presentation skills are weak - get a staff member who loves to present and close cases.

This information ties in closely with every phase of your practice. Utilize it to the maximum.

COMMUNICATING WITH THE PATIENT

In our office, much of the communication is delegated. Certain dental assistants communicate more successfully with most patients for a variety of reasons:

A.   A dental assistant is willing to take as much time as necessary to chat with the patient.

B.   The patient may feel at ease asking more questions of the dental assistant.

C.   The dental assistant's vocabulary and understanding are usually closer to that of the patient and therefore her ability to "connect" with the patient is often superior.

Always remember the patient does not have the vocabulary or the background to understand technical dental terms. Therefore, we must communicate in terms which are familiar to the patient. (We must show them examples of partials and crowns and dentures and bridges.)

Even though the patient and the dental assistant think they have communicated, the ultimate responsibility to see that communication has occurred always rests totally on the dentist. If and when a patient does not understand a procedure or a charge or additional appointments to complete a root canal treatment this is the dentist's problem.

COMMUNICATING WITH THE PATIENT
WHO IS IN A COMPROMISED POSITION

Communicating with the patient while the patient is in a compromised position, such as:

    --   a rubber dam in place in the patient's mouth

    --   the patient has a mouthful of impression material

    --   after an extraction while the patient is under instruction to continue biting on a 2 x 2 gauze and unable to open his mouth

    --   the patient's mouth is anesthetized

In these situations all questions can be structured so that the appropriate answer is yes - an affirmative nod - or no - a negative nod.

Instead of saying, "Would you like just that one broken tooth restored today or would you like all of your cavities on that side completed while you are numb?"

Say: "Would you like all of your cavities on that side completed while you are numb?"

Instead of saying: "Would you like this prescription called into Range Drug or Keeley Drug?

Say: "Would you like this prescription called into Range Drug?

If you get a negative...then inquire **"Keeley?"**

Instead of asking the patient after multiple extractions: "Would you like to sit here awhile or are you all right to get up?

Say: **"Would you like to sit here a while?"**

Instead of asking after nitrous oxide/oxygen analgesia, "Are you feeling okay or would you like to breathe some more oxygen?"

Say: **"Are you feeling okay now?"**

While it may take a little thought and practice, structuring your questions to be answered easily with an affirmative or negative nod will facilitate communication with the patient whom we have in a compromised condition.

This can be a helpful, fun and challenging project for the entire staff. Making a game out of it and helping one another learn to structure questions for the patient's convenience will facilitate communication.

YOUR TECHNICAL SKILLS VS.
YOUR COMMUNICATION SKILLS

Reflecting back to Dale Carnegie's assertion that success is perhaps 15% due to technical knowledge and 85% due to personality, and recognizing that the dentist's training is perhaps 85% technical skills with relatively little emphasis on communication skills, it is no wonder that some dentists become frustrated with the private dental practice.

While these numbers are obviously subjective, they are very interesting and pertain as well to our dental environment.

> I was much enlightened as well as amused and informed many years ago when a patient presented with a filling out. (Our registration forms have

always included date of last dental examination and the previous dentist's name.)

The previous dentist had a good reputation among patients and was located in a town about 50 miles away.

When the patient opened her mouth it was a sight to behold. Talk about amalgams with thumbprints on them! The FBI files had nothing on her. All amalgam restorations were functional. No high spots but no carver had distorted the thumbprint amalgams either. This was many, many years prior to latex gloves. As you have discovered, amalgam carvings by any one individual are as unique as is handwriting -- just as you can recognize one's penmanship so can you recognize one's amalgam carvings.

The patient readily offered that the only other dentist that she had ever seen was the one reported on her chart. She added that her "real dentist" was the "best dentist in the world," but he was away on vacation. She needed treatment immediately and was seeking a "pinch hitter" to get her by until his return.

So you pick the number, be it 15%, 10%, 20% or 5% or whatever is attributable to technical skills (clinical skills). Obviously, that very successful dentist had a great personality or superior communication skills.

This is a hard lesson to swallow for those of us who pride ourselves in clinical excellence; however, we are all aware at some level that a patient's ability to evaluate what was done in their mouth is miniscule, at best.

Clinically, it is essential that we are proficient at relieving pain and at doing restorations. Also, we must not leave a high restoration. These, along with esthetics, (patients pick their own shade, laboratory contours and crowns) are the extent of a patient's ability to evaluate our work!! He basically just knows what feels good and is aware of what shows in the mirror.

Personality and communication skills play a large part in the very successful dental practice. These are skills which can be readily improved and developed through conscious effort. Get going, get growing!

On to our next Chapter - Third Party Payment!

CHAPTER 19

THIRD PARTY PAYMENT

Discover a need in your community. When you are successful in filling the need, you are a success.

The proper management of third party payment patients as well as the prompt and efficient handling of their related paperwork is an important function of dental practice management.

In this Chapter we will address THREE types of third-party payment:

1.   **DENTAL INSURANCE**

        THIS IS WHEN AN INSURANCE COMPANY HAS A CONTRACT WITH A PATIENT'S EMPLOYER - For instance, Delta or Equitable or Prudential or John Hancock Insurance Company has a contract with 3-M, Control Data or Riverwood International. In this scenario the insurance compa-

243

ny, depending on the fine print in the contract, agrees to reimburse some percentage, let's say 80% of the dentist's fee for operative dentistry (up to a given percentile of the fees in the dentist's area).

The insurance company may well pay 50% on crown and bridge and partial or full dentures with prior authorization and perhaps 100% on preventative (examination every six months; x-rays - 4 bite wings per year and a panoramic film every three years - as well as a prophylaxis on adults and prophylaxis and fluoride treatment on children every six months).

This type of an insurance program usually has an annual deductible amount -- often $50. Therefore, the patient has to pay the first $50 every calendar year.

When dealing with this type of an insurance plan, it is best to have the patient pay his portion of the daily charges as dental procedures are completed. When he pays for 20% of his restoration charges and 50% of his crown and bridge at each appointment, the minimal cash outlay at the time often leaves the patient content with the modest amount required to get his mouth in good condition again.

MAXIM

ALWAYS OBTAIN A WRITTEN PRIOR AUTHORIZATION FROM THE INSURANCE COMPANY ON CROWN AND BRIDGE AND REMOVABLE PROSTHETICS PRIOR TO BEGINNING TREATMENT

With crown and bridge work we ask the patient to pay 1/2 of his anticipated portion at the time of the preparation and the other 1/2 when the crown is cemented.

Most insurance companies require periapical x-rays of all root canal teeth, extractions and crown and bridge teeth prior to commencing treatment.

MAXIM

ALWAYS HAVE A PERIAPICAL X-RAY OF ALL ROOT CANAL TEETH, EXTRACTIONS AND CROWN AND BRIDGE TEETH PRIOR TO COMMENCING TREATMENT

Bear in mind that once the eligibility and/or prior authorization has been established, the insurance company will contribute 50% or 80% or whatever the contract specifies.

Knowing that 50% or 80% of the funds will definitely be received we can proceed. If the patient does need a little time to make his portion of the payment we may accept monthly payments for a month or two. Obtain a duplicate of the agreement with the patient's anticipated portion in writing. Keep a copy of the agreement in the patient's chart and give the original to the patient.

MAXIM

ALL PROCEDURES MUST BE AGREED TO BE PAID IN FULL WITHIN 90 DAYS MAXIMUM.

Now in real life---thanks partly to tradition, partly to the historical lack of business savvy of most dentists, and partly to the patient's propensity to not want to part with his funds, many patients wish to keep their money as long as possible.

Typically, patients request that we bill their insurance companies for payment and bill them only after we receive payment from their insurance carriers.

> This traditional method of handling insurance, which never was very great in the first place, is even less satisfactory today. As the pace of our society is accelerating and so much more is going on in patient's lives, their recollection of an event such as a restoration or a crown is to a degree numbed by the time the insurance company has settled and the remaining balance has been communicated to them.

> One patient we treated recently had been half way around the world on business three times in the preceding two months.

The method we have developed to counter this "bill the insurance company and then let me know what the balance is" mind set is to offer a significant discount for payment at the time of service. If the patient's portion is 50% and he pays his 50% at the time of service, offer him a discount on his portion.

This plan often stimulates interest in payment at the time of service. This is better for cash flow and has an improved psychological affect on the patient. It is better for the patient to pay at the time of service when he is aware of the service received (still numb). At the end of the insurance company's final payment, often 30 or 60 days later, or longer, the patient may barely remember being at the dental office. By this time the patient's financial situation and priorities may have changed considerably.

2.   DIRECT PAYMENT TO THE DENTIST

> **A SECOND TYPE OF THIRD PARTY PAYMENT IS DIRECT PAYMENT TO THE DENTIST** - This is an arrangement where the third party pays the dentist (usually a significantly reduced fee) and the patient has no financial obligation.

MEDICAL ASSISTANCE paid by some states is an example of this type.

This scene presents an entirely different ball game. With this group of patients one has opportunity to address and conquer some unique challenges.

MAXIM

BY CONQUERING CHALLENGES
AND STRETCHING WE GROW

Some of the challenges frequently presented by this group are:

A. A high percentage of failed appointments.

B. Patients tend to present for treatment only when in pain.

C. Dentistry is often a low priority in their value system.

D. Due to the low priority of dentistry, cooperation with recommended home care practices may be neglected or overlooked.

E. Chronic Irreversible Detrimental Diet Syndrome (CIDDS).

F. Gross neglect of the dentition - "...haven't seen a dentist for over 12 years."

Working with this group is where skill, efficiency, effectiveness, flexibility and ability to complete a long series of procedures in a single appointment can create a win-win situation.

One can ask the patient whether he would prefer to "come back several times or get as much needed work completed today as possible." When put this way the answer from the patient is almost always to get as much completed today as possible and avoid having to come back many times. Once one has the go ahead and the assistants are organized we can proceed without the need for consultation on any further financial arrangements.

For the well-organized and highly efficient operator, the incremental time required to complete additional restorations after the initial restoration is minimal. By utilizing this multiple procedure principle to the maximum one can create a win-win scene. Unless everybody wins we won't play!

Doing from one to four quadrants of dentistry per setting allows one to accept a lesser fee as dictated by the governmental agency, in our case, and still do all right.

Some dentists, and at times even an entire society of dentists, occasionally pride themselves in not accepting patients from this segment of the population.

Inadvertently, this group of dentists is creating a window of opportunity for the energetic, industrious, hard-working dentist who is willing to help patients that need help! Watch closely for such needs in your community; evaluate the possibility of serving any segment of the population which is not being served.

MAXIM

DISCOVER A NEED IN YOUR COMMUNITY.
WHEN YOU ARE SUCCESSFUL
IN FILLING THE NEED
YOU ARE A SUCCESS

3.   **CAPITATION**

A third type of third party payment is CAPITA-TION.

Through a capitation program, the dental office receives a monthly fee per patient for all patients who choose the office for treatment. The capitation patient is provided with a list of possible member dentists and must make a selection from the list.

In return for this monthly compensation, the dentist agrees to adhere to a predetermined reduced fee schedule.

It is very important to closely review the proposed fee schedule prior to signing an agreement.

The trend in fee schedules, as of this writing, seems to be more palatable than they were a handful of years ago.

Keep in mind one must be very busy in order to advance rapidly on the learning curve.

Capitation is one of the ways to get and keep the patient flow going and to get and keep very busy!

If one had absolutely all the fee-for-service patients one could possibly handle at maximum efficiency, the decision to not accept capitation patients would be automatic.

However, in real life, especially when starting a new dental practice, this is seldom the case. Therefore, capitation can help keep you and your staff busy (a must). It can significantly add to the number of satisfied and happy patients in your community -- advertising by "word of mouth." Happy capitation patients often refer friends and relatives who are fee-for-service, or insurance patients, who also add to your happy patients.

249

Besides, with most of the current capitation plans one can show a profit on the individual patients by treating them efficiently.

Capitation programs can be of much benefit to the start-up practice in the early stages of growth. If and when one must cut back on the patient flow, the capitation programs can be reduced to make more room in the schedule for some other segment of the dental patient population.

You learn to work efficiently by staying busy and constantly fine tuning the dental machine. (The tray set up, the mobile arrangements, the operatory equipment, continual training of the dental assistants, instituting some of the dental assistants' suggestions, etc.)

Capitation has received a bad rap by some who either do not fully understand it, do not see the Big Picture or who are not too far advanced along the efficiency learning curve.

While the subject of capitation could fill an entire volume, let it rest for now in the best interest of time and space that capitation can play an important role in the development of a successful dental practice.

In the next Chapter we will take a look at Expenses.

CHAPTER 20

EXPENSES

"A Penny Saved is a Penny Earned."

Benjamin Franklin

Controlling expenses is at least as important to the success of the dental practice as reducing accounts receivable or increasing production.

Here we are walking the tightrope again - balancing between FRUGALITY, which cuts into production and being a SPENDTHRIFT, to the detriment of the practice!

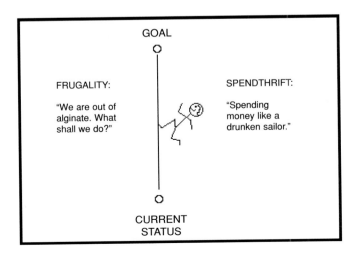

THE SOLUTION OBVIOUSLY IS TO FIND A LOGICAL POINT
SOMEWHERE NEAR THE MIDDLE OF THE ROAD.

For instance, let's take a look at one specific expense -- <u>Dental
Supplies</u>.

Dental supplies are a big expense -- 6% to 9% of your monthly collections and increasing steadily -- and require constant monitoring to
keep them in check. Reducing expenses increases profits!

Start out by doing some comparison shopping to find your best deals,
then constantly monitor those prices as they seem to have a way of
creeping up when unwatched.

Non-perishables - alginate, laboratory stone, amalgam, film which is
kept refrigerated, gauze 2 x 2s, paper products, disposable needles,
etc., often can be purchased in volume at a sizeable discount. All dental supply flyers should be directed to the dental supply purchasing
staff member for careful review and comparison. Companies often
send out flyers with specials near, at, or below their cost, in an attempt
to stimulate their business. Your purchaser can pick the bargains out
of these flyers and record a substantial savings.

We purchase alginate impression material and dental stone in bulk
drums out of which we refill our smaller containers. We also purchase etchants in bulk. Cements, anesthetics, needles, amalgam,
gauze 2 x 2s, impression materials all are purchased on sale in sufficient quantity to carry us through until the next anticipated sale.

Have someone responsible for the dental supply scene...delegate and
monitor...and keep monitoring. This monitoring is an ongoing management responsibility in the successful dental office.

Keeping the number of instruments, burs, and supplies to a minimum
and ordering the limited number of supplies in large quantities takes
maximum advantage of quantity discounts as well as making the
whole office run more smoothly. For instance, when the new dental
assistant is sent to the "cupboard" to get a sterilized scalpel blade, if

there are four different style blades it will, according to Murphy's Law, require her four trips to get the right one. While, on the other hand, if there is only one style blade she has the correct one on the first trip.

We charge our dental supplies on our VISA card for VISA volume bonuses and send a check to VISA in the total amount the same day to maintain a zero balance. In fact, we strive to keep all account balances at "zero." No service fees that way!

Minimizing expenses without jeopardizing production is a challenge to even the most astute.

A MORE GLOBAL VIEW OF DENTAL EXPENSES:

Expenses can be grouped into three categories:

FIXED
VARIABLE
SEMI-VARIABLE

Let's look at each group separately:

FIXED EXPENSES include those expenses which are constant whether you go to work or go fishing.

These are:

Building mortgage payment or rent or lease payment
Property taxes
Utilities
Equipment payment or lease payment on equipment
Malpractice insurance
Building and contents insurance

VARIABLE EXPENSES include those expenses which increase with increased production.

These are:
Dental laboratory fees
Dental supplies
Office supplies
Postage expense

SEMI-VARIABLE EXPENSES include (some fixed and some variable components):

These are:
Salaries
Repairs and maintenance
Education and books

SALARIES: A skeleton crew is necessary to answer the telephone when you take off to go fishing. Therefore, a portion of the salary expense is fixed. As your production increases the need for more employees becomes apparent. This component of salaries is variable.

REPAIRS AND MAINTENANCE: Some repairs and maintenance always will be required. The more the building and equipment are used, the more repairs and maintenance are required.

EDUCATION AND BOOKS: Basic continuing education is necessary to remain qualified to practice dentistry. Those dentists who go above and beyond the basic requirements to learn more about the latest technology and more efficient methods increase their expenses slightly. However, by going the extra mile and learning to become more efficient and effective they reap rich rewards for the extra effort both professionally and monetarily.

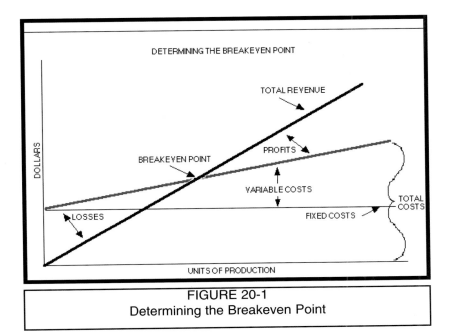

FIGURE 20-1
Determining the Breakeven Point

As the above graph illustrates, keeping expenses to a minimum and units of production to a maximum are the keys to creating profits.

Strategies for trimming expenses:

- Train, delegate and monitor. Three well-trained dental assistants can accomplish more than five untrained or poorly trained dental assistants.

- Minimize the number of different instruments and supplies you use. For instance, minimize the number of different burs on the bur block to, let's say, 10 ... (some offices have 60 different burs) then order those 10 burs in volume and reap discounts on a limited number of different burs. This minimizes time in selecting burs, setting up trays, scrubbing instruments, etc.

- Another example -- if you use rubber base impression material - instead of stocking heavy, medium, and light bodied try cutting down to just one weight and ordering it in quantity at a discount.

- The fewer the number of different instruments and the fewer the number of different supplies means being more cost effective, less confusing and more efficient. For example, let's take amalgam carvers. If you have only one and always use the same end your assistant will always snap it in your hand like clockwork. If you have eight double ended carvers your dental assistant has a one in sixteen chance of being correct in her choice of which end of which amalgam carver to pass to you.

- The more efficient the procedure becomes the less stressful and the more enjoyable is your day.

Next -- the Chapter we have all been waiting for -- Marketing!

CHAPTER 21

MARKETING

You have to let potential patients know you are there.

WHAT IS MARKETING?

The American Marketing Association defines marketing as:

> "Marketing is the process of planning and executing the conception, pricing, promotion and distribution of ideas, goods and/or SERVICES (emphasis added) to create exchanges that satisfy individual and organizational goals."

Marketing has also been defined as:

> "Marketing consists of individual and organizational

activities that facilitate and expedite satisfying exchange relationships in a dynamic environment through the creation, distribution, promotion, and pricing of goods, SERVICES (emphasis added) and ideas." MARKETING CONCEPTS AND STRATEGIES, William Price and O. C. Ferrell, 8th Edition, p.4.

Many argue that marketing has no place in dentistry. Others believe that it is an integral link in the chain of the successful dental practice.

In a recent study of marketing managers it was agreed that "creating customer satisfaction" was the most important concept in the definition of marketing. MARKETING CONCEPTS AND STRATEGIES, William Price and O. C. Ferrell, 8th Edition.

Establishing and maintaining a constant positive rapport with the patient is an important goal of the dentist.

We have a total 100% satisfaction guarantee in our office. If you are our patient we will not rest until you are TOTALLY SATISFIED with any treatment performed. If we can't satisfy you, you get a full refund... (we get the denture). While taking the denture and giving the patient a refund sounds extreme, it is indeed the best solution at times. We insist on patient satisfaction!

A patient who feels he has been treated fairly in a difficult situation is a great asset. Having virtually all patients to whom you are exposed be sources of referral is to insure your success.

The marketing concept stresses that an organization can best achieve its goals by providing **TOTAL PATIENT SATISFACTION!**

MARKETING STRATEGY
(Find a need and fill it!)

Select and analyze a target market (that group of people you want to reach) for which you offer services which will satisfy this group's needs!

Factors to Consider in Selecting a Target Market:

1. Doctor's abilities and inclinations - if children drive him to distraction do not promote services for children.

2. Demographics of community - if you are in Sun City, Arizona, where, by city ordinance, individuals must be at least 55 years old to purchase a property, do not market to children.

3. Other professionals in the area - what is the gap in services in your community? If there are six other dentists and none will see children, maybe you should let the other dentists know you will be happy to treat their young patients.

4. Company insurance plans in your area - perhaps you want to market to employees of a particular company or corporation.

5. Geriatric dentistry - nursing homes often struggle to fill their dental needs. Nursing home regulations require their patients to have periodic dental examinations. Since transportation is often a challenge, some nursing homes may be willing to set up an operatory at their facility if you were to staff it for them on a part-time basis.

6. Ethnic group - perhaps there is a sizeable ethnic group in your community you would like to market to. This can at times be very effective through radio stations which broadcast in their language or via ethnic newspapers.

7.   Surgery - If you particularly like oral surgery and the community's surgical needs are not being met, promote this service by notifying your colleagues and patients that you also take out wisdom teeth and/or difficult extractions.

8.   Emergency patients - If emergency patients are waiting several days to several weeks to see a dentist, let the public, as well as other dentists, know that you will treat emergency patients on the same day!

9.   Denture repair - If denture patients have to wait a long time in your area to get their dentures repaired, advertise "Same Day Denture Repair." Most repairs can be completed in an hour. (See Chapter 31.)

10.   Extended Hours - patients appreciate evening, early morning and Saturday dental appointments; If you dislike getting up early in the morning...work from 1:00 p.m. until 9:00 p.m.

Concentration Strategy Approach is picking a single market segment and marketing to this particular market segment.

Promoting to geriatric patients is an example of Concentration Strategy Approach.

Undifferentiated Approach or Total Market Approach is when one defines the entire market for all their dental needs as the target market.

CONCENTRATION STRATEGY APPROACH:

The following examples of the concentration strategy approach are designed to communicate the concept of how it works and stimulate your thinking for the segment you desire to address.

Market segments which you may choose to explore are limited only by your imagination:

1.	Pediatric Dentistry - We may consider addressing this market segment by:

   A.	Informing school authorities and/or parents of availability of Saturday or after school appointments.

   B.	Volunteering to conduct educational programs in the school, Dental Health Week, etc.

   C.	Informing day care staff of availability of extended hours.

   D.	Sponsoring "Best Picture Coloring Contests" - with a new bicycle or some other significant prize.

   E.	Giving out free treats - helium balloons or burger and malt coupon to patients.

   F.	Having a kiddy area in the waiting room.

   G.	Giving out special stickers or "in" toys.

   H.	Advertising a daycare drop off - Mom can drop Susie off and shop for two hours while Susie is getting her teeth filled - 45 minute appointment. The staff watches while Susie plays with waiting room toys for 15 minutes prior to her appointment. And an hour afterward. WARNING...consult with your staff first on this one.

2.	Suppose your market segment is the blue collar

worker. You may choose to:

A.   Offer evening appointments.

      i.   Tuesday and Thursday open until 8:00 p.m.

      ii.   Open daily until 8:00 p.m.

B.   Offer Saturday appointments - open 8:00 a.m., until 5:00 p.m., or open 8:00 a.m. until noon.

C.   Conduct company seminars - seminars in the company classroom informing workers about their dental insurance coverage.

      Explain how the patient can come in for the initial visit, get x-rays, examination, and cleaning, and his insurance company will pick up the tab.

      Explain how the insurance company pays 80% of the cost of restorations on the employee and his family.

      Explain how the dental office personnel will complete their insurance forms and submit them to the insurer.

      Become personally acquainted with the employees through seminars.

D.   Hold an Open House at the dental office for all your target company's employees:

      tea and cookies
      wine and cheese

outdoor grill - brats and soda
balloons for the kids

E.   Offer a FREE gift to a certain company's
new patients who visit this month. (Check
with any local governing bodies you do not
want to offend before starting this type of a
promotion.)

electric toothbrush
wrist watch
SONY Walkman® stereo headphones

Once you have chosen a market segment you must take a look at dentistry from the perspective of that market segment. Interview several members of this market segment either with a written form to fill out or a very casual chat with existing patients. Discover what would make their dental visits more convenient or more enjoyable. Your patients and potential patients will tell you what you need to do to succeed in attracting their group if you listen carefully to what they say! The better we listen the more we learn.

UNDIFFERENTIATED APPROACH :

A market segment can be defined as the entire market for all their dental needs. This is the total market approach.

"Complete Family Dentistry" and "Total Dental Care" - are examples of total undifferentiated market approach.

This strategy is to get as many patients as possible into the dental office. The patients' ages and treatment requirements are not issues. This approach is fine when the dentist is comfortable with all phases of dentistry and all age groups.

THE CONSUMER BUYING DECISION PROCESS CONSISTS OF FIVE STAGES:

STAGE 1.   <u>PROBLEM RECOGNITION</u>

- pain

- teeth have not been checked for 20 years

- a chipped tooth

- a filling out

- have not had teeth cleaned recently

- dentures are loose

STAGE 2.   <u>INFORMATION SEARCH</u>

- ask friends and neighbors where they go for their dental needs

- consult the telephone directory for advertisements

- facility recognition - (drive by nice looking professional dental building daily on their way to work)

- newspaper, professional directory or advertisement

- call medical clinic for information and referral

- received coupon in the mail

STAGE 3.   EVALUATION OF ALTERNATIVES

- patient analyzes how quickly he can receive treatment if his needs are urgent

- availability of evening appointments - if it is difficult to get off work

- is this office open on Saturdays?

- does this office accept new patients?

- does this office accept insurance patients?

- does this office accept other third-party pay patients?

- does this office accept capitation patients?

- is this a "full service dental office, for example, does this office perform all dental needs, i.e., preventative dentistry, operative, endodontic, crown and bridge, dentures, surgical extractions, and so forth?

STAGE 4.   PURCHASE OF SERVICES

- patient visits and is treated by the dentist

- hopefully had a pleasant experience

STAGE 5.   POST PURCHASE OF SERVICES EVALUATION

- after the dental visit the patient begins evaluating the services received

The outcome of this stage is either satisfaction or dissatisfaction.

265

PROMOTION

Promotion is communication in an effort to persuade patients to accept your services.

Promotion and the product/service adoption process involves the following stages:

STAGE 1.   AWARENESS STAGE - Individuals become aware that a product or service exists.

STAGE 2.   INTEREST STAGE - Consumers enter the interest stage when they are motivated to get information about the products/service features, uses, advantages, price and location.

STAGE 3.   EVALUATION STAGE - Individuals consider whether the product or service will satisfy certain criteria that are crucial for meeting their specific needs.

STAGE 4.   TRIAL STAGE - They experience product/service for the first time by taking advantage of a free sample or demonstration.

STAGE 5.   ADOPTION STAGE - Individuals move into the adoption stage by choosing the specific product/service when they need a product/service of that general type.

Do not assume, however, that because a person enters the adoption process she or he will eventually adopt the new product. Rejection may occur at any stage, including adoption. Both product/service adoption and product/service rejection can be temporary or permanent.

PUBLICITY

Publicity is communication that is transmitted through a mass media at no charge. There are several types of publicity such as:

1. News Release - usually fewer than 300 words

2. Feature Article - longer than the news release

3. Captioned Photograph - explains photograph

4. Press Conference - to announce major news event

Publicity can be especially helpful in the start-up phase because potential patients are much more likely to notice publicity than advertising.

> In 1983 Dr. Herman Boehme and I opened a dental office in Glendale, Arizona, 24 hours a day, 365 days a year. In a ceremony we literally "threw away the keys to our dental office." Twenty-nine hospitals and/or emergency facilities very eagerly welcomed this schedule and were very supportive. We were filling a NEED. The hundreds of physicians on call on weekends had had no place to send their dental emergencies.
>
> We had all three major television stations present at our ceremonies.
>
> The free press was wonderful -- we even made the national news!
>
> (You think you have staffing problems -- count your blessings!! Thirty, forty or fifty hours of staffing is much easier than 168 hours weekly - Thanksgiving, Christmas, New Year's.)

I tell you this story not to impress you but to impress UPON you the power of creating some newsworthy happening. Invent a new dental instrument! Become active in your community! Become a philanthropist!

But most of all -- let your potential patients know you are there! Your best marketing device is happy patients. But when starting out you must get patients in to make them happy in the first place.

MARKETING DENTISTRY

One of the goals of marketing in dentistry is to attract patients into the dental office for treatment. There are nearly as many ways to market as there are dentists. Use your imagination! Think about various scenarios and how you would fit into them. See yourself acting out the various roles and experience what it feels like. Go with what is comfortable or at least semi-comfortable for you.

Following are a few suggestions; you will devise your own unique method. The more unusual the better so let your imagination run wild!

1. Coaching - Little League baseball, soccer, basketball, football, tennis, hockey, etc.

    When the participants and parents know you, they will be more likely to become your patients.

2. Radio and television - talk shows - often welcome presentations on specific topics - sealants, TMJ, esthetic restorations, etc. Participate only if you are comfortable with these media. If not, your nervousness will probably show.

3.   Publicity - news story - create something unique or exciting -- invent a new dental instrument -- and let the media know about it.

4.   Advertising - must have something which will bene-fit the patient or which he perceives as a benefit. Telling him there is one more dental office in the community is a little "Ho-Hum."

On the other hand, informing the public that there is now a dental office **OPEN UNTIL 8:00 P.M. daily and/or SATURDAYS** may stimulate responses.

5.   Television - tends usually to be expensive and often addresses too broad a geographic area - too far from the dental office. If one had many dental satellite offices, then television may become an effective tool.

6.   Radio - less costly - again, many listeners may be too far away geographically to be serious potential patients.

7.   Newspapers - can be effective - again look at distrib-ution geography. The cost per household may be quite small, but if the majority of households are too far away and the potential patient would be driving past dozens of other dental offices to reach yours, it simply will not pay.

8.   Direct mail - even though much more costly per household it can be targeted to zip codes or geo-graphic boundaries which makes sense.

9.   Door knob flyers - can be effective in high density locations - potential patients tend to be more curious of door knob flyers than direct mail and are more likely to read it or at least glance at it.

10.   Telephone book - Always a good potential source of patients. Must plan ahead as advertising deadlines are considerably earlier than distribution.

The telephone book is an annual commitment and therefore must be evaluated on an annual basis. Once it goes to print you are locked in for a year.

All other modes of advertising offer the luxury of being able to do a sample batch and observe the results - not the telephone book.

11.   Free standing building - A freestanding building looking clean and neat in a high traffic location is an important marketing strategy. The first stage is **awareness.**

12.   Parking - parking right up to the front door is advantageous - make it as convenient for the patient as possible.

13.   Signage - important to passersby. We have an 8' x 10' lighted sign with our logo on it. Most of the local population became aware of the new dental facility soon after our opening.

Experiment with different methods and pursue those most effective for you.

TOTAL PATIENT SATISFACTION

Total patient satisfaction is another element of marketing. The patient is *always right no matter whether he is reasonable or unreasonable!*

Some of our most unreasonable, ridiculous, cantankerous patients have become some of our very best referral sources because they were treated kindly when they were obstinate. Keep your cool...it pays!

When a patient is upset, it frequently is our fault. We probably failed to fully explain the possible consequences or complications of treatment prior to treatment. For example, the patient comes in late in the day with tooth number 30 grossly decayed. You take a deep breath and ask the patient if she wants to attempt to save it. This is the time to inform the patient the tooth may require a root canal treatment or may become painful after restoration. With proper explanation up front you have given the patient the information required for her active participation in the treatment decisions. She also will understand the cause of the pain when it wakes her up in the middle of the night. Without proper explanation the dentist appears to be at fault.

The denture patient also requires thorough explanations. Prior to making a denture we must always explain to the patient the limitations of dentures. The patient should be aware before we begin the process that the end product will be less stable than their natural dentition. When the patient's completed denture is not the same as her real teeth, we can refer to our previous discussion. If she has no post-insertion problems and loves her denture (which, in most cases is true), the dentist is a hero!

The more time spent explaining the treatment and possible consequences to the patient before treatment begins, the fewer the problems later on. No matter how busy you perceive yourself to be, take the time to explain the situation to the patient prior to treatment.

Patients really appreciate special attention when time permits.

As an illustration, shortly after opening this dental office a horizontally impacted lower third molar was removed from one of the construction workers who was involved in constructing our building. After the tooth was removed we used the chalkboard to explain how the tooth was sectioned and what the various noises were that he heard during the tooth removal.

No fewer than two dozen new patients have mentioned they were referred by this individual -- that is powerful!

The more patients you are able to treat in your office and the fewer you have to refer out for treatment, the faster your practice will grow.

This is not down playing the specialists ... they are wonderful to have; however, the general practitioner who refers out all surgery, all endodontics, all orthodontics, all periodontics, all removable prosthodontics, and all fixed prosthodontics may get really tired of doing restorations. He may also get pretty hungry!

TELEPHONING PATIENTS AFTER TREATMENT

Patients love being called after treatment! I know of a dentist who claims he calls every patient whom he anesthetized that day before he leaves his office for the day.

This is admirable. If you can do it, go for it. It will pay off handsomely.

On the other hand, if one is a firm believer in delegating and a firm believer as well in the dentist's efforts being directed to duties which only the dentist can perform, **DELEGATE POST-TREATMENT CALLS TO A FLUENT, CARING, WELL-TRAINED RECEPTIONIST.**

We circle selected patients on our daily schedule which we would like our front office to call the next day to see how well they are doing.

When we leave at night we put the copy of the day's schedule with the circled names on the front desk for the receptionists to call the following day.

The next day the receptionist calls the patients saying exactly, "Hello, this is 'Jan' from The Smile Center and Dr. Silker has asked that I call and see how well you are doing." She then logs each call in a notebook designated for that purpose. She clears up any questions and consults with me, if necessary, to get the patient content or comfortable.

MORE ON MARKETING

Of all the ingredients necessary for developing a successful dental practice marketing is probably the least familiar or perhaps the least comfortable for most dentists. However, marketing is a necessary element of any business -- including Dentistry!!! Dentistry is a business today. Now that we are a service-oriented economy and we are all competing for market share, some form of marketing is essential.

Marketing comes in a myriad of forms:

In dentistry the primary purpose of marketing is to attain sufficient patient flow to make the practice profitable.

With this in mind let your imagination go wild. Come up with what is right for you.

What someone else does may only be good for stimulating your thinking.

Maybe Dr. Sweet joins a softball league and meets scores of people that way. Maybe you hate softball!

You say softball? Marketing? Yes, indeed. Whatever works to get patients into your office is marketing. You get to know Kim the pitcher on an opposing team. His son gets hit in the mouth by a ball

273

when playing Little League. Who does he call? You, of course!

Perhaps you choose to join the "Lions", "Rotary" and six other orga-
nizations. Any or all of these may help.

The goal is to let people know you are there, **FOR THEM,** you are
ready, willing and able...IT MAKES LITTLE DIFFERENCE HOW
YOU DO THIS. JUST BE SURE YOU DO IT!

Starting a new practice may be construed as a newsworthy event if it
is done properly. Strive for this position.

Perhaps you have extended hours - patients can now get their teeth
fixed after work.

Perhaps Saturday appointments.

Perhaps dentures are your forte'.

Perhaps a Panoramic x-ray machine in your office, if there is not one
in your area, would be a draw to patients. You may commit yourself
to $15,000 for a new Panoramic x-ray machine and get $20,000 worth
of free advertising.

Now that we've been to the extreme let's explore some more subtle
ways of letting the community know you are there.

Dentistry in the past has historically been in the "We'll see you at our
convenience" mode. The patient calling the dental office in pain on
Thursday was at times informed the dentist would see him at 2:30
p.m. next Tuesday. Considering that the excruciating pain from an
abscess can be at least equal in magnitude to that of a broken limb and
that a physician would not think of letting their patient suffer over the
weekend with a broken limb, who gave dentists this privilege?

Today our society is more and more in a service mode. The dentist
who is flexible enough to get the patient in quickly when he is hurting often **EARNS** the patient's respect for years to come. The patient

generally tells many people who got him in right away and relieved his discomfort.

WE ALWAYS SEE PATIENTS IN PAIN RIGHT AWAY -- IT'S OUR POLICY!!

INTERNAL MARKETING

That which is done within the dental office to promote new patients, more dentistry and happier patients

INTERNAL MARKETING FACTORS:

1. Physical plant - clean, neat, modern dental office

2. Friendly staff

3. Prompt service

4. Efficient service

5. Quick pain relief

6. Competent dental treatment

7. Well-trained, clean and neat appearing staff

8. The staff's positive perception of the dentist

   One of the most important aspects of internal marketing is the staff's perception and feelings about the dentist - not the dentist personally, but the dentist's ability to treat patients successfully and in the patient's best interest with total concern for the needs of the patient.

The dentist who practices with competence and integrity has a staff who promotes the practice 24 hours a day.

The dentist's personality becomes irrelevant when the staff recognizes **the dentist operates successfully with the patient's best interest as his top priority.** They are quick to get their friends, family, and acquaintances to come in when they feel confident these people will be well cared for.

YOUR LOGO

LOGO

Lo-go (lo'go') n. pl. -gos. A name, symbol, or trademark designed for easy and definite recognition. - The American Heritage Dictionary of the English Language 1992 - Third Edition.

The benefit of a logo cannot be overemphasized because it identifies your office and reinforces patient recognition.

It connotes organization.

Developing a logo can be viewed as a fun spare time doodling project. Simply carry a note pad with you for a few days. When you are put on hold by the telephone company or when you are waiting for lunch, just doodle. Have your friends and relatives do the same. Compare doodlings and build on one another's best ideas.

Once you have sketched a potential logo, show it to people in your environment and observe their reactions. Their facial expressions will let you know when you have it right! A logo which brings a smile to people's faces is a great logo!!

You can, on the other hand, contact a professional agency to create a logo for you.

Even though marketing is a serious part of the business of dentistry, it is also an interesting part of the business. Now that you have a background and understanding of what marketing is, experiment with different approaches and observe what works. Build on your successes and always remember to have fun in the process.

MAXIM

WHATEVER WORKS, WORKS!

Now let's move on to our next Chapter -- Accounting!

CHAPTER 22

ACCOUNTING AND THE BUSINESS OF DENTISTRY

"Remember the Bookkeeper, perched on his stool, green eyeshade tilted, quill for a tool? He wasn't too fast, but nowhere in town, did you hear the excuse, "Our computer is down."

(Author unknown)

While it may be tempting to utilize software and do your accounting on-site, this is nearly as ludicrous as the accountant attempting to fix his own teeth. Some figures are better kept out of the office and not on the computer where employees may have access to them.

The benefits received from a competent and savvy accountant far outweigh the cost. A CPA with experience in the dental field is a preferred choice.

Your accounting may be done on a CASH BASIS or an ACCRUAL BASIS. It is customarily to your benefit to be on the cash basis.

In tax planning and retirement planning as in dentistry "An ounce of prevention is worth a pound of cure." Or maybe we should say a "ton of cure" in this case.

SELECTING YOUR ACCOUNTANT

When interviewing an accountant, helpful questions to ask may include:

1. Education - degrees

2. Years of experience

3. Type of accounting most familiar with - who are your clients?

4. References - other clients

5. Experience in the dental field

6. Involvement in financial planning

7. Monthly charges for services rendered

Services required of an accountant:

1. Monthly profit and loss statements

2. Monthly balance sheet

3. Monitor payroll taxes, state and federal

4. Depreciation schedules

5.   Quarterly reports

6.   Income taxes filed - corporate, individual

7.   Quarterly consultation on progress

--   discuss growth

--   compare expenses of office to national averages which are constantly changing.

--   compare current period to previous year's figures to be aware of trends.

National averages recently observed were:

Collections		98.5%
Payroll Expense	25.2%	
Benefits	1.8%	
Laboratory Fees	8.1%	
Rent	6.3%	
Dental Supplies	8.2%	
Office Supplies	2.6%	
Utilities	1.8%	
Other	11.4%	
Interest, Depreciation and Income Taxes	6.2%	
TOTAL OPERATING EXPENSE	71.6%	71.6%
NET AVAILABLE		**28.4%**

IN-HOUSE ACCOUNTING:

In-house accounting consists of the daily computer output which is:

1.   **DAYSHEET**

The daysheet details individual charges for the day in detail, for example:

PATIENT	DENTIST #	TREATMENT	CHARGE
Carmela Sweet	1	Emergency Exam	$ 20.00
Carmela Sweet	1	Analgesia	$ 10.00
Carmela Sweet	1	Resin, Tooth #E - MI	$ 90.00
Carmela Sweet	1	Resin, Tooth #F - DI	$ 90.00

TOTAL CHARGES . . . .$ 4,720.00

TOTAL PAYMENTS . . . .$ 2,497.45

Yesterday's Accounts Receivable Balance $ 218,860.17

Increase (or decrease) in Accounts Receivable $ 2,222.55

TODAY'S ACCOUNTS RECEIVABLE BALANCE $ 221,082.72

MONTH-TO-DATE PATIENT CHARGES: $ 19,872.00

TODAY'S TOTAL PAYMENTS $ 2,497.45

Each provider's production is listed:

PROVIDER #	PROVIDER NAME	TOTAL CHARGES
1	Edward L. Silker, DDS	$ 4,318.00
13	Sue Clean, Hygienist	$ 139.00

14   Flossie Wright, Hygienist $ 263.00

2.   **SUMMARY DAYSHEET**

The summary daysheet lists each patient treated for the day. It shows the total charges for the day for that patient and ALL payments received for that day.

The totals at the end of the report show --

TODAY'S TOTAL CHARGES: **$ 4,720.00**

TODAY'S TOTAL PAYMENTS: **$ 2,497.45**

MONTH-TO-DATE CHARGES: **$19,872.00**

3.   **BANK DEPOSIT**

The bank deposit lists all funds received by category:

A.   Cash received ....$ 210.00

B.   Personal checks received......................$ 558.45

C.   Insurance checks received....................$ 1,620.00

D.   Credit card payments............................$ 109.00

      TOTAL BANK DEPOSIT...................$ 2,497.45

After the day's transactions have all been entered the three preceding printouts are placed on the dentist's desk.

The next day the printouts are reviewed by the dentist prior to the arrival of the first patient.

This way daily progress toward accuracy of the computer printout and goal achievement are monitored.

1. The printout is reviewed for accuracy as to having: all charges entered -- (most find it easy to review the following morning - the only better way might be to monitor it at the end of the day - whatever works for you).

2. The dentist can review payments received.

3. The dentist can review month-to-date charges.

 FOR EXAMPLE, by about the 10th of the month one can project where the month's totals are headed at the current pace by using a factor of three.

 By the 15th of the month, one can simply double the month-to-date figures mentally to project the anticipated monthly outcome.

4. The dentist can review the accounts receivable balance - monitoring accounts receivable is an important aspect of management. But note that overemphasis on minimizing accounts receivable may have a dampening effect on production.

ALAS!
ONE IS WALKING THE
TIGHTROPE AGAIN!!

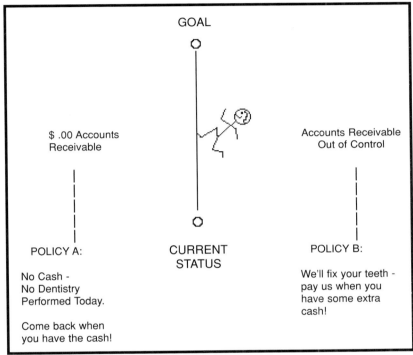

POLICY "A"

WHEN ONE IS TOO STRICT ABOUT
EXTENDING CREDIT
ONE RISKS A SERIOUS CUT IN PRODUCTION!

POLICY "B"

WHEN ONE IS TOO LENIENT ON
EXTENDING CREDIT
ONE CAN END UP WITH A CASH FLOW INSUFFICIENT
TO MEET ONE'S MONTHLY OBLIGATIONS!

This appears to be a Catch-22! - What is a soul to do?

You must establish a sound financial policy. With specific guidelines you can make appropriate decisions on an individual basis. Suppose, for example, patient "X" presents for an examination and prophylaxis. He has insurance, has not had a dental examination for four years and now has the time because of a job-related back injury.

Today an examination, a Panorex x-ray, four bite wing x-rays, a prophylaxis, and periodontal evaluation are completed.

The examination reveals the need for the following dental care:

4 quadrants periodontal scaling	$ 480.00
3 extractions	$ 120.00
6 2-surface restorations	$ 300.00
2 1-surface restorations	$ 100.00
1 removable partial denture	$ 630.00

His insurance company pays 100% of today's charges of $118.00 (minus his deductible). Further, his insurance will pay 80% of the periodontal scaling, extractions, and fillings and 50% for the removable partial denture.

Suppose the patient's portion of the fee will be $565.00 and your policy is that all accounts must be paid in full within 60 days of service. Further suppose the patient feels that he can only pay $100.00 per month until he returns to work.

Now a management decision must be made. Does one help this patient get his teeth restored, and accept the insurance company's $1,223 and be patient with the patient's abilities to pay, or does one insist on cash up front?

The savvy dentist may decide to help the patient and take some slight risk. But the accounts receivable rise in the process.

By helping a number of patients in similar situations, the accounts receivable may rise to the point where some well-meaning but naive consultant will suggest that the accounts receivable are "out of control." Actually, if the bottom line is healthy and doing well the accounts receivable balance is of only secondary concern.

When your **SINCERE CONCERN** is to help a large number of people your accounts receivable may be higher than "standards" set by some "experts". **That's okay! For your bottom line may well blow these same "experts" right out of the water!!!**

So when your accounts receivable are running in the 2 to 2-1/2 times your average month's production figure and you are showing a satisfactory profit on your monthly profit and loss statements you are doing just fine!

MONTH-END ACCOUNTING:

Following the daily entries from the last day of the month, the month-end report can be run on the in-house computer.

This is real review time for the dentist!

The month-end figures, as well as the check stubs, complete payroll information and the monthly bank statement go to the C.P.A. for monthly compilation.

All supplies and parts (we do all our own repairs) are ordered by telephone and put on a VISA card. This VISA card accumulates free miles for airplane tickets. As soon as an item is ordered a check is sent to VISA to keep a zero balance on the card. No service fees!!

One dental supplier delivers bulk alginate and dental stone -- we save the freight and he is competitive on price -- and is not allowed to leave without a check.

Our dental laboratory charges are recorded by number of units sent out of our laboratory during the week and a check is sent every Friday to maintain a zero balance with our dental laboratories.

Our C.P.A. even shows a credit balance on our account. Now, that's good accounting!

Therefore, the cash position of the practice is always synchronous with the balance in the checking account. No surprises at the end of the month.

THE BUSINESS OF DENTISTRY

Private practice dentistry is a business just as banking or McDonald's or your corner grocery store.

BUSINESS COURSES - If you currently are in a dental practice or intend to start a dental practice get as much business training as soon as you can. Whether it is attending a night school, correspondence school or any other school, get as much as soon as possible.

MARKETING - It would be wonderful for you to take some marketing courses. You would find them enjoyable and informative.

TIME MOTION - You can become your own time/motion expert. Pretend you are an observer. To get a good look at this dentist/dental assistant team take a seat preferably above the operatory where you can view from above and watch this dentist (you) along with his assistant and observe all the wasted motions. Then coach this team on becoming more efficient. It is fun and profitable.

FLEXIBILITY - While you won't find any courses

on flexibility or perhaps any books other than this one, your development of a flexible attitude greatly stimulates your successful practice. When one patient fails to show up for an appointment and you have a patient in the chair who needs more dentistry than was scheduled, give your current patient an opportunity to finish up today. As indicated previously, there are many, many patients that like to get as much completed as possible in one sitting.

Use lines like - "Would you like to get as much completed today as possible?" Flexibility has another side - the side when you are running a little behind or is it the clock is running a little ahead today? "We're going to let you off easy today and just clean your teeth or just do one restoration or just rinse out and medicate the root canal treatment tooth which we started last week."

UNIFORMITY - ALL OPERATORIES THE SAME - it is essential for maximum efficiency that all operatories are equipped the same. All with x-ray capabilities, all with nitrous oxide/oxygen analgesia and sonic and ultrasonic scalers and ultraviolet lights and all high speeds, and on and on.

THE DAY'S SCHEDULE SHOULD BE SEEN AT A GLANCE FROM ALL OPERATORY POSITIONS.

In the next Chapter we will discover how a Trip to the Banker can actually be enjoyable!

CHAPTER 23

A TRIP TO THE BANKER

"Always bear in mind that your own resolution to success is more important than any other one thing."

Abraham Lincoln

This may well be the trip for which the dentist is least prepared. However, by following this outline and doing your homework in advance you can obtain your objective.

Prior to your first meeting with the banker, get yourself well organized.

Have neatly prepared the following items:

     1.   **Last three (3) years' income tax returns**

     2.   **Current financial statement**

     3.   **Other cash sources available**

4.   **Location for dental office**

5.   **Construction plan and costs if your plan is to build**

6.   **Building to lease if your plan is to lease**

7.   **Complete list of dental equipment**

8.   **List of office equipment**

9.   **Office furniture**

10.   **Business plan**

11.   **Projections**

12.   **Total amount of desired loan**

When you go in having all your ducks in a row, obtaining your objective is the most likely outcome.

If, for some unforeseen reason, Mr. Banker does not like your plan, simply go across the street and cut a deal with a more insightful competitor.

PREPARATION, DETAILS AND EXAMPLES:

1.   **Last three (3) years income tax returns:**

> The previous three years may have been during Dental School. Do not let this concern you because the banker realizes your focus during this period was your education. On the other hand, if your returns show some income, so much the better.

> Have with you a set of clean copies of your last three

years' tax returns in chronological order with the most recent year on top so the bank does not need to do any copying - this is an unusual gesture on your part and impresses the banker favorably.

2. **Personal financial statement:**

A personal financial statement form is available from any bank teller or secretary and can be obtained a day or two prior to your meeting with the banker.

The financial statement should be on a form provided by the bank you are pursuing. It is more convenient for the banker to work with a form with which he is familiar.

3. **Other cash sources:**

(Example: Your wife's Aunt Jill McGill - $70,000 for 5 years interest free.)

4. **Location for dental office:**

Have a location selected, preferably for new construction (patients are impressed by a new building and new equipment). Have demographics on the location.

Have traffic counts.

Have available the population within a 7-mile radius. Dental practices typically draw the bulk of their patients from within a seven mile radius of the practice. Guestimate, if necessary - present what your research shows - be as accurate as possible.

Obtain a plot plan of the building site.

Have a copy of the plot plan with a sketch of the building, the landscaping and parking lot laid out so the banker can see how it all fits together.

If possible, have the lot purchased - or a down payment, or an option to purchase or contract subject to...or at least the cost of the lot or something concrete you can present.

5.   **Construction plan and costs if your plan is to build:**

Use the plan in this book, a modification of the same, or use an entirely different plan. Have something, however, to show the banker that you are going to build - with their help - or without it!

Your draftsman, architect, lumber yard, or brother-in-law, depending upon your local ordinances, can construct a set of working drawings from which you can get bids on the building construction costs.   (See Chapter 26.)

Have your plans and total building costs organized so they can be displayed smoothly. Have building costs broken down, if possible, into:

Foundation and Basement	**$11,300**
Lumber and Millwork	**$34,000**
Electrical	**$ 6,600**
Plumbing & Heating	**$ 8,200**
Floor Covering	**$ 3,900**
Cabinetry	**$ 7,100**
Carpentry	**$12,200**
Landscaping	**$ 1,600**
Parking Lot and Sidewalks	**$ 9,300**
TOTAL COST OF CONSTRUCTION	**$94,200**

6.   Building to lease if your plan is to lease:

If you are going to lease have the plan and total costs of leasehold improvements. Follow the same format as Building (above). Also have a copy of the building Lease.

7.   Dental equipment:

Make a complete equipment list using the list in Chapter 29 as a guide.

Make the list - exact to every specification - model numbers, etc., and retail costs. (You will be able to trim considerably from your retail costs in your actual purchase. This gives you a little latitude for unexpected costs and there will be some...trust me.)

Include a complete equipment list. Any local dental supplier will gladly figure you a cost on all equipment. Tell them you need a list to present to your banker for loan purposes. They will come up with this list quickly. Get brochures for the banker and briefly explain the merits of the state-of-the-art dental equipment. Inform the suppliers to sharpen up their pencils for the real order as they will be up against competing bids. They will understand.

8.   Office equipment:

A.   Telephone system - you will want the capability of at least four incoming lines with a rotary system

B.   Typewriter

C.   Computer and printer, with adequate capabilities

D.   Photocopy machine

E.   Telecopy (Facsimile) machine

F.   Calculator

G.   Office supplies for the front office including stationery, envelopes, etc.

Figure costs of each item with a total office equipment cost at the bottom.

9.   Office furniture:

Eight chairs and a table for magazines will usually suffice for the waiting room.

Some miscellaneous funds for framed pictures, etc., in the waiting room.

10.   Business plan:

Create a business plan - **A Blueprint to Success**

Preparing this for the banker may well be your key to success because it makes you think about how you are going to succeed.

This is something that you must do for yourself! Following is only a sample:

You recognize dentistry as a service business and realize that the traditional 9:00 a.m. to 5:00 p.m. hours are not ideal for the convenience of many potential patients.

Further, you are young and energetic and have spent many years of schooling in preparation for your private dental practice.

Now that opportunity exists, you are committed to have "The New Concept Dental Care Center" open from 8:00 a.m. until 8:00 p.m., daily so patients can come in after work.

You further plan to construct a building which has been designed specifically for dentistry by a very successful dentist who has proven that a million dollars annually can be generated in this facility.

You further plan to use similar equipment to that which was used in the Model and has been tested and proven to be efficient and effective.

Your business plan includes a publicity campaign in which all the local newspapers will be provided with a news release about "The New Concept Dental Care Center": From now on patients do not need to have the pain from missing work added to their dental discomfort. Now evening and Saturday appointments are available.

In addition, multi-media marketing will inform the public of the new facility and extended hours. This will be done in the form of newspaper and radio advertising. Also, new patient introductory coupons for a free examination and x-rays will be direct mailed to all local residents.

Further, to stimulate cash flow a 10% discount will be offered to patients who pay at the time of service.

THIS PROGRAM WILL EXCITE THE BANKER - and having a business plan reduced to writing is most important to your success!

11.   Projections:

Create your own projections using the format and paper similar to that used in the sample projections herein. Actual paper size was 8-1/2 x 14 prior to reduction for print. Obtaining the large size paper is well worth the effort. Do all projections in pencil (accountants always use pencil) and spread it out on the banker's desk pointing out how the bottom line accelerates rapidly. Make projections impressive but do-able. (See FIGURE 23-1 at the end of this chapter.)

Your banker, even though he may not comprehend all the figures right at that moment, will be dazzled by your homework being done so astutely.

12.   Calculate the total amount of the loan desired.

This is a figure totally dependent upon your needs!

The result of this exercise is very effective for its presentation to the banker. However, its most important function is that strong psychological advantage of having a set of monthly goals to achieve or even surpass on your part!

NEGOTIATING YOUR BEST DEAL

Now that your homework is completed you will walk into the bank with your head held higher because you know you are going to succeed.

Practice your presentation several times at home before your scheduled meeting with Mr. Banker. Go through the entire list in the EXACT order you have prepared it. Go through all the details just as we did in the outline above.

Now Mr. Banker has viewed your last three years tax returns, your personal financial statement, other cash sources, if any. He has looked over your building lot site plan, has admired your building plans with detailed analysis of costs including parking lot and landscaping.

Your banker has also seen brochures and costs on all of your proposed dental equipment. He has seen costs for office equipment and furniture. He has seen your business plan and your projections. Chances are excellent he will propose that they finance your endeavor. Turn him down! Not flatly, but more in the tone of "Your interest rate sounds pretty steep." The banker will almost never quote you his very best shot the first time.

Before going into this meeting you will, of course, have checked on the prime lending rate. (This information is available in the <u>Wall Street</u> <u>Journal</u> or from many other sources and it changes from time to time.)

Your banker may propose, for instance, 2-1/2 points over prime which means 2-1/2% over the current prime rate. What he is telling you is that for the life of your loan the interest rate will fluctuate each time the prime rate changes. When the prime rate goes up 1/2% your interest rate goes up 1/2%.

Therefore, if the prime rate is 6.75% at the time and he offers 2-1/2% over prime he is offering you a 9.25% rate.

Perhaps the best you can hope for is about 1-1/2% or 2% over prime. One-half percent on a sizeable loan is a very significant savings.

If you ask for 1-1/2% over prime he may settle on 2% over prime and you have struck a deal.

A better strategy may be to leave with the statement that you were hoping to obtain a loan at 1-1/2 points over prime and you will have to think it over and he can think it over also.

Very politely thank him for his time and express that it has been enjoyable as it most certainly will be when you are well prepared.

Shop other sources to compare interest rates.

Contact your original banker in a few days to see what he has come up with. In negotiations, always allow the other party to speak first. You may be hoping for 2% over prime while he may be thinking 1-3/4% over prime.

If two points over prime is the best deal you can obtain from any lender, you have to take it, if you need the financing.

Your banker probably will want the bank to be the beneficiary of a life insurance as well as a disability insurance policy on you because it is your earning power on which they are loaning their money. This is customary and reasonable!

Once you have struck a deal on the interest rate your banker may tell you the entire $200,000 will be transferred to your account tomorrow.

You say "No" again.

Explain that what you want is a **Line of Credit** not a loan! With a line of credit you pay interest on the money only after you have written a check against the line of credit and the check has cleared. The banker would prefer to have interest accumulating on the entire $200,000 from day one.

If you are on a 90-day construction schedule you can avoid interest on a portion of the building costs until the building is completed. Further, the equipment requires only a small down payment with the order. Sometimes you can even negotiate to make final payment from 30 to 60 days after receiving the dental equipment and usually without additional charges.

You have saved as much as 5 months' interest - 3 months' construction time, plus 2 months after the equipment arrives.

The general strategy with a line of credit during the start-up phase of a dental practice is to make payments to contractors, subcontractors, dental suppliers, telephone companies, etc., as slowly as possible while keeping everyone happy or at least amiable. You often can negotiate up front with the building contractor for the final payment to be made 30 days after occupancy. This all helps contribute to a successful and effective start-up.

With prudent use of this information, you will be successful at the bank and in your dental practice.

In the next Chapter we will take a look at creating your Mission Statement...

CASH FLOW PROJECTIONS

	APRIL 90 (1)	MAY 90 (2)	JUNE 90 (3)	JULY 90 (4)	AUG 90 (5)	SEPT 90 (6)	OCT 90 (7)	NOV 90 (8)	DEC 90 (9)	JAN 91 (10)	FEB 91 (11)	MAR 91 (12)
INCOME	3500	4500	6500	8500	10500	10500	12500	13000	13500	14000	14500	15000
EXPENSE	3620	4340	5180	8560	9930	9930	11170	11375	11580	11785	11990	12395
(net)	⟨1120⟩	160	1320	⟨60⟩	570	570	1330	1625	1920	2215	2510	2605
MORTGAGE	1000	1000	1000	1000	1000	1000	1000	1000	1000	1000	1000	1000
SALARIES	1000	1500	1900	2400	2800	2800	3200	3200	3200	3200	3300	3400
UTILITIES	275	275	275	275	275	275	275	275	275	275	275	275
LAB FEES	270	405	585	765	945	945	1125	1170	1215	1260	1305	1350
MISC	500	500	500	500	500	500	500	500	500	500	500	500
SUPPLIES	325	410	560	630	710	710	770	780	790	800	810	820
ADVERTISING	250	250	350	450	550	550	550	550	550	550	550	550
PAY DR.												
DUE DR.												
DUE DR TO DATE	750	1350	1950	2550	3150	3150	3750	3900	4050	4200	4350	4500
INCOME	15500	16000	16500	17000	17500	17500	18000	18500	18500	19000	19500	20000
EXPENSE	12700	13125	13380	13715	14050	14050	14385	14720	14720	15055	15390	15725
(net)	2800	2875	3120	3485	3450	3450	3615	3780	3780	3945	4110	4275
MORTGAGE	1000	1000	1000	1000	1000	1000	1000	1000	1000	1000	1000	1000
SALARIES	3500	3600	3630	3790	3850	3850	3960	4070	4070	4180	4290	4400
UTILITIES	275	275	275	275	275	275	275	275	275	275	275	275
LAB FEES	1395	1440	1485	1530	1575	1575	1630	1665	1665	1710	1755	1800
MISC.	500	500	500	500	500	500	500	500	500	500	500	500
SUPPLIES	830	960	990	1020	1050	1050	1080	1110	1110	1140	1170	1200
ADVERTISING	550	550	550	550	550	550	550	550	550	550	550	550
PAY DR.	4650	4900	4950	5100	5250	5250	5400	5550	5550	5700	5850	6000

FIGURE 23-1
SAMPLE
PROJECTION SHEET

CHAPTER 24

YOUR MISSION STATEMENT

"We are prophets unto ourselves and we fulfill our prophecies."
(Author unknown)

A mission statement is a statement of the purpose or course to which a person or a group is dedicated. In order for a mission statement to be effective it must be created by those it serves.

Get your staff together and, with a little guidance, have them create a mission statement they can GET EXCITED ABOUT.

DEVELOPING YOUR MISSION STATEMENT:

Developing a mission statement can be fun as well as very rewarding. It is essential that it be developed <u>by</u> the staff as opposed to being developed <u>for</u> the staff. Just as the patient clings to her shade choice staff members become involved and emotionally charged by a mission statement which they have created.

"To be available to take care of the dental needs of our community at the convenience of the patient in a friendly, loving environment."

OR

"To provide quality dental care in comfortable surroundings for the convenience as well as the benefit of the patient."

These are very important statements because they identify a certain market segment by offering evening and/or Saturday appointments. This addresses the following patients:

1.   **Working class - works 8 to 5 ... can come in after work or on Saturdays.**

2.   **Children - do not need to miss school - let school authorities know this service is available.**

3.   **Moms - can have a dental appointment in the evening or on Saturday while Dad watches the kids.**

4.   **Dads - can come right after work while Mom watches the kids.**

Your mission statement could include phases of dentistry like:

1.   **To develop primarily a crown and bridge practice.**

2.   **To be known as the Denture Center.**

3.   **Fill the need for root canal therapy in the area.**

4.   **Emphasis on preventive or periodontal treatment.**

5.   **To produce $1,000,000 by CARING for your patients!**

Your mission statement may be time specific -- to work only 3-1/2 days per week or 30 hours per week.

To love making dentistry fun.

Whatever best fits your desires and needs.

While it is important that the staff creates the mission statement, it is also necessary that they do it with your guidance and in a direction which is compatible with your goals, and developed in a spirit of camaraderie.

An ideal setting for the creation of your mission statement might be for the dentist to be writing on the marker board, facilitating the session and receiving at least one component of the mission statement from each staff member. The next step is to have all staff members endorse the final mission statement. Once the staff is all in unison you have created a powerful tool!

Once your Mission Statement has been prepared, you will want to take a look at our next chapter on Goal Setting.

CHAPTER 25

GOAL SETTING

"Goals are as essential to success as air is to life."
David Schwartz

The famous follow-up study on 4% of the Yale graduates with written goals whose net worth 20 years after graduation exceeded the net worth of the 96% of their classmates without written goals is so impressive it is hard to believe there are still some people who operate without goals.

As Earl Nightingale would say when referring to those without goals "...navigating like a ship without a rudder." "Highly unlikely to reach any worthwhile destination."

The apparent magic of goal setting combined with the vivid picturing of the result produce amazing clarity of vision and incredible results.

Goals are best when reduced to writing. They must be realistic so the subconscious mind can accept them as reasonable and do-able. Yet the subconscious mind appears often to be more aware of potential than is the conscious mind.

Goals should be stated in measurable terms (dollars will do) and set to be accomplished within a specific time frame.

Assume we have a practice grossing $220,000 in the current year and that we want to gross $1,000,000 in the following year. Our subconscious mind sees this as unrealistic and will not participate in this folly.

On the other hand if you do your accounting on the calendar year (which is recommended by most accountants and is great for goal setting) and you are doing $220,000 in year one and you write out a plan for year two as follows:

1. Fee schedule increase of 10% effective January 1, Year Two.

2. Marketing plan which calls for 8% of gross receipts designated for bringing in new patients in Year Two.

3. Adding an additional certified and registered dental assistant in Year Two.

4. Extending the hours to include one evening a week.

5. And setting a <u>realistic</u> goal of $280,000 for Year Two, which breaks down to $70,000 per quarter.

It may be believable and do-able.

Even though this is a 27% increase in a single year, which is quite ambitious, it may well be possible because a systematic plan for the goal achievement has been laid out.

It is a good idea to evaluate the year by quarters; at the ends of March, June, September, and December, as well as monthly, weekly and daily so that a single month's activity does not skew your projections. It is possible to have a great or not so great month, but by the quarter you have a much better feel for your general direction. If, at the end of your first quarter, you are running behind your desired quarterly projections, you may want to make changes in your marketing or promotional plans for the second quarter. On the other hand, if your first quarter or second quarter has far exceeded your projections, adjust your annual goals upward.

Goal setting methods, strategies, and philosophies are as varied as are techniques in dentistry. Most agree that it is important to have short term, intermediate and long term goals.

For now, let us set ONE YEAR goals, TEN YEAR goals and TWENTY YEAR goals.

Adjust these to fit your own situation.

Obviously, if one is nearing retirement one might choose to do 1-year, 3-year and 5-year goals while at the other end of the scale, if one is currently in dental school just about to launch into an exciting career in dentistry, one may choose to set 1-year, 5-year, 10-year, 20-year and 30-year goals.

Goals need not be totally related to dentistry or to production. They can apply to other aspects of one's life. However, numerical goals are ideal for demonstrative purposes.

Let's assume a goal of creating a million dollar practice, be it in year twenty, ten, five, three or next year.

Bear in mind you must be realistic, but recognize the incredible powers of your subconscious mind as well as your conscious mind. We are walking the tightrope again!

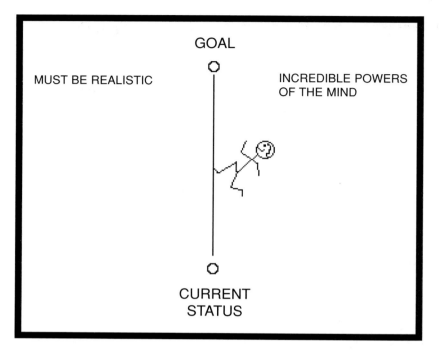

As the Quote Goes, "Inch by Inch - Life's a Cinch."
Robert Schuller

Rather than saying on January 2nd that the goal is one million dollars for the year, working like a crazy person all year and then observing how close you came on December 31st, it is more realistic to create manageable chunks which can be monitored and adjusted during the year.

Here is one way to approach this project:

Let's assume your desire to create your own million dollar practice is so strong that you are willing to work 52 weeks to accomplish this and will limit your vacations to long weekends. Your goals might look like this:

GOAL FOR THE YEAR	**$1,000,000**
GOAL FOR EACH QUARTER	**$ 250,000**
GOAL FOR EACH MONTH	**$ 83,333**
GOAL PER WEEK*	**$ 19,231**
GOAL PER DAY**	**$ 3,846**

* **$1,000,000 divided by 52 = $19,230.77**

** **This figure does not account for holidays and long weekends. To aim for $4,300 per day gives nice allowance for recreation time.**

Now you have an objective method for monitoring your progress.

But note that even the most productive dentist has days when so little is accomplished it is ridiculous. Observe this fact and let yourself be amused by it for it will always be a fact of dentistry. Therefore, do not let a single day or even a week overly concern you. When you are operating efficiently and effectively, another day or another week will be so tremendously productive you will hardly be able to believe those figures either.

Just focus on each day, concentrate on what is the best for your patients and how you can best serve them and eventually the numbers will pleasantly surprise you.

This is by no means saying to ignore the daily, weekly or monthly results. It is only saying that practices produce in waves, and quarterly production is much more indicative of trends. In fact, some weeks we do so many of the same procedures our assistants are accused of "hanging the 'special on root canal treatments' shingle" outside our door. Other weeks it seems to be all crown and bridge and another week just a ton of kids.

If at the end of January you are not on course, adjust your marketing, presentation, scheduling, recall, staff, hours open or all or part of the above until you are obtaining figures compatible with the goals you set.

Graphs are an ideal way to monitor progress.

Graph 25-1 is set up for you to plot your production right in this book or you can photocopy the page, white out the figures, and fill in your goals - be they $500,000, $200,000 or whatever is practical. Plot your progress monthly.

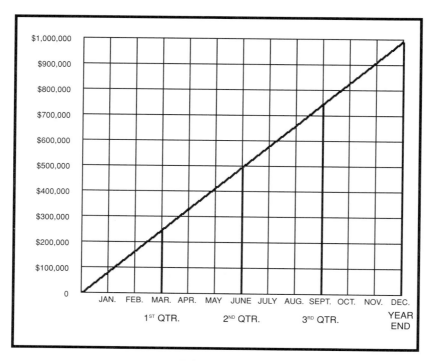

FIGURE 25-1
Yearly Goals

With the use of Graph 25-1 you can plot your progress toward your goal on a monthly basis. Don't be discouraged if you are falling a bit behind in the early months. All the time you are ascending the learning curve and it is customary for the later months to be considerably more productive than the earlier months. This is evidenced by your learning how to be more efficient, more effective, and more productive; your ability to serve more patients.

Remember as Winston Churchill said, **"Never, Never, Never, Never give up."**

Below find Graph 25-2 for your 10 year goals and on the following page find 25-3 for your 20 year goals. Write in the book or photocopy them, alter them to fit your needs, but do yourself a favor and set goals, monitor them, work toward them, and your rewards will be phenomenal!

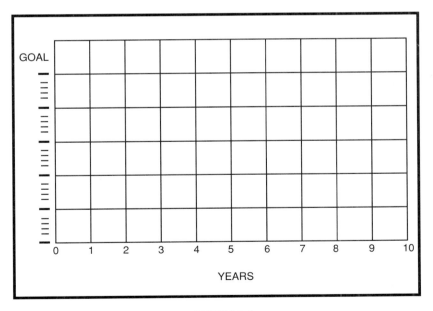

FIGURE 25-2
10 Year Goals

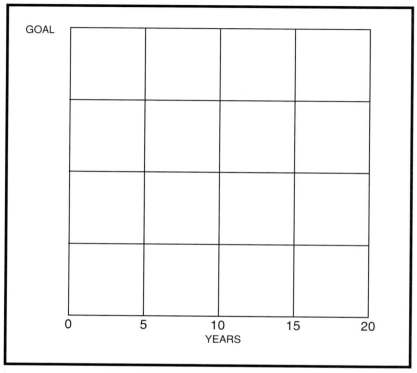

FIGURE 25-3
20 Year Goals

GOAL SETTING SUMMARY

The seemingly magical powers of setting goals, reducing your goals to written form, and developing a plan for achieving these goals will put you into a position to achieve beyond your fondest expectations.

Also bear in mind your goals do not need to be monetary. You can use the same process to achieve goals of spending more quality time with a loved one or physical achievements such as running a marathon or working less or taking more vacation time or whatever.

Just remember the principle is to:

1. Set a REALISTIC goal which is achievable.

2. Reduce it to writing.

3. Establish a plan for its accomplishment.

4. Monitor your progress toward your goal - graphs work best.

5. Make adjustments in your plan, if necessary, to assure your success.

Now that you have the armament for achieving whatever it is that is most important in your life, pause a moment --

-- Write down your fondest goal,

-- Establish a plan for its achievement; and

-- **Walk your Talk** right down the path you have prepared -- to have your goal become a REALITY!

CHAPTER 26

THE PHYSICAL PLANT

"The thing always happens that you really believe in; and the belief in a thing makes it happen."

Frank Lloyd Wright

I remember a meeting years ago with a real estate tycoon. He stated to be successful in real estate you have to know only three things. Those three things are LOCATION, LOCATION, LOCATION!

We all laughed at the time as the presentation was amusing. However, the content was serious.

Where to locate your dental office is of significant importance.

LOCATION:

In our analysis of location we want to explore the following:

1. **Demographics** - Pay special attention to the market segment you intend to pursue, as well as growth patterns in your area.

2. **Visibility** - a great asset. High visibility means that the building and/or sign can be viewed for a long distance while approaching the location. In contrast, a building site with adjacent commercial buildings built right out to the street gives minimal visibility and should be avoided.

3. **Traffic count** - the main arterial street is best - the higher the traffic count the better.

4. **Access from street** - patients must be able to have easy access from the street. A boulevard or a divided street with an inaccessible divider for one direction of traffic is a definite detriment. We once studied a location off the cloverleaf of a busy freeway which had phenomenal traffic count, but which was very difficult to access. It was turned down because of the difficulty of access.

5. **Proximity to school, college, factory, hospital, etc.** - where patients can get to your facility with minimal travel time. This also affords a high-density marketing target.

6. **Dentist population** - plot the dentists within a 7 or 10 mile radius on a map.

7. **Dentists' ages** - determine the surrounding dentists' ages and anticipated retirement ages. Some retire at age 50 and some at age 80.

8. **Dentist's willingness to refer** - visit several dentists in the proposed area and chat about needs in the area. Would they refer their children patients, denture patients, etc., to you? Are they taking new patients?

9. **Cost of land, office space, building** - check to see what office space rent would cost. Calculate the cost of land and building, the current interest rates and determine approximately what your mortgage payment would be. From these calculations make a decision on renting-vs-building a new facility.

For several reasons I personally strongly prefer a free-standing building. This is surely somewhat related to personality as the results-oriented personality prefers not to be dependent on a landlord if something needs to be accomplished.

REASONS FOR A FREE-STANDING BUILDING:

1. VISIBILITY - far superior visibility to a strip mall or office complex or above the drug store.

2. SIGNAGE - By having a free standing building one can have sufficient signage on the street to display your logo and let the public know you are there.

3. PARKING - Parking at your front door - convenience for the patient makes it as effortless as possible.

4. FUNCTIONALITY - Building designed for dentistry; as opposed to trying to adapt existing space to dental use.

5. ESTHETICS - Able to create a nice, neat clean-looking building, landscaping, sidewalk and parking lot.

6.   ELIMINATE LANDLORD AND LEASE COMPLI-CATIONS - You are in control of your own destiny.

7.   PATIENT ACCEPTANCE - Patients are very favorably impressed by a total facility devoted to the care of their dentition.

8.   EQUITY POSITION - As you make your monthly payments you are creating an equity position and you can pay off your mortgage in 10 years or 5 years, if you so desire.

9.   COMMITMENT - This is a two-edged sword -- the dentist's commitment (psychological) to make this work and the community's perception of the dentist's commitment to serve the long-term needs of the community.

YOUR BUILDING LOT

Your building lot size requirement would be dependent upon your local requirements and must be researched for your particular situation and through your local authorities: Planning & Zoning, City Hall, Courthouse, City Clerk, Building Inspector, etc.

The cost of a building lot may vary greatly. A building site in a small town may run as little as $10,000 or less while the costs of a downtown location in an urban area may be prohibitive.

If the core city lots are too expensive, explore the peripheral locations for a building site that makes sense. Finding a building site in a suburban area which is in the direction the city is growing may be much less costly and be in an area where many new families are moving.

This Deerwood building is on a lot 100 feet wide by 150 feet deep, 15,000 square feet. Since an acre is 43,560 square feet, our lot is .34 acre or just over 1/3 acre. Your prospective building lots will often be represented in terms of acres or a fraction thereof.

You may well need more space. Your local authorities are generally very helpful when you are anticipating a new building in their jurisdiction. Simply call the governing office and inform them you are anticipating building a 28' x 52' dental building 1,456 square feet. Ask what the lot requirements are. They will probably tell you over the telephone.

THE PRIMARY EFFECT OF THE PHYSICAL PLANT --The patient's reaction --

Empirical evidence has shown that the physical plant can be a very big factor in the rapid development of a successful dental practice.

This is both good and bad. It is **good** in that we know what to do to get off to a fast start. It is **bad** in that it takes capital to create an impressive physical plant.

However, by following a proven design which is functional, practical, efficient, and by following the guidelines in this chapter you will be able to build a dental office you are proud of and your patients think is great. You can do this within a reasonable budget.

The physical plant makes a statement to the patient who drives by and to the patient who enters. This statement most appropriately says..."Wow, this is a nice, clean, warm, bright, cheery dental facility." And if the logo makes them smile - so much the better. In most cases it is important to have the decor nice but not too nice. If it is too nice, too plush, too beautiful, too expensive, the patients immediately think they are going to pay too much and regardless of your fee schedule, their minds are made up. "It's too high!" This depends, of course, on the market segment you are addressing.

Approach this physical plant scenario with your own plan, get bids from several general contractors (a list of which any building material supplier will furnish to you), check with homeowners (this building is not that different from residential construction) or commercial contractors (possibly higher in price). By comparing square footage costs to similar residential new construction, one may be able to create a really nice facility and keep the cost within reason.

Being your own general contractor, you can probably save an additional 10% to 12% on the building costs. However, it could turn into a fiasco if you are not qualified. Undertake this task only if you are knowledgeable about construction and have the time to devote to it.

If you have a general contractor, include a completion date and a penalty for each day beyond the completion date in your agreement with him. If the opening of the office is delayed, the penalty should be substantial. Perhaps $200 to $500 per day. Be reasonable in your interpretation of completion...if you can function by completion date, go for it. Things can happen in construction just like in dentistry.

Open on your opening date. If the contractor has to come in some weekend and do some touch-up or a little trim or swap out some door knobs or fixtures, treat him with understanding and compassion -- as you would like that patient whose crown did not fit to treat you.

On the other hand, if your building is 60 days late getting into operation you have bought a building at 60 x $500 = $30,000 less than the original bid.

As of this writing (1994-95) this building could be constructed here in northern Minnesota for approximately $65.00 per square foot or $94,640 on your lot.

Regional variations, local ordinances and codes, parking space requirements, union vs. non-union craftsmen all play a significant role in construction and in the actual cost.

If you do decide to build your own building---let me be the first one to congratulate you! Construction is great fun, exciting and rewarding.

Follow these guidelines...seek qualified help for any phase of the construction you need help with. Keep the costs down. Get competing bids. Don't be talked into a lot of extravagances and you will be ever grateful you did it this way.

STEP I   Check with local authorities on zoning requirements and lot size requirements for the building you desire.

STEP II   Land - If you are going to build you must first have a lot to build on. Refer to the beginning of this chapter - LOCATION.

This is big decision time -- while location is very important some "ideal" locations may be cost prohibitive.

You want a good location with high visibility and good traffic volume passing by daily to see your sign and building but you do not want to totally distort your overhead in the process.

If the core city costs are unreasonable take a look at locations more toward the edge of the city in the direction the city is growing.

In this way you may be able to get a good buy on a lot and be right in a neighborhood where new families are moving. Carefully check out many possibilities and then make a decision. You must take action! Purchase a lot which is at least slightly larger than your minimal requirements and up to twice the size of your minimal requirements if the price is right. You may choose to expand some day.

STEP III   Consider an architect - meet with a couple of architects and discuss your plans. Ask what they can do for you and what the cost will be.

You may choose not to use an architect, but you still will learn much by meeting with them.

STEP IV   Check local building codes and local building procedures. You don't want to try to put in a basement if you are in solid granite!! If you have an architect he or she will address these issues. If you do not have an architect it will be necessary for you to do your homework.

STEP V   Get a plan - use the one from this book, have this one modified or use an entirely different plan.

Have an architect, a draftsman, a builder or yourself, if you are qualified, draw a working plan to include:

> Foundation
> Framing
> Electrical
> Plumbing
> Heating and air conditioning
> Cabinets and countertops
> Nitrous oxide and oxygen
> Air lines and vacuum lines
> Landscape and parking
> Signage

Specify all materials for inside and outside walls, ceilings and floor coverings, cabinets, and countertops.

STEP VI   Select a general contractor --

Get bids from several contractors - look at their recently completed projects.

Talk to owners of recently completed projects.

Find out where the contractor buys his lumber, then find out from the lumber yard where the contractor's last few projects have been completed. This way you get the real picture. The contractor himself will only lead you to his most satisfied customers.

Examine the contractor's finished product while visiting with his previous customers. This is a most critical process -- once you are committed to a contractor you are married to him - do your homework first.

When selecting a contractor and entering into an agreement insist that a part of that agreement be a time frame for a completed project. Ninety days should be sufficient; never consider going over 120 days!

Our "million dollar" office was completed -- from breaking frost to dig the basement to patients being treated -- in seven weeks. To accomplish this, I was on the site constantly during construction to avoid any decision delays.

Once the deal is struck, do everything you can possibly do to help the contractor and build a great rapport. By working together, being available to him for quick decisions and checking in regularly you can both have a good time and create a very nice facility in which to practice dentistry.

THE SECONDARY EFFECT OF THE PHYSICAL PLANT -- on the Community --

While the primary effect of the physical plant (the patient's reaction to it) is sufficient to justify the cost, the secondary effect is an unspoken subjective realization of commitment. This beautiful nice new single purpose facility is a statement to the community that there is a strong intention to provide dental care for a long time into the future.

This is important because patients do not like to switch dentists and also do not like to switch dental facilities. Even if the dentist did move and the staff remained the same, patients would find it to be less traumatic than moving to a new facility <u>and</u> a new dentist.

CONSTRUCTION NOTES:

-- washable interior walls are necessary.

-- we used vinyl wrapped gypsum board - your lumber supplier will show you samples.

-- high light intensity in the operatories as per the specifications -- so if the dentist takes his eyes out of the patient's mouth to look at the instrument tray his pupils do not need to readjust from the high intensity dental light.

-- windows where patient and staff can see out -- to see the sunshine (or snow)!

-- curved wall in the waiting room is of high esthetic value.

You will probably receive much opposition from your contractor to the radius wall in the waiting room/operatory area. Do not give in! This soft curve has a very soothing effect on the first impression of the patient as she enters the waiting room. You have sufficient room in the operatory and the challenge is good for the craftsmen for as they "stretch they grow" also.

An alternative to the vinyl wrapped gypsum board is to sheet rock, tape, size and wallpaper. This alternative gives much more color and pattern selection because the choices of washable wallpaper are approaching infinity.

The cost of vinyl wrapped gypsum vs. drywall: tape, size and wallpaper is very close to the same. Wallpaper is more time consuming and creates more of a mess with taping and sanding joints.

The vinyl wrapped gypsum finished product is superior because it is more durable and no paper seams open as time goes on. Also, the construction time is far less for the vinyl wrapped gypsum. Having done it both ways several times, we find the vinyl wrapped gypsum more satisfactory for most applications.

Hard surface floor covering is recommended for the entry way, the waiting room side of the receptionist desk, the laboratory, the bathrooms and the operatories. The remainder can be carpeted.

Put in a basement, if possible, for the mechanical room where you can store your evacuation system, air compressor, nitrous oxide and oxygen tanks, hot water heater, furnace and extra supplies.

If a basement is not practical in your location, add a room at least 8 x 12 in the rear of the building for your mechanical components.

ON THE FOLLOWING PAGES FIND FLOOR PLANS,
ELECTRICAL PLAN, PLUMBING PLAN,
JUNCTION BOX, FLUORESCENT LIGHTING,
SOUND SYSTEM, LANDSCAPE
AND SIGN PLANS

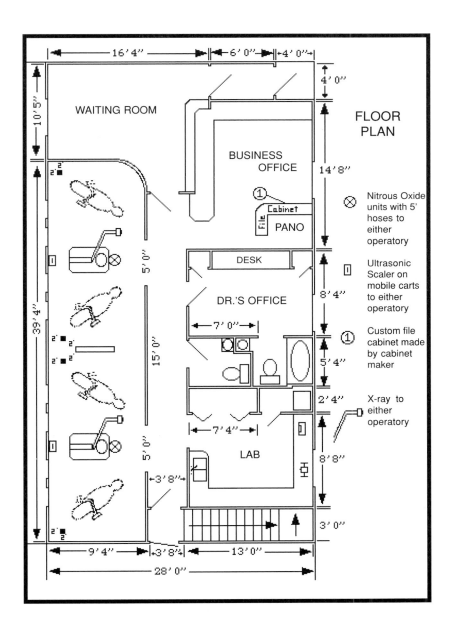

FLOOR
PLAN

Nitrous Oxide units with 5' hoses to either operatory

Ultrasonic Scaler on mobile carts to either operatory

Custom file cabinet made by cabinet maker

X-ray to either operatory

WAITING ROOM

BUSINESS OFFICE

Cabinet

PANO

DESK

DR.'S OFFICE

LAB

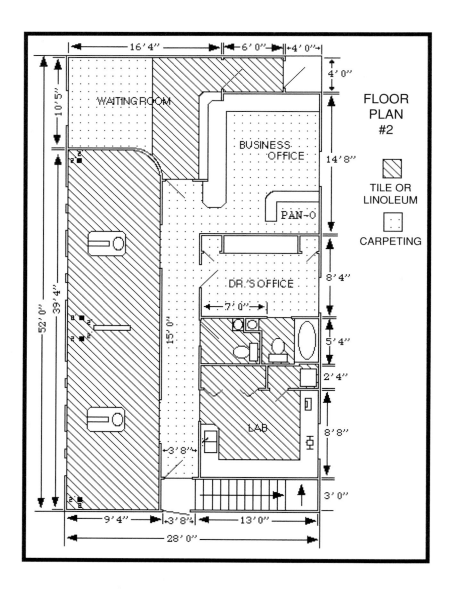

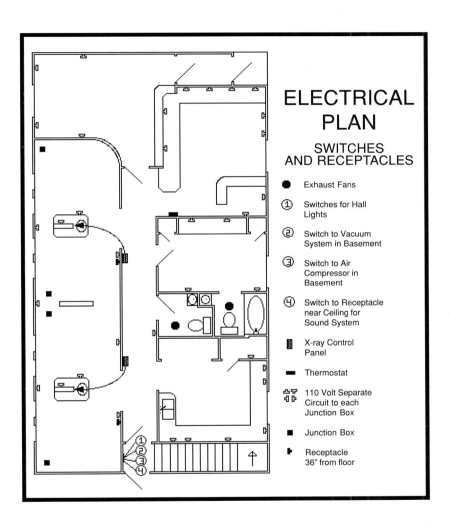

ELECTRICAL PLAN

SWITCHES AND RECEPTACLES

●   Exhaust Fans

①   Switches for Hall Lights

②   Switch to Vacuum System in Basement

③   Switch to Air Compressor in Basement

④   Switch to Receptacle near Ceiling for Sound System

▌   X-ray Control Panel

▬   Thermostat

  110 Volt Separate Circuit to each Junction Box

■   Junction Box

▶   Receptacle 36" from floor

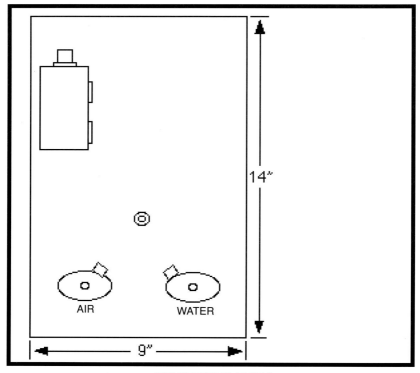

JUNCTION BOX

AIR - 1/2" pipe N.P.T. protruding 1" from floor or wall. Supplied by contractor. Manual shut-off valve supplied by dental dealer to be installed by contractor. Air pressure 80-100 P.S.I. Air plumbing should be flushed clean before making final connections to dental equipment.

WATER - 1/2" pipe N.P.T. protruding 1" from floor or wall. Supplied by contractor. Manual shut-off valves supplied by dental dealer to be installed by contractor. Water pressure 40-80 P.S.I. Water plumbing should be flushed clean before making final connections to dental equipment.

ELECTRICAL - 1/2" conduit and box with quad or equal receptacle supplied by contractor. Wire box as per Code with top of the box no higher than 4" above finished floor. Voltage: 110 volts, 3 wire.

CENTRAL VACUUM - plumbing up to utility center should be specified by central vacuum supplier and terminated in utility center with 5/8" O.D. tube perpendicular to floor similar to drain connection.

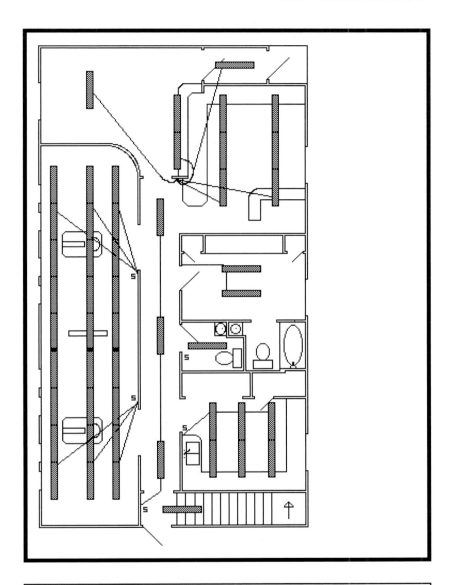

FLUORESCENT LIGHTING PLAN

Dual Bulb 4' Panels

S = Switch

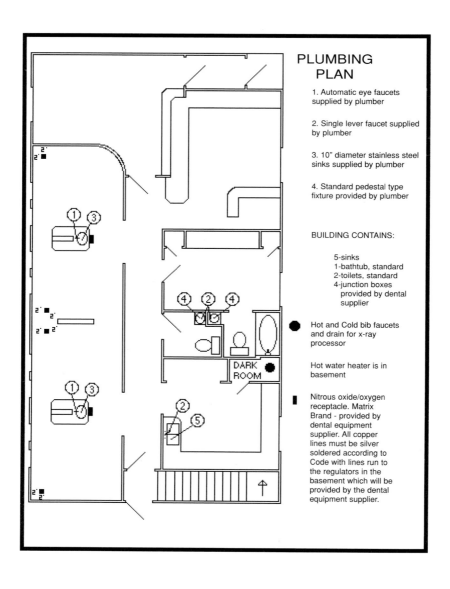

PLUMBING PLAN

1. Automatic eye faucets supplied by plumber

2. Single lever faucet supplied by plumber

3. 10" diameter stainless steel sinks supplied by plumber

4. Standard pedestal type fixture provided by plumber

BUILDING CONTAINS:

5-sinks
1-bathtub, standard
2-toilets, standard
4-junction boxes
  provided by dental
  supplier

Hot and Cold bib faucets and drain for x-ray processor

Hot water heater is in basement

Nitrous oxide/oxygen receptacle. Matrix Brand - provided by dental equipment supplier. All copper lines must be silver soldered according to Code with lines run to the regulators in the basement which will be provided by the dental equipment supplier.

DARK ROOM

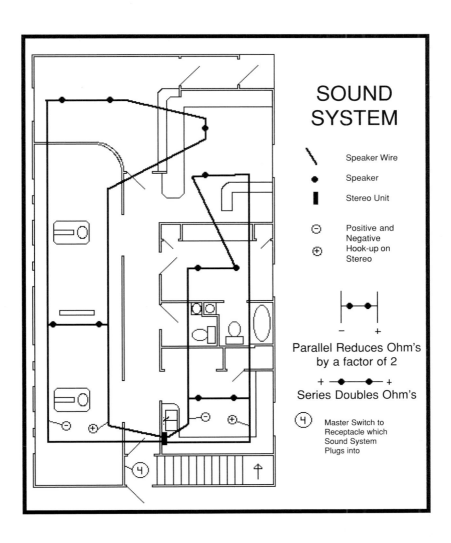

SOUND SYSTEM

╲	Speaker Wire
●	Speaker
▮	Stereo Unit
⊖	Positive and Negative
⊕	Hook-up on Stereo

Parallel Reduces Ohm's by a factor of 2

Series Doubles Ohm's

④ Master Switch to Receptacle which Sound System Plugs into

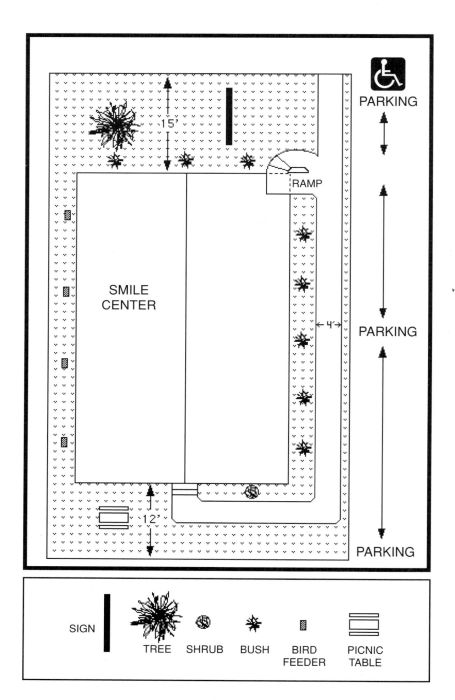

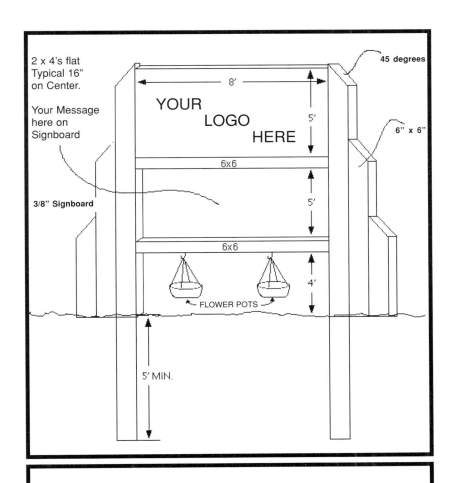

2 x 4's flat
Typical 16"
on Center.

Your Message
here on
Signboard

3/8" Signboard

45 degrees

6" x 6"

8'

YOUR
LOGO
HERE

5'

6x6

5'

6x6

4'

FLOWER POTS

5' MIN.

OUTDOOR SIGN

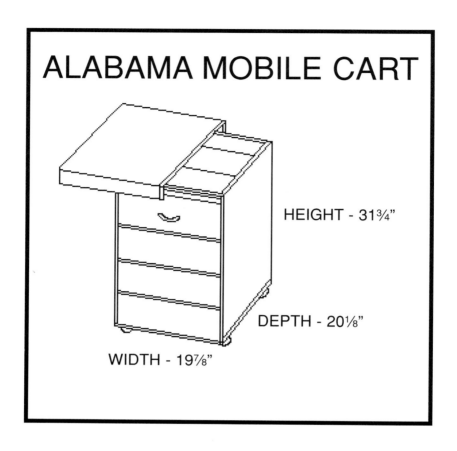

CHAPTER 27

THE TELEPHONE SYSTEM

"We are not creatures of circumstances; we are creators of circumstances."
Benjamin Disraeli

Since initial contact with the dental office is usually by telephone, the telephone system is very important.

The telephone companies recommend that the telephone should be answered by the third ring in a friendly, uniform, helpful way, with a smile on the receptionist's voice which carries over the phone. It is a great idea to have a mirror by each telephone as a constant reminder for the receptionists to smile while answering the telephone.

When building an office, well before printing appointment cards, business cards or stationery, contact the telephone company and notify them of your plans to open a dental office. Tell them that you are interested in selecting a telephone number which will fit into your marketing plans. Ask them for a list of possible telephone numbers. Their first list may not include all of the available numbers, so persist for more selection until you get a number you can work with. Make your search for a good telephone number an EARLY priority in your dental office plans.

WHAT TO LOOK FOR IN A TELEPHONE NUMBER:

What you want in a telephone number is one which the patient can remember and you can promote. It is effective when patients can recall the number and can tell their friends the number as opposed to having their friends look in the telephone book. And since the telephone book is only published once a year, generally, there may be a delay before your number appears. Look for anything catchy! Assume that your area code is 222. If you could get 222-2222 your patients might relate two to tooth and never have to look up your number. Just dial 1-222-222-2222.

Zeroes are good - 920-0000 or 922-2000, 534-3434 or anything which is easy, catchy, fun and most of all --- easy to remember!

Once you have the number, print it on all forms, letterhead, appointment cards, balloons, outdoor signage, etc.

YOUR TELEPHONE SYSTEM:

The telephone *system* should be studied carefully --

We have four lines coming into our office. The fourth line doubles for the FAX machine. We would not recommend any fewer for a busy office. You may choose to start with two live lines but be sure your initial system is capable of adding a third and fourth line without additional major expense.

It is imperative that the patient gets through immediately when he finally gets up the courage to call the dental office. We do not want the patient to have to dial two, three or four different numbers.

Therefore the additional lines (2nd, 3rd, 4th) must be on what the telephone people call a rotary which is the ability of the system to roll over the calls coming to the 222-2222 number to the 2nd line when the 1st line is in use and to the 3rd line when lines 1 and 2 are in use and so on. When your FAX machine is not in use, this line also is available for rollover use as necessary.

In this way the publicized number rings in whenever any of the lines are open. Monitor the lights on your telephone system and if all the lights are on often, you must do something. Discuss the phone situation with the receptionists to see how they feel, then either coach them on being more brief or add another line.

There is absolutely no excuse for a patient not to reach a receptionist 98% of the time. It is our responsibility as managers of a successful dental practice to keep a line open for incoming calls.

If you are in an area where a considerable percentage of your patients are charged for their telephone calls to your office, it may be of benefit to look into the cost of an 800 number.

We have an 800 number in our office since we are in a relatively sparsely populated area where the various local calling districts are divided up in such a way that the majority of our patients are charged long distance fees to call our office.

Making it convenient and free to call for an appointment and being greeted by a friendly and compassionate voice by the third ring will help get more patients into your office.

The easier you make it for your patients, the more patients you will serve.

One of the substantial benefits of our open office design is the ability of the dentist to be aware of the receptionists' end of many telephone conversations during the course of the day while treating patients.

Therefore, when time allows he can assist the receptionists in fine tuning their telephone techniques.

For more advantages of the Open Operatory Concept proceed to Chapter 28.

CHAPTER 28

OPEN OPERATORY CONCEPT

"A man can succeed at almost anything for which he has unlimited enthusi-asm."

Charles M. Schwab

The open operatory arrangement is where several dental chairs are in a single room with dividers separating them.

THE OPEN OPERATORY IS EFFICIENT --

The open concept adds so much to efficiency, flexibility, and effec-tiveness, allowing the potential for increasing production by as much as 70%, while helping the patients feel more at ease.

The fact that the dentist supervises the dental assistants and hygien-ists while at the same time performing his regular functions, affords opportunity for the team to serve significantly more patients in a day.

When the dentist is in the same room, it allows him to constantly monitor the dental assistants' steps through "pre-diagnosis," consult as necessary so the dental assistants can set up for the appropriate procedure and, consequently, save a tremendous amount of time.

When the dentist arrives in that operatory, he has only to confirm the "pre-diagnosis" and proceed with treatment.

With the dental assistants' "pre-diagnosing" two or three times simultaneously and off and on all day long, the end result is empowering. This is what we call Leveraging the Dentist's Time! We are expending much more of the dental assistants' time and effort to conserve the dentist's time.

MAXIM

THE PRINCIPLE OF LEVERAGING IS FOR THE DENTAL ASSISTANTS TO PERFORM ALL OF THOSE FUNCTIONS WHICH DO NOT REQUIRE A DENTIST TO PERFORM

The dentist performs all of those functions which only a dentist can perform!!

The open operatory concept allows maximum leveraging of the dentist's time. Since the dentist's time is the most precious of the limiting factors in treating the maximum number of patients per unit of time, the contribution of well-trained dental assistants to the OVERALL EFFICIENCY IS PRODIGIOUS!

This open operatory concept is often quite a shock to those viewing it for the first time. Anything new or different from the norm is expected to receive some opposition, just like the horseless carriage or the first wireless communication systems. The strongest opposition usually is heard from those practitioners who have never operated in the open operatory setting while many younger more progressive dentists appear to be moving toward the open operatory concept.

The open operatory is designed so that no patient has a view of any other patient's mouth either when entering, when seated, or when leaving his operatory.

Therefore, when Sally Jones has her dentures out Nancy Smith cannot see her in her edentulous condition.

At the same time, the dentist, from his operating position, can keep abreast of all that is happening in the other operatories. For example, let's assume that an assistant is making an alginate impression or taking an x-ray in another operatory and is having a problem with a gag reflex. The dentist is aware of the challenge and can excuse himself to assist if necessary.

The dentist also can be aware of any verbal communications going on in the other operatories at all times. A hygienist has a patient experiencing discomfort from her root planing in a quadrant you have just anesthetized. But how can this be?

A dental assistant is asking Johnnie if he ever brushes his teeth!

Another assistant is quizzing Susie about the symptoms from her fractured anterior tooth, attempting to determine whether a root canal treatment will be required prior to her restoration.

When you finish with your portion of the crown preparation you are focused on, you can choose to re-anesthetize the mysterious periodontal patient, discuss brushing with Johnnie or start root canal treatment on Susie, as you are aware of the status of all three from being in the same room with them while their conversations are unfolding.

With all of this information you may choose to start the nitrous oxide/oxygen analgesia for Susie's assistant, re-anesthetize the mysterious periodontal patient, then examine and reinforce brushing with Johnnie, in that order.

The open concept allows the dental staff to work as a team while offering the patients a much more comfortable and less isolated environment.

The open concept also allows the convenience, economy and functionality of having ultrasonic scaler capacity, nitrous oxide/oxygen, and radiography availability to all four operatories with only two x-ray machines, two ultrasonic scalers, and two nitrous oxide/oxygen units. By having all operatories equipped the same, any patient can be placed in any operatory and the work day goes on very smoothly.

The less planning and thinking the dental assistants have to do about which patient goes in which operatory the more efficient the office becomes and the more patients can be served in a given day.

While some may criticize equipping the hygiene rooms the same as the other operatories, the smoothness with which the dentist can do a restoration or two or a crown preparation on a hygiene patient far outweighs the cost involved.

THE PSYCHOLOGY OF THE OPEN OPERATORY CONCEPT

Now that we are using the open design it is amazing how many patients volunteer that it is so much "nicer" or "more fun" or "easier" or "less threatening" or "more friendly" ... having the open feeling ... as opposed to the "small room", "closed door", "the way it used to be."

Imagine what's going through an 8-year-old boy's mind when his 10 and 12-year-old sisters are brought into adjacent operatories at the same time. No way is he going to make a peep with his sisters listening and no way are the young girls going to let their little brother hear a noise out of them.

On very rare occasions when a patient (almost always an older one) expresses shock at the open concept, we josh them out of it by expressing something like "We thought those carpenters forgot something. It must have been those walls!" "But we'll just make the best of it, won't we?" Then we explain that no other patients will be able to see in her mouth. Without exception, the patients agree that all is well after all.

The amusing conversations heard from patients in adjacent operatories talking back and forth over the years has brought us all much delight.

In the next Chapter we will take a look at the Dental Equipment utilized in this facility!

CHAPTER 29

DENTAL EQUIPMENT

"In all human affairs there are efforts, and there are results, and the strength of the effort is the measure of the result."

James Allen

The research and purchase of your dental equipment are very important aspects of setting up your new office. It is critically important that you make wise decisions. This guide will assist you in getting the most value for your expenditure.

Even though you will undoubtedly be offered many temptations to lease dental equipment, your BEST value will almost always be to purchase your equipment.

Any lease entered into will necessarily include the cost of the equipment (normally at full retail price) plus the use of the money (usually at a rate well above current averages) for the length of the lease. It's easy to see how some dentists pay twice as much for their equipment as is necessary and therefore, why so many "salesmen" have these "unbelievable deals" on THEIR NEW LEASE PROGRAMS. Once these deals are properly dissected by a savvy accountant they usually are "unbelievable deals."

MAXIM

DO NOT ENTER INTO ANY EQUIPMENT
LEASE PROGRAM UNLESS YOUR TRUSTED
ACCOUNTANT HAS THOROUGHLY
CALCULATED THE TOTAL COSTS AND
SUGGESTED IT TO BE
YOUR BEST STRATEGY

So let's look into our BEST purchase options. Since this is one of the largest expenditures, all possible options are to be researched.

Armed with your equipment list (a sample of which is enclosed in this Chapter) start getting prices on the entire package. Have your suppliers itemize all components of your package.

These initial equipment costs serve as a reference for later.

While the dental equipment people are working on their bids, it is time for you to get to work! This is an area where thousands of dollars can be either SPENT or SAVED.

A good way to start your research is to understand the mechanics of the equipment and how it works. If you have at least average aptitude for mechanical things you may choose to contact a manufacturer or two and tell them you are considering purchasing their equipment and would like to see a schematic of how they are made, how they work and what the installation procedures are. They may well recommend, in an effort to protect their dealers, the equipment be dealer-installed. Agree for the time being, but insist that they send you the requested information because you are considering their equipment and comparing it to another manufacturer. Once you understand the general concept of how the equipment works, installation and/or repair becomes quite trivial.

Contact a mail order company such as Schein equipment (1-800-645-6594) and have them send the information also.

You will soon realize, after you look over the schematic and installation instructions, that it is quite simple. (Or, if you do not have the aptitude or the desire, have a friend or relative -- any mechanic type or construction type -- do it for you.)

Another alternative is to contact a dental equipment service technician. Look in the Yellow Pages. These freelance technicians are usually former employees of one of the large dental supply houses who have started their own business. They will install four operatories quickly and at a relatively modest cost.

Once you are in a position where you no longer are concerned about the installation you are in an entirely different ball game! You are ready to get some bids on your dental equipment.

Give your bidders the dental equipment list (or your modification from the list that follows in this chapter.) Just the equipment F.O.B. their dock, no installation! Then tell them "You'll have a truck at their dock to pick it up and use a sharp pencil to keep the cost to a minimum as the competition is stiff and you would like to see them get the bid."

If you don't know anyone with a pick-up truck you can hire someone for a modest fee or your installer will pick it up for you.

Where many dentists incur much expense is in buying the equipment installed. You will be able to see this from your initial cost estimates.

The dental supply houses grossly overplay the complexity of the installation in most cases.

There are many sources of dental equipment and you are now in the driver's seat. This is a favorable position and a very enjoyable part of the project.

The first time I talked F.O.B. their dock, no installation, many years ago, I was offered an immediate 28% discount from the company's previous bid. This revised bid was offered over the telephone without my even being there.

Twenty-eight percent (28%) on $50,000 or $100,000 can reduce the initial investment considerably which in turn lowers the monthly overhead -- which, of course, with the increase in efficiency and production produces a bottom line which is awesome.

There usually is no problem with installation, but the factory is always very helpful if you do need assistance. (See the listing of 800 numbers at the end of this book.) Also, as I have noted, without exception, that companys' telephone numbers have always been on the installation instructions.

As I have mentioned several times previously in this text, it is important to have all operatories equipped the same right down to the most minute detail. This way no one needs to think about which patient has to go in which operatory thereby facilitating efficiency.

Following find an Equipment List which was taken from our office.

Even though you may choose to alter some items or add as you go, this equipment has been proven to be able to produce a million dollars annually.

(See next page for Dental Equipment List)

DENTAL EQUIPMENT LIST

4 - Belmont Lights - CLESTA Model - 2650 foot candles at 29", 3" high-7-1/2" wide, Focal Band

4 - Belmont Chairs - Serial # L0501 34, Model #-BEL-7, Rating 115V 6A 60Hz

4 - Assistant Stools with Arms - Deltube

4 - Doctor's Stools - Deltube

4 - Engle Units - appear similar to ADEC * - each with:

    3 - High Speed Fiberoptic coiled hoses
    1 - Slow Speed coiled hose
    1 - Condensaire Pneumatic Amalgam Plugger
    1 - Air/Water Syringe

4 - Midwest Shorty Slow Speed Handpieces

1 - Lifecycle Air Station which goes in the sterilization area

36 - Fiberoptic Air Turbine Handpieces
(Three sets - one set in use, one set in the Autoclave, One set being lubricated and ready to go.)

4 - Assistant's Arms - each with:

    1 - Air/Water Syringe
    1 - Saliva Ejector
    2 - HVE (High Volume Evacuators)

2 - Parkell Clean Machine Turbo 25-30 Ultrasonic Scalers

2 - Sedatron Nitrous Oxide/Oxygen Units with Stands, Hoses, and Matrix
Quick Disconnects
Scavenger Systems

2 - Matrix Wall Mount Nitrous Oxide/Oxygen Receptacles

2 - X-ray Belmont Acuray - Model 071 A 70 KVP 10 MA

1 - X-ray Panoramic Corporation - PC - 1000
(1/800-654-2027)

4 - Ultraviolet Lights - DEMETRON - Optilux 400

4 - Amalgamators (get the quick mix 2 or 3 second mix)
(Schein or comparable)

4 - Carpule Warmers - PREMIER

4 - ALABAMA Mobile Carts

1 - DENTSPLY Evacuation System - Model SEU-8,
Dual 2 HP, 230 VOLTS, 14 AMPS

1 - PERIO-PRO Automatic Film Processor
with Daylight Loader

1 - Phillips 620 Film Processor with Daylight Loader

1 - SANBORN 5 HP Air Compressor, Springfield, MN,
Model G500 BPL 60V 1 STAGE 60 Gallon Tank,
Factory Setting 90-120 PSH **

1 - TUTTNAUER^{TM} - Model # 2340, Autoclave

2 - Cold Sterilizers - GETZ

1 - ULTRASONIC Cleaner - (Schein or comparable)

1 - Red Wing Lathe - 1/4 HP

1 - Vibrator - HENRY SCHEIN, BUFFALO (or equivalent)

1 - Vacuum Forming Machine (Henry Schein)

Laboratory Supplies

MISCELLANEOUS SUPPLIES AND MATERIALS

*   We started in May of 1990 with Schein dental units. In the fall of 1992 as momentum was building a fire destroyed all of our equipment. The disaster occurred on a Sunday night about 6:00 p.m. It was Wednesday late evening, three days later, before the insurance adjusters would let us in to start the clean-up. The adjusters words were "You'll be lucky if you are back in business in 90 days." The adjuster knew little about determination. All the walls had to be stripped, the smoky insulation taken out and replaced, new ceiling, new walls, new floor coverings, as well as all dental equipment replaced.

If there has ever been a supreme lesson in the power of rapport in this Universe, this may well have been the lesson.

The construction team, the electricians, plumbers, carpenters, painters, floor covering contractor, who built the building in record time two and a half years earlier, dropped what they were doing, came to the rescue and -- just 16 days later - we were back in business. Also, our entire incredible dental staff worked day and night salvaging our charts, and so forth, to get us operational again. Since Schein Equipment was not available on our time frame we equipped with Engle units the second time around. They both appear to be similar to the ADEC Equipment and are both equally serviceable. ANOTHER wonderful opportunity to stretch and grow!

**   Your supplier will have a great deal on a dental air compressor for only a few thousand dollars. Air is Air! An in-line air filter and you are set! This unit was on sale for $385.00.

CHAPTER 30

A CHALK BOARD or MARKER BOARD is a great adjunct for demonstrative and training sessions for staff as well as for patients at times.

The more educated, better informed staff member is the more enthusiastic, more team-oriented staff member.

As dentists, we had the opportunity to learn much. We owe it to our staff and to ourselves to pass some of this pertinent information on to our staff. Our office accomplishes this through CHALK TALKS! The typical staff is eager to learn more and more about dentistry.

Occasionally or periodically, depending on your style, give a "chalk talk" on a single topic and answer questions of your staff. Some dentists prefer to schedule regular staff meetings for this purpose; others prefer to take advantage of breaks in the schedule because they thrive on spontaneity. Any way is fine!

Following are some examples of "CHALK TALKS." You can create many more or invite your staff to suggest topics for future meetings.

CHALK TALK #1

Dental caries - how, why, when? Even though you could go on for hours, just hit some high spots:

I.   Genetic Predisposition

      A.   Enamel thickness
      B.   Enamel quality
      C.   Dentinogenesis imperfecta; amelogenesis imperfecta
      D.   Saliva
            -       Viscosity
            -       Flow
      E.   High energy, nervous-type individual tends to snack more

II.   Familial Traits - traits which run in families

      A.   Much snacking - mid-morning, mid-afternoon and bedtime snacks are a way of life in some families
      B.   Lots of sugar in diet
      C.   Always sweets in the home
      D.   Get the "all day sucker" treat as a reward for good behavior
      E.   Flossing vs. no flossing
      F.   Brushing habits or lack of same

III.   General oral hygiene

IV.   Frequency of exposure to sweets -- can range from never to constant!

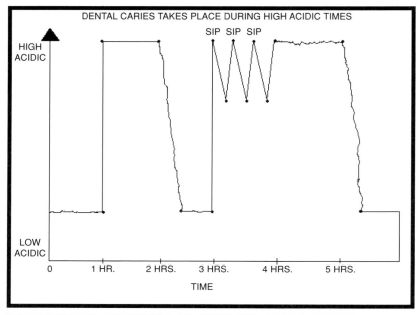

FIGURE 30-1
Showing effect of exposure to sweets

DENTAL CARIES TAKES PLACE
DURING HIGH ACIDIC TIME

TIME PERIODS
HOUR

0-1   no food intake with low acid environment for teeth

1-2   all day sucker

2   hours 20 minutes acidity drops

3   hour three open cola - sip every 10 minutes during hour

4-5   sipping cola every minute

5-6   no exposure to sweets

The more time spent in the high acid zone the more prone to dental caries development.

The point of the graph is that after exposure to refined carbohydrates (sugars) the acidity in the mouth (don't get into ph with this group) spikes and stays high for approximately 20 minutes.

Therefore, having dessert with a meal, then brushing is of very little detriment, but sipping a cola every 5-10 minutes maintains a high acidic environment for the teeth for hours at a time. The all-day sucker is the grand daddy of all...constant exposure.

Restorations   -   The more restorations the more tooth/enamel margins, the higher the probability of decay.

CHALK TALK #2

ASK YOUR STAFF THE FOLLOWING QUESTIONS:

1. WHO IS THE MOST IMPORTANT PERSON IN YOUR DENTAL OFFICE?

    Write suggested answers on the Chalk Board. Perhaps as follows:

    A. The receptionist
    B. The dentist
    C. The dental assistant
    D. The cleaning lady
    E. The patient

    It is fun to see their input and how long it takes for them to "See the Light."

2. Who makes it possible for us to get paid every two weeks? (For the remaining questions put marks by answers on the board - /////.)

3. Who has to have pleasant experiences here in our office?

4. Who has to leave the office happy?

5. Who is always right - about trivial matters?

6. Who is a guest in our house - who do we treat like a guest - (walk to the front desk)?

7. Who is our best possible advertising source?

8. Who is this facility set up for?

9.   Who did we go to school to learn to serve?

10.   Who do we want to get to know better?

11.   Who do we want to record more information about? (On upper right hand   corner of the chart - pets, hobbies, jobs, where they winter, children names, etc.?

12.   Who do we want to spend more time with? (Assistants are to chat with patients if the dentist is running late.)

13.   Who brings us flowers, berries, homemade bread and jams?

14.   Who...(you can go on and on as long as time permits).

As you go through each of these questions you can expand on the content. Of course the answer is ALWAYS - THE PATIENT!

CHALK TALK #3
ROOT CANAL TREATMENT

Root Canal Treatment is often quite intriguing and mysterious to the staff -- THIS MAKES FOR A GREAT SESSION! You can share some of the challenges faced in our daily lives. The more understanding the staff has the more supportive they tend to become.

Why Root Canal Treatment -

1. Pain
2. Radiolucency at apex

Why Pain -

1. Tooth is alive and the patient is experiencing pulpal hypersensitivity
2. Nerve died - bacteria "set up housekeeping" in the pulp chamber - no blood supply in chamber to combat the bacteria. Bone is destroyed around the apex by bacteria migrating from the apex.
3. The pain is from the bacteria and pressure in the bone.
4. Gangrenous pulp - pressure from expanding gases - cold soothes.
5. Pain at night when lying down.

Discuss:

A. X-rays with radiolucencies or thickened periodontal ligament spaces
B. Access to the pulp chamber
C. Instrumentation
D. Medication
E. Filling - sealing the apex
F. Crowning - to protect the more brittle tooth

G. The staff will ask questions to the extent of the available time.

They love it!

CHALK TALK #4
TOOTH REMOVAL

Discuss

1. Periodontal attachment

2. Elevation - The physics of leverage with elevators

3. Forceps

4. Ankylosis

5. Raising a flap - flap design

6. Osseous reduction

7. Suturing

8. Removal of sutures

9. Post operative complications

    -   Dry socket - alveolar osteitis

        CAUSES:
        A. Smoking
        B. Over-exertion
        C. Tongue playing with area
        D. Sucking

CHALK TALK #5
TOOTH DESIGNATION SYSTEMS

PALMER SYSTEM FOR PERMANENT TEETH

8 7 6 5 4 3 2 1 | 1 2 3 4 5 6 7 8

----

8 7 6 5 4 3 2 1 | 1 2 3 4 5 6 7 8

We seldom see the **PALMER SYSTEM** any more - 20 years ago it was quite often used.

ADA OFFICIAL FOR PRIMARY TEETH

E D C B A | A B C D E

E D C B A | A B C D E

This **ADA OFFICIAL SYSTEM** is still used in our deciduous stainless steel crown kit.

UNIVERSAL TOOTH NUMBERING SYSTEM
MOST COMMONLY USED IN 1995

1 2 3 4 5 6 7 8 9 10 11 12 13 14 15 16

A B C D E F G H I J

RIGHT--LEFT

T S R Q P O N M L K

32 31 30 29 28 27 26 25 24 23 22 21 20 19 18 17

Explain how specific permanent teeth cause individual primary teeth to exfoliate.

Show how the permanent teeth replace the deciduous teeth by causing resorption of the roots of the deciduous teeth.

The importance of the deciduous molars in holding the first permanent molars from coming forward.

Several sets of mixed dentition x-rays will best illustrate this.

The importance of care of the primary dentition -- this could be another Chalk Talk.

CHALK TALK #6
PERIODONTAL THERAPY

PERIODONTIUM = The tissues investing and supporting the teeth, including cementum, periodontal membrane, alveolar bone, and gingiva.

Healthy gingiva - 2-3mm gingival pocket maximum.

Attachment (explain the attachment).

Periodontal ligament is composed of: 1) alveolar group; 2) horizontal group; 3) oblique group; 4) apical group; radiate apically.

Interdental papilla (sharp in healthy dentition).

Gingival color:

> Normal color - coral pink
> Texture - stippled
> Contour - Papilli

Pocket Depth

Bleeding and exudation

Bone loss

Migration of teeth

Occlusal disturbances and how they affect the periodontium

Radiographic changes: Use patient x-rays from charts for demonstrative purposes.

A. Gingivitis - none

Marginal periodontitis - as inflammatory process extends in an apical direction.

B. Alveolar crest disturbance on radiograph

C. Occlusal traumatism -

Thickening of periodontal ligament space due to resorption of tooth structure and alveolar bone.

CHRONIC ALCOHOLISM - fiery-red tissue is often diagnostic.

CHALK TALK #7
PERIODONTAL DISEASE

Did you ever wonder why some 40-year-old patients present with bone support and tissue which looks as great as an ideal teenager and when others present and all we can do for them is remove their teeth and make them dentures?

Periodontal disease is an invasive destructive process which can start in early childhood and totally destroy the alveolar bone by early adulthood -- even by late teens.

FACTORS:

1. **Genetic Predisposition** - while this factor exists it most assuredly can be overcome.

2. **Familial Traits** - It becomes apparent from observation that familial traits play by far the greatest role in periodontal disease. For example, in one family the entire diet may consist primarily of refined carbohydrates washed down with pop while at the other end of the spectrum another family may have a great diet and consider an apple or banana at the end of their meal to be a satisfying dessert.

   Patients raised in these contrasting environments have entirely different views of dentistry, dental care, their dentition and individual teeth as the teeth become painful.

3. **Eating Habits** - Frequency of exposure to sweets, sipping cola all day long. All day suckers.

371

4.   **Nutrition**

5.   **Dental Hygiene**

Discuss periodontal surgery.

CHALK TALK #8
HOW TO STRUCTURE QUESTIONS
FOR THE COMPROMISED PATIENT

COMMUNICATING WITH THE PATIENT WHO
IS IN A COMPROMISED POSITION

Communicating with the patient while the patient is in a compromised position, such as:

        --   a rubber dam in place in the patient's mouth

        --   the patient has a mouthful of impression material

        --   after an extraction while the patient is under
                  instruction to continue biting on a 2 x 2 gauze
                  and unable to open his mouth

        --   the patient's mouth is anesthetized

In these situations all questions can be structured so that the appropriate answer is yes - an affirmative nod - or no - a negative nod.

Instead of saying, "Would you like just that one broken tooth restored today or would you like all of your cavities on that side completed while you are numb?"

Say: "Would you like all of your cavities on that side completed while you are numb?"

373

Instead of saying: "Would you like this prescription called into Range Drug or Keeley Drug?

Say: "Would you like this prescription called into Range Drug? If you get a negative...then inquire "Keeley?"

Instead of asking the patient after multiple extractions: "Would you like to sit here awhile or are you all right to get up?

Say: "Would you like to sit here a while?"

Instead of asking after nitrous oxide/oxygen analgesia inhalation, "Are you feeling okay or would you like to breathe some more oxygen?"

Say: "Are you feeling okay now?"

While it may take a little thought and practice, structuring your questions to be answered easily with an affirmative or negative nod will facilitate communication with the patient whom we have in a compromised condition.

This can be a helpful, fun and challenging project for the entire staff. Making a game out of it and helping one another learn to structure questions for the patient's convenience will facilitate communication.

CHALK TALK #9
PRIORITIES FOR DENTAL ASSISTANTS

Ask the assistants what they see as their top priority. Often they will do the entire session. You simply write their priorities down so they can see them. If they need some help or refreshing, here are some items you may choose to suggest:

List on the Chalk Board:

PATIENT CARE - treatment is top priority.

PATIENT DISMISSAL - RESCHEDULE - COLLECTION

PATIENT COMFORT PRIOR TO DENTIST'S ARRIVAL - Sit and chat with the patient or give radio headset or magazine to the patient.

PATIENT GREETED WITH A SMILE AT THE FRONT DESK AND WHEN TAKEN BACK TO THE OPERATORY.

PATIENT **CONSTANTLY** ATTENDED AND MONITORED WHILE UNDER NITROUS OXIDE/OXYGEN ANALGESIA.

OPERATORIES MUST BE IMPECCABLY CLEAN.

FOLLOW RULES OF INFECTION CONTROL.

SET UP OPERATORY FOR THE NEXT PATIENT.

SIX-HANDED DENTISTRY - ITS GREAT BENEFITS!

BRINGING PATIENT BACK **ON TIME** - If patient's appointment is at 2:15 bring the patient back at 2:15, not 2:16 or 2:17, or 2:30.

ASSISTANTS ARE <u>ALWAYS</u> NEAT AND CLEAN.

We prefer assistants who have their priorities focused around the PATIENT rather than other interests they may have.

There are a multitude of subjects which the staff would be interested in. At the end of one session ask what they would like to discuss next session. Then you can prepare for the topic or ad lib which ever is more your style.

CHALK TALK #10
SCHEDULING

Scheduling is immensely important. Keep an eye on it. Coach the schedulers. When a day goes particularly well (you know when things just seem to flow smoothly), keep the schedule and take a look at it for one of your Chalk Talks. Have the receptionist use the sample schedule as a pattern to attempt to duplicate. Have your staff analyze and discuss it, particularly the receptionist. Discuss this pattern at your Chalk Talk staff meetings.

These Chalk Talks will prove to be most beneficial to staff education and enthusiasm. The more well informed assistants or receptionists are, the better they are.

CHAPTER 31

IN HOUSE LABORATORY

"Find a need and fill it."

Ruth Stafford Peale

A cracked or broken denture or a tooth cracked or broken out of a denture is a DENTAL EMERGENCY to the denture wearing patient.

Therefore, following through with our philosophy of "Dental Emergencies Treated the Same Day," we have set up an in-house dental laboratory. We repair broken dentures within an hour while the patient reads a magazine in our waiting room.

This added service has been very well received and the initial investment is modest. The only additional equipment which is required to get started with the denture repairs is: A pressure cooker, an air line connection from your existing air pressure line to your pressure cooker -- your plumber can have this installed in an hour or two -- some denture repair polymer and monomer and an assortment of denture teeth.

379

As you service more and more dentures your equipment will naturally expand. However, the above list allows you to offer the service initially.

We now have added a sandblaster and hood, metal bonding acrylic, lathes and a model trimmer. This all can come later after you are in the denture repair business for a while.

In our fast moving society patients appreciate prompt service.

Same day denture repair or one hour denture repair are GREAT SERVICES to be able to offer your patients.

We have set up a laboratory in our basement for this purpose and are pleased with the results.

On many occasions we had patients present with a broken denture, or a tooth out of their denture or a tooth broken in half and various other dilemmas. It was explained to our patients that it would be necessary for us to send the denture out for the repair and that the turnaround time would be a minimum of 24 hours but more likely a couple of days. Seeing the absolute dismay and panic-stricken look in their eyes at the prospect of "going without my teeth" moved us to open our own in-house laboratory.

Our in-house laboratory is small, very compact, but very serviceable. It measures 8' X 10', has painted sheetrocked walls, one large overhead light, 8" white ceramic tile on the floor, a lot of counter space, a sink, an air hose, a pressure cooker, and various other items of equipment, a complete list of which will follow the text in this chapter.

A denture repair takes approximately 1 hour --

Always have your assistant get an alginate impression of the opposing arch so a model can be poured and occlusions checked during and after making the denture repair.

BROKEN TEETH REPAIR

Drill out the old broken tooth using your Dremel tool - be sure to roughen up all areas around the hole where the replacement tooth will be placed. Trim the new tooth so that it fits snugly. Begin with monomer using the salt and pepper method, to start refilling the acrylic. Set the new tooth in place, checking the occlusion to make sure the new tooth will fit properly. Follow directions on the acrylic.

Place the repaired denture into a disinfected beaker and place the beaker in very hot water inside the pressure cooker for the time period stated with your brand of acrylic.

After the specified amount of time in the pressure cooker remove and clean the excess acrylic with either your Dremel tool or the lathe.

Polish using copious amounts of pumice and water.

**(FIND EQUIPMENT LIST FOR IN-HOUSE
LABORATORY ON NEXT PAGE)**

EQUIPMENT LIST FOR IN-HOUSE LABORATORY

Lathe - 2 speed

Model trimmer

Burs - vulcanite - large round

Torch

Waxes - utility, base plate, alu and sticky

Polishing wheels - rag and chamois

Soldering iron and solder

Sandblaster

Hood for sandblaster

Dremel® handtool with all attachments

Stone

Plaster

Acratone liquid separator

Alginate

Beale's wax carver

X-acto knife

Pressure cooker

Face masks

Gloves

Heat cure acrylic

Self cure acrylic

Air line installed

Polishing agents

2 large beakers

Generous supply of teeth of various sizes and shades

About the Author

Dr. Silker, author, inventor, entrepreneur, may have viewed his dental education from a slightly different perspective for he was a very successful businessman prior to dental school. Upon graduation he entered into private practice from 1973 through 1979 when he relocated from Minnesota to Arizona. From 1980 through 1989 Dr. Silker joined forces with Dr. Herman H. Boehme in Phoenix, Arizona to create a group practice empire. They started with a single dental office and expanded to three other locations. Their fully staffed 24-hour-a-day, 365-days-a-year approach to serve the dental needs of the community received national attention.

Dr. Silker received his Doctor of Dental Surgery from the University of Minnesota School of Dentistry in 1973 and did his post-graduate work in World Business and International Studies at the American Graduate School of International Management in Glendale, Arizona.

Dr. Silker is a goal-directed, success-oriented, innovative thinker who combines a positive approach with sound business principles to achieve his goals.

ACKNOWLEDGMENTS

Most hearty thanks to D who took the illegible notes and created a manuscript out of them. Without her efforts this book would not have happened.

This book would not have been possible without the multitude of colleagues, assistants, receptionists and patients who have contributed to these findings.

Thanks to all University of Minnesota School of Dentistry professors and particularly, Dr. Robert Gorlin, Dr. James Beck and Dr. James Donahue.

A special thanks to Drs. William Berger and C. Ferdinand Benzie, my mentors during the critical two year period following graduation from Dental School, who helped me get started on a phenomenal career in Dentistry.

A great big thank-you to Dr. Herman H. Boehme for his contributions to my education in business, marketing, purchasing and finance.

Thanks also to Kevin Rients for his illustrations and help on the "Mac."

To Jackie Gellhorn for her contributions.

To Christina Riewer who gave us the "roadmap."

Thanks to Doug Peterson and Judy Morgan for their special friendship and encouragement.

To Dr. Fredrick Eichmiller, a long term friend and consultant.

AND TO MY PHENOMENAL STAFF at The Smile Center where this all came together:

Tricia Lundberg, RDH - for her contributions to our periodontal program.

Louise Dvorak - for her teaching skills in training in the new recruits, her amazing organization, sense of humor and loyalty.

Gail Britton, CDA, RDA - for her dedication, ingenuity and ability to fix anything that needs fixing so we have zero down time.

Jan Anderson - for her wonderful smiling face and pleasant handling of our patients at the front desk.

D Silker, CDA, RDA - for constructing and giving our in-house lab its start-up.

Anna Nyberg - for her extraordinary effort and versatility of being able to fill in wherever needed from start to present.

Sheryle Eastman, CDA, RDA - for her assistance with the start-up and continuing support of The Smile Center.

Sue Johnson, CDA, RDA - for keeping things light and lively at the office.

Amy Gibson, CDA, RDA - for her alert assisting on the evening shift.

Heather Papenfuss - for her long-term dedication and sincere interest in Dentistry.

Patricia Ralipak, RDH - for her continued excellent care and education of our hygiene patients.

LIST OF MAXIMS

Strive to discover your patient's priorities and value system and integrate their desires with your broad knowledge of Dentistry to develop a treatment decision which is in your patient's best interest and your practice will flourish.

Word of Mouth -- Your Best Advertising!

Advance on as many dental learning curves as possible as soon as possible.

Learn to be flexible enough to serve the patient spontaneously.

Complete the patient's dentistry in a single appointment, when possible.

The ability to remain flexible may well be your greatest asset.

Things will never be perfect and that is wonderful -- for we can always seek improvement.

The better we listen the more we learn.

When patients know why you are placing a rubber dam -- that it is for their benefit -- they tend to be much more cooperative.

Work in a room without the tongue and cheek -- use rubber dam.

The more you use the rubber dam the happier your "dental life" will be.

You cannot do well what you cannot see well.

Rubber dam is to dentistry what flossing is to home dental care.

Always consider placing survey crowns with rests on abutment teeth prior to partial denture construction.

When you really don't feel you can help the patient tell them you don't feel you can help them.

We owe it to our patients to suggest crown and bridge treatment whenever it is indicated.

If you try something which is a compromise in an attempt to save the patient some money or buy the patient some time, you own it!! It becomes your restoration and it will eventually come back to haunt you!! -- Do it right the first time. Crown it!

On all posterior crowns instruct the laboratory to take the crown "out of occlusion."

Show your patients the alternatives then help them make the decision.

It is the dentist's responsibility to present the best possible solution first.

Always obtain a written prior authorization from the insurance company on crown and bridge and removable prosthetics prior to beginning treatment.

Always have a current periapical x-ray of all root canal teeth, extractions, and crown and bridge teeth prior to commencing treatment.

All procedures must be agreed to be paid in full within 90 days maximum.

By conquering challenges and stretching we grow.

Discover a need in your Community. When you are successful in filling the need, you are a success.

Whatever works, works!

The principle of leveraging is for the dental assistants to perform all of those functions which do not require a dentist to perform.

Do not enter into any equipment lease program unless your trusted accountant has thoroughly calculated the total costs and suggested it to be your best strategy.

FAMOUS QUOTES TO REFLECT UPON

Inspiration and motivation are Essentials for Success.

'Though inspiration and motivation come from within, an outside spark may be responsible for igniting the fire!

Let us take a look at some favorite quotes left by others who have traveled or are currently traveling our same path.

Following are 52 favorite quotes - one for each week of the year --

We hope you enjoy and are as inspired by them as we are:

---

1)   WE ARE PROPHETS UNTO OURSELVES AND WE FULFILL OUR PROPHECIES.
            - Unknown

2)   REPETITION IS THE MOTHER OF SKILL
            - Anthony Robbins

3)   NOTHING GREAT WAS EVER ACHIEVED WITHOUT ENTHUSIASM.
            - Ralph Waldo Emerson (1803 - 1882)

4)   EVERY GREAT MAN, EVERY SUCCESSFUL MAN, NO MATTER WHAT THE FIELD OF ENDEAVOR, HAS KNOWN THE MAGIC THAT LIES IN THESE WORDS: EVERY ADVERSITY HAS THE SEED OF AN EQUIVALENT OR GREATER BENEFIT.
            - W. Clement Stone

5)   INCH BY INCH, ANYTHING'S A CINCH.
            - Dr. Robert Schuller

6)   SUCCESSFUL PEOPLE MAKE DECISIONS QUICKLY (AS SOON AS THE FACTS ARE AVAILABLE) AND CHANGE THEM VERY SLOWLY (IF EVER).   UNSUCCESSFUL PEOPLE MAKE DECISIONS VERY SLOWLY, AND CHANGE THEM OFTEN AND QUICKLY.
            - Napoleon Hill

7) THE MAN WHO DOES NOT WORK FOR THE LOVE OF WORK BUT ONLY FOR MONEY IS NOT LIKELY TO MAKE MONEY NOR TO FIND MUCH FUN IN LIFE.
   - Charles Schwab

8) GOALS ARE AS ESSENTIAL TO SUCCESS AS AIR IS TO LIFE.
   - David Schwartz

9) YOU CAN GET EVERYTHING IN LIFE THAT YOU WANT...IF YOU'LL JUST HELP ENOUGH OTHER PEOPLE GET WHAT THEY WANT.
   - Zig Ziglar

10) DON'T LET THE OPINIONS OF THE AVERAGE MAN SWAY YOU. DREAM, AND HE THINKS YOU'RE CRAZY. SUCCEED, AND HE THINKS YOU'RE LUCKY. ACQUIRE WEALTH, AND HE THINKS YOU'RE GREEDY. PAY NO ATTENTION, HE SIMPLY DOESN'T UNDERSTAND.
    - Robert G. Allen

11) PROGRESS ALWAYS INVOLVES RISK. YOU CAN'T STEAL SECOND BASE AND KEEP YOUR FOOT ON FIRST.
    - Frederick B. Wilcox

12) THE WINNERS IN LIFE THINK CONSTANTLY IN TERMS OF I CAN, I WILL AND I AM. LOSERS, ON THE OTHER HAND, CONCENTRATE THEIR WAKING THOUGHTS ON WHAT THEY SHOULD HAVE OR WOULD HAVE DONE, OR WHAT THEY CAN'T DO.
    - Dr. Dennis Waitley

13) IT IS A ROUGH ROAD THAT LEADS TO THE HEIGHTS OF GREATNESS.
    - Lucius Annaeus Seneca (4 B.C. - A.D. 65)

14) THE HEIGHTS BY GREAT MEN REACHED AND KEPT WERE NOT ATTAINED BY SUDDEN FLIGHT, BUT THEY, WHILE THEIR COMPANIONS SLEPT, WERE TOILING UPWARD IN THE NIGHT.
    - Henry Wadsworth Longfellow (1807 - 1882)

15) THE GREATEST USE OF LIFE IS TO SPEND IT FOR SOMETHING THAT WILL OUTLAST IT.
    - William James (1842 - 1910)

16) OPPORTUNITY IS MISSED BY MOST PEOPLE BECAUSE IT IS DRESSED IN OVERALLS AND LOOKS LIKE WORK.
- Thomas A. Edison (1847 - 1931)

17) IN ALL HUMAN AFFAIRS THERE ARE EFFORTS, AND THERE ARE RESULTS, AND THE STRENGTH OF THE EFFORT IS THE MEASURE OF THE RESULT.
- James Allen (1849 - 1925)

18) STRONG PEOPLE ARE MADE BY OPPOSITION LIKE KITES THAT GO UP AGAINST THE WIND.
- Frank Harris (1856 - 1931)

19) I WOULD NEVER HAVE AMOUNTED TO ANYTHING WERE IT NOT FOR ADVERSITY. I WAS FORCED TO COME UP THE HARD WAY.
- J. C. Penney (1875 - 1971)

20) WE HAVE A PROBLEM. "CONGRATULATIONS." BUT IT'S A TOUGH PROBLEM. "THEN DOUBLE CONGRATULATIONS."
- W. Clement Stone (1902 -   )

21) HE DID IT WITH ALL HIS HEART, AND PROSPERED.
- 2 Chronicles 31:21

22) OUR GRAND BUSINESS IN LIFE IS NOT TO SEE WHAT LIES DIMLY AT A DISTANCE, BUT TO DO WHAT LIES CLEARLY AT HAND.
- Thomas Carlyle (1795 - 1881)

23) THOSE THINGS WHICH ARE IMPOSSIBLE JUST TAKE A LIT-TLE LONGER.
- Lyle H. Silker (1917 - 1989)

24) WE ARE NOT CREATURES OF CIRCUMSTANCES; WE ARE CREATORS OF CIRCUMSTANCES.
- Benjamin Disraeli (1804 - 1881)

25) PERSEVERANCE IS A GREAT ELEMENT OF SUCCESS. IF YOU ONLY KNOCK LONG ENOUGH AND LOUD ENOUGH AT THE GATE, YOU ARE SURE TO WAKE UP SOMEBODY.
- Henry Wadsworth Longfellow (1807 - 1882)

26)   THE GREAT THING IN THIS WORLD IS NOT SO MUCH WHERE WE ARE, BUT IN WHAT DIRECTION WE ARE MOVING.
        - Oliver Wendell Holmes (1809 - 1894)

27)   ALWAYS BEAR IN MIND THAT YOUR OWN RESOLUTION TO SUCCESS IS MORE IMPORTANT THAN ANY OTHER ONE THING.
        - Abraham Lincoln (1809 - 1865)

28)   THE GREATEST DISCOVERY OF MY GENERATION IS THAT A HUMAN BEING CAN ALTER HIS LIFE BY ALTERING HIS ATTI-TUDES OF MIND.
        - William James (1842 - 1910)

29)   IN ANY PROJECT THE IMPORTANT FACTOR IS YOUR BELIEF. WITHOUT BELIEF THERE CAN BE NO SUCCESSFUL OUT-COME.
        - William James (1842 - 1910)

30)   DESTINY IS NOT A MATTER OF CHANCE; IT IS A MATTER OF CHOICE.   IT IS NOT A THING TO BE WAITED FOR; IT IS A THING TO BE ACHIEVED.
        - William Jennings Bryan (1860 - 1925)

31)   A MAN CAN SUCCEED AT ALMOST ANYTHING FOR WHICH HE HAS UNLIMITED ENTHUSIASM.
        - Charles M. Schwab (1862 - 1939)

32)   THE THING ALWAYS HAPPENS THAT YOU REALLY BELIEVE IN; AND THE BELIEF IN A THING MAKES IT HAPPEN.
        - Frank Lloyd Wright (1869 - 1959)

33)   NEVER, NEVER, NEVER, NEVER GIVE UP.
        - Winston Churchill (1874 - 1965)

34)   ENTHUSIASM IS A KIND OF FAITH THAT HAS BEEN SET AFIRE.
        - George Matthew Adams (1878 - 1962)

35)   TO BE HAPPY, DROP THE WORDS IF ONLY AND SUBSTITUTE INSTEAD THE WORDS NEXT TIME.
        - Smiley Blanton, M.D. (1882 - 1966)

36) MY MOTHER SAID TO ME, "IF YOU BECOME A SOLDIER YOU'LL BE A GENERAL; IF YOU BECOME A MONK YOU'LL END UP AS THE POPE." INSTEAD, I BECAME A PAINTER AND WOUND UP AS PICASSO.
- Pablo Picasso (1881 - 1973)

37) FLAMING ENTHUSIASM, BACKED UP BY HORSE SENSE AND PERSISTENCE, IS THE QUALITY THAT MOST FREQUENTLY MAKES FOR SUCCESS.
- Dale Carnegie (1888 - 1955)

38) I RATE ENTHUSIASM EVEN ABOVE PROFESSIONAL SKILL.
- Sir Edward Appleton (1892 - 1965)

39) AN ENTHUSIAST MAY BORE OTHERS, BUT HE HAS NEVER A DULL MOMENT HIMSELF.
- John Kieran (18892 - 1981)

40) ACT AS IF IT WERE IMPOSSIBLE TO FAIL.
- Dorothea Brande (1893 - 1948)

41) FIND A NEED AND FILL IT.
- Ruth Stafford Peale (1906 -   )

42) SHOOT FOR THE MOON. EVEN IF YOU MISS IT YOU WILL LAND AMONG THE STARS.
- Les Brown (1928 -   )

43) EVERY TOMORROW HAS TWO HANDLES. YOU CAN TAKE HOLD OF THE HANDLE OF ANXIETY OR THE HANDLE OF ENTHUSIASM. UPON YOUR CHOICE SO WILL BE THE DAY.
- Anonymous

44) IF YOU HAVE FAITH AS A GRAIN OF MUSTARD SEED...NOTHING SHALL BE IMPOSSIBLE UNTO YOU.
- Matthew 17:20

45) YOU CAN MAKE MORE FRIENDS IN TWO MONTHS BY BECOMING MORE INTERESTED IN OTHER PEOPLE THAN YOU CAN IN TWO YEARS BY TRYING TO GET PEOPLE INTERESTED IN YOU.
- Dale Carnegie (1888 - 1955)

46)   OUR LIFE IS WHAT OUR THOUGHTS MAKE OF IT.
             - Marcus Aurelius (121 - 180)

47)   EVERY MAN'S WORK, WHETHER IT BE LITERATURE, OR
       MUSIC, OR PICTURES, OR ARCHITECTURE, OR ANYTHING
       ELSE, IS ALWAYS A PORTRAIT OF HIMSELF.
             - Samuel Butler (1612 - 1680)

48)   A MAN IS WHAT HE THINKS ABOUT ALL DAY LONG.
             - Ralph Waldo Emerson (1803 - 1882)

49)   THE SECRET TO SUCCESS IN LIFE IS FOR A MAN TO BE
       READY FOR HIS OPPORTUNITY WHEN IT COMES.
             - Benjamin Desraeli (1804 - 1881)

50)   IF YOU WANT A QUALITY, ACT AS IF YOU ALREADY HAD IT.
       TRY THE "AS IF" TECHNIQUE.
             - William James (1842 - 1910)

51)   ADVERSITY CAUSES SOME MEN TO BREAK; OTHERS TO
       BREAK RECORDS.
             - William A. Ward (1893 - 1959)

52)   NOTHING IN LIFE IS MORE EXCITING AND REWARDING THAN
       THE SUDDEN FLASH OF INSIGHT THAT LEAVES YOU A
       CHANGED PERSON -- NOT ONLY CHANGED, BUT FOR THE
       BETTER.
             - Arthur Gordon (1912 -   )

SUGGESTED READING and LISTENING LIST

1. As a Man Thinketh (Robert Allen), Family Inspirational Library

2. Think and Grow Rich (Napoleon Hill), 1966

3. Success Through a Positive Mental Attitude (Napoleon Hill and W. Clement Stone), Nightingale-Conant Corp., Audiocassettes

4. The Power of Thinking Big (David J. Schwartz) 1986

5. The Road Less Traveled (Scott Peck)

6. Megatrends (John Naisbitt)

7. Magical Mind, Magical Body, (Mastering the Mind/Body Connection for Perfect Health and Total Well-Being (Deepak Chopra), Nightingale-Conant Corp. Audiocassettes

8. The One Minute Manager (The Quickest Way to Increase your Own Prosperity) (Kenneth Blanchard, Ph.D, Spencer Johnson, M.D.) 1984

9. Pulling Your Own Strings (Wayne Dyer)

10. Awaken the Giant Within (Anthony Robbins), First Fireside Edition, 1992

11. The 7 Habits of Highly Effective People (Stephen R. Covey)

12. First Things First (Stephen R. Covey, A. Roger Merrill, Rebecca R. Merrill), 1994

13. How to Make Love All the Time (Barbara DeAngelis), February, 1991 - Audiocassettes

14. Handbook to Higher Consciousness (Ken Keyes) - Audiocassettes

15. Clinical Research Associates Newsletter, 3707 North Canyon Road, Suite 6, Provo, UT 84604 - Phone: (801)226-2121

16. Dr. Mollen's Anti-Aging Diet (Dr. Art Mollen with Judith Sachs), 1992

17. Psychology of Winning (Dr. Dennis Waitley), Nightingale-Conant Corp., Audiocassettes, 1987

18. Quality is Free (Philip B. Crosby), 1979

19. Do What You Love, The Money Will Follow (Dr. Marsha Sinetar), 1987

20. Global Paradox (John Naisbitt)

21. Personal Excellence (Where Achievement and Fulfillment Meet) (Kenneth Blanchard, Ph.D) Nightingale-Conant Corp., Audiocassettes

22. Lead the Field (Earl Nightingale), Nightingale-Conant Corp., 1990 Audiocassettes

21st CENTURY HEALTH CARE PRODUCTS, INC.   (800) 325-0277
3CI COMPLETE COMPLIANCE CORP.   (800) 937-4324
3M DENTAL PRODUCTS DIVISION   (800) 634-2249
3M UNITEK CORPORATION   (800) 423-4588
7L CORPORATION   (800) 468-4927

A

AALBA DENT INC.   (800) 227-1332
ABIODENT, INC.   (800) 648-1802
ACCU BITE DENTAL SUPPLY, INC.   (800) 248-2746
ACCU-DENT RESEARCH & DEV. CO.,, INC   (800) 344-5457
ACTION EYEWEAR   (800) 285-3937
ADAM DENTAL MFG., CORP.   (800) 232-6810
ADCOA, INC.   (800) 876-8276
A-DEC, INC.   (800) 547-1883
ADIUM DENTAL PRODUCTS, INC.   (800) 892-2150
ADVANCED DENTAL CONCEPTS, INC.   (800) 369-3698
ADVANCED IMPLANT TECHNOLOGIES   (800) 876-4620
ADVANTAGE DENTAL PROD., INC.   (800) 388-6319
AEROSPACE LUBRICANTS, INC.   (800) 441-9160
AFFORDABLE DENTAL PRODUCTS   (800) 666-9008
AIR TECHNIQUES, INC.   (800) 822-2899
ALGIPAK COMPANY   (800) 272-5517
ALLIANCE SUPPLY CORPORATION   (800) 283-1688
ALLIED PHOTO PRODUCTS CO.   (800) 262-9333
ALLPRO, INC.   (800) 243-2285
ALMORE INTERNATIONAL, INC.   (800) 547-1511
ALPHADENT   (800) 942-4884
ALPHAHEALTHCARE™   (800) 283-0004
ALPHA PROTECH, INC.   (800) 527-7689
AMADENT/AMERICAN MEDICAL & DENTAL CORP. (800) 289-6367
AMBU, INC.   (800) 262-8462
AMDENT CORPORATION   (800) 833-7432
AMERADENT INC. OF NEVADA   (800) 959-8517
AMERICAN DENTAL ASSOCIATION   (800) 947-4746
AMERICAN DENTAL LASER   (800) 359-1959
AMERICAN DENTAL SUPPLY, INC.   (800) 558-5925
AMERICAN DENTECH CORPORATION   (800) 462-7990
AMERICAN DIAMOND INSTRUMENTS   (800) 537-7474
AMERICAN DIVERSIFIED DENTAL SYSTEMS   (800) 637-2337
AMERICAN LINEN   (800) 339-1691
AMERICAN MEDICAL ASSOCIATION   (800) 621-8335

AMERICAN ORTHODONTICS CORP.	(800) 558-7687
AMERICAN SOC. OF DENTISTRY FOR CHILDREN	(800) 637-2732
AMERICAN TOOTH INDUSTRIES	(800) 235-4639
AMINODERM LABORATORIES, INC.	(800) 426-1681
AMMEX	(800) 274-7354
AMSCO STERILITY ASSURANCE PRODUCTS	(800) 444-9009
ANALYTIC TECHNOLOGY CORP.	(800) 428-2808
APM-STERNGOLD	(800) 243-9942
APO HEALTH COMPANY	(800) 365-2839
APOLLO DENTAL PRODUCTS	(800) 233-4151
ARTUS CORPORATION	(800) 535-0086
ASEPTICO, INC.	(800) 426-5913
ASH/DENTSPLY	(800) 877-0020
ASKO INC.	(800) 367-2444
ASTRA USA, INC.	(800) 225-6333
ASTRON DENTAL CORPORATION	(800) 323-4144
ATHENA TECHNOLOGY, INC.	(800) 253-1771
ATTACHMENTS INTERNATIONAL INC.	(800) 999-3003
AUDRA, INC.	(800) 445-0170
AUKLAND MEDICAL PLASTICS, INC.	(800) 468-2363
AUTHENTIC PRODUCTS, INC.	(800) 683-1025
AUTOMATED DIAGNOSTIC DOCUMENTATION	(800) 257-6298
AUTOMATED SOFTWARE	(800) 259-9616
AVITAR, INC.	(800) 225-0511
AVTEK	(800) 423-2868

B

BALDOR ELECTRIC COMPANY		(800) 888-0360
BALSTON, INC.		(800) 343-4048
BANDITT DENTAL INSTRUMENT CO.		(800) 222-0961
BANYAN INTERNATIONAL CORP.		(800) 351-4530
BARRIER CONCEPTS, INC.		(800) 822-2854
BARRIER PROTECTION CO., INC.	CA	(800) 237-0097
		(800) 367-5432
BARRIERS FOR DISEASES		(800) 233-1006
BAUSCH & LOMB ORAL CARE DIVISION		(800) 633-6363
BAXTER HEALTHCARE CORPORATION		(800) 423-2311
BENCHMARK PROFESSIONAL, INC.		(800) 332-4274
BEST MANUFACTURING COMPANY		(800) 241-0323
BILSOM INTERNATIONAL, INC.		(800) 733-1177
BIO AESTHETICS CORPORATION		(800) 677-4432
BIO-CIDE INTERNATIONAL, INC.		(800) 323-1398
BIO-MEDICAL/DENTAL CORPORATION		(800) 444-1765
BIO-PROBE INC.		(800) 282-9670
BIO-RESEARCH, INC.		(800) 251-2315
BIOSAFETY SYSTEMS, INC.		(800) 421-6556

BIOTROL INTERNATIONAL	(800) 822-8550
BISCO DENTAL PRODUCTS	(800) 247-3368
BLOCK DRUG CORPORATION	(800) 365-6500

C

CADCO DENTAL PRODUCTS, INC.	(800) 833-8267
CALCITEK, INC.	(800) 854-7019
CALGON VESTAL LABORATORIES	(800) 243-5799
CALTECH INDUSTRIES, INC.	(800) 234-7700
CAM VAC	(800) 327-4401
CARLISLE DENTAL	(800) 392-2652
CENTRIX INC.	(800) 235-5862
CERAMCO INC.	(800) 487-0100
CHALLENGE PRODUCTS, INC.	(800) 322-9800
CHAMELEON DENTAL PROD., INC.	(800) 366-0001
CHATSWORTH MEDICAL SUPPLY, INC.	(800) 752-6919
CLEARCHEM CORPORATION	(800) 523-1328
CLINICAL RESEARCH DENTAL SUP. & SVCS., INC.	(800) 265-3444
CMP INDUSTRIES	(800) 833-2343
COAXCO, INC.	(800) 637-0001
COBB DENTAL SYSTEMS	(800) 541-8108
COLGATE ORAL PHARMACEUTICALS	(800) 225-3756
COLLA-TEC INC.	(800) 762-1574
COLORADO BIOMEDICAL, INC.	(800) 962-2272
COLTENE/WHALEDENT	(800) 221-3046
COLUMBIA WORLD CORPORATION	(800) 852-7519
COMLITE SYSTEMS, INC.	(800) 426-5291
COMMAND DENTAL SYSTEMS	(800) 221-4256
COM-PAC INTERNATIONAL	(800) 824-0817
COMPRESSOR TECHNOLOGIES, LTD.	(800) 847-0694
CONFI-DENTAL PRODUCTS COMPANY	(800) 383-5158
COOKE & ASSOCIATES, INC.	(800) 231-3058
COSMEDENT, INC.	(800) 621-6729
COTTRELL, LTD.	(800) 843-3343
COX STERILE PRODUCTS, INC.	(800) 247-6493
CRESCENT DENTAL MFG. COMPANY	(800) 323-8952
CREST ULTRASONICS CORPORATION	(800) 441-9675
CURA PHARMACEUTICAL, INC.	(800) 326-5690
CYGNUS INSTRUMENTS, INC.	(800) 626-2664

D

DEL-TUBE	(800) 558-8934
DEMETRON RESEARCH CORP.	(800) 444-3589
DENBUR, INC.	(800) 992-1399
DENDEV LABORATORIES, INC.	(800) 331-4437
DENERICA DENTAL CORPORATION	(800) 336-7422
DENLINE	(800) 336-5463
DEN-MAT CORPORATION	(800) 433-6628
DENOVO	(800) 854-7949
DENTACO PRODUCTS	(800) 925-8696
DENTAL ARTS LABORATORY, INC.	(800) 322-2213
DEN-TAL-EZ, INC.	(800) 275-3320
DENTAL HEALTH PRODUCTS, INC.	(800) 828-6868
DENTAL INVISIONS, INC.	(800) 322-7207
DENTAL/MEDICAL OPTICS MFG., INC.	(800) 423-7688
DENTAL NETWORK OF AMERICA, INC.	(800) 323-6840
DENTAL RESOURCES, INC.	(800) 328-1276
DENTAL SERVICES/DENTAL DYNAMICS	(800) 788-9174
DENTAL SLEEP DISORDER PREVENTION	(800) 477-6673
DENTAL VENTURES OF AMERICA	(800) 228-6696
DENTA-SLEEVE	(800) 535-4370
DENTAURUM, INC.	(800) 523-3946
DENTELLIGENT CORPORATION	(800) 535-3955
DENTICATOR INTERNATIONAL, INC.	(800) 227-3321
DENTO-PROFILE SCALE COMPANY	(800) 336-8610
DENTREX, INC.	(800) 344-2223
DENTRONIX, INC.	(800) 523-5944
DENTSPLY INTERNATIONAL, INC.	(800) 877-0020
DENT-X	(800) 225-1702
DESIGNS FOR VISION, INC.	(800) 345-4009
DEXIDE INC.	(800) 645-3378
DIAMOND CAMERA	(800) 477-3686
DINE, LESTER A., INC.	(800) 237-7226
DIO0PTICS MEDICAL PRODUCTS, INC.	(800) 959-9040
DISCUS DENTAL, INC.	(800) 422-9448
DISPOMED, INC.	(800) 873-4776
DISTRON SYSTEMS	(800) 453-4362
DMV CORPORATION	(800) 522-9465
DOLAN-JENNER INDUSTRIES, INC.	(800) 833-4237
DREXAM LABORATORIES, INC.	(800) 237-3926
DU-MORE, INC.	(800) 643-3447
DW TECHNOLOGY	(800) 448-4417
DYNA FLEX LTD.	(800) 489-4020
DYNATRONICS RESEARCH CORP.	(800) 874-6251

E

E. A. BECK & COMPANY		(800) 854-0153
EASTMAN KODAK COMPANY		(800) 933-8031
ECONO SYSTEMS		(800) 527-2076
E. C. MOORE COMPANY, INC.		(800) 331-3548
E & D DENTAL PRODUCTS, INC.		(800) 526-4911
EFOS, INC.		(800) 826-8701
ELECTRONIC WAVEFORM LAB, INC.		(800) 874-9283
ELLMAN INTERNATIONAL, INC.		(800) 835-5355
EMERY DENTAL		(800) 637-6611
EMF CORPORATION		(800) 456-7070
ENGELHARD CORP./BAKER DENTAL		(800) 631-5599
ENGLER ENGINEERING CORP.		(800) 445-8581
ENVIRO-AMERICAN, INC.		(800) 729-2048
ENVIROLUBE, INC.		(800) 233-5823
ENVIRO SENSE, INC.		(800) 995-8800
EQUIMED CORPORATION		(800) 451-7470
ESPE-PREMIER SALES COMPANY		(800) 344-8235
ESSENTIAL DENTAL SYSTEMS, INC.		(800) 223-5394
E-Z FLOSS	CA	(800) 227-0208
		(800) 458-6872
E-Z JECT SYRINGE		(800) 323-7922

F

FAIRFAX DENTAL INC.	(800) 233-2305
FISHER-SCIENTIFIC	(800) 766-7000
FISCHER-SCIENTIFIC CORPORATE	(800) 926-8877
FLORIDA PROBE CORPORATION	(800) 443-2756
F-M DENTAL	(800) 338-5077
FLOW X-RAY	(800) 356-9729
FLUID ENERGY INC.	(800) 756-2590
FOREMOST DENTAL MFG. INC.	(800) 662-6383
FOREST MEDICAL PRODUCTS, INC	(800) 423-3555
FRINK DENTAL SUPPLY CO.	(800) 373-3746
FUJI OPTICAL SYSTEMS, INC.	(800) 634-6244

G

GAC INTERNATIONAL, INC.	(800) 645-5530
GARLIC-GO U.S.A., INC.	(800) 548-8686
GASTON MEDICAL INSTRUMENTS, INC.	(800) 231-1547
GC AMERICA INC.	(800) 323-7063
GEBAUER COMPANY	(800) 321-9348
GENDEX CORPORATION	(800) 769-2909
GEN-STAT	(800) 870-7118

GENT-L-KLEEN PRODUCTS INC.	(800) 233-9382
G. HARTZSELL & SON	(800) 950-2206
GILCOM TECHNOLOGY, INC.	(800) 872-6444
GINGI-PAK	(800) 437-1514
GIRRBACH DENTAL GMBH	(800) 638-6041
GLENROE TECHNOLOGIES	(800) 237-4060
GLIDDEN PAINTS	(800) 221-4100
GLIDEWELL LABORATORIES	(800) 854-7256
GLOBE MEDICAL, INC.	(800) 237-4456
GNATHOS DENTAL PROD., INC.	(800) 325-0285
GOJO INDUSTRIES	(800) 321-9647
GOLDSMITH & REVERE	(800) 662-6383
G.P. DENTAL PRODUCTS, INC.	(800) 236-7677
GRESCO PRODUCTS INC.	(800) 527-3250
GUARD AID	(800) 225-4002

H

HALL SURGICAL	(800) 235-5713
H.A.L. PRODUCTS	(800) 962-7056
HANDLER MFR. CO., INC.	(800) 274-2635
HASCO, INC.	(800) 348-7747
HDK: MARKLINE BUSINESS PRODUCTS CO	(800) 343-8572
HEALTHCARE COMMUNICATIONS	(800) 888-4344
HEALTH CAREER LEARNING SYST.	(800) 829-4257
HEALTHFIRST CORPORATION	(800) 331-1984
HEALTHPAK, INC.	(800) 777-4725
HEALTH SCIENCE PROD., INC.	(800) 237-5794
HEALTH SONICS CORPORATION	(800) 342-3096
HEALTH TECHNOLOGY SYST., INC.	(800) 457-3997
HEALTH-TECH SYST., INC.	(800) 288-7691
HGM INC.	(800) 942-2119
HOBON	(800) 521-7721
HO DENTAL COMPANY	(800) 635-0555
HOLMES DENTAL COMPANY	(800) 322-5577
HOOKER SALES COMPANY	(800) 359-5180
HU-FRIEDY MFG. CO., INC.	(312) 975-6100
HUNTINGTON LABORATORIES	(800) 537-5724
H.W. ANDERSEN PRODUCTS, INC.	(800) 523-1276
HYDRO FLOSS, INC.	(800) 322-7955

I

ICN PHARMACEUTICALS, INC.	(800) 548-5100
I.C. PUBLICATIONS	(800) 426-6588
I.D.E.A.S., INC.	(800) 877-4332

IDE-INTERSTATE, INC.	(800) 666-8100
I.E.A. (ISHIYAKU EURO/AMERICAN INC., PUB.	(800) 633-1921
IMPLANT INNOVATIONS INC.	(800) 443-8166
IMPLANT SUPPORT SYSTEMS, INC.	(800) 338-5620
INDISPERSE DOSTRIBUTOR, U.S.A.	(800) 755-7720
INFECTION CONTROL SYSTEMS	(800) 835-3003
INFECTION CONTROL TECHNOLOGY	(800) 551-8008
INGLIS DENTAL SUPPLY, INC.	(800) 346-4547
INNOVATORS, INC.	(800) 347-0985
INSIGHT IMAGING SYSTEMS	(800) 654-0200
INTECARE INC.	(800) 548-9089
INTERPORE INTERNATIONAL	(800) 722-4489
ISLAND POLY	(800) 338-4433
IVORY	(800) 343-5336

J

JAVA CROWN, INC.	(800) 322-5282
JAZZ DENTAL PRODUCTS, INC.	(800) 676-4421
J.B. DENTAL SUPPLY COMPANY	(800) 777-0577
JELENKO DENTAL HEALT PROD.	(800) 431-1785
JENERIC/PENTRON INC.	(800) 243-3969
JENSEN INDUSTRIES, INC.	(800) 243-2000
J & J RESEARCH & DEVELOPMENT LTD	(800) 444-9254
J. MORITA USA INC.	(800) 752-9729
J.M. NEY COMPANY	(800) 243-1942
JOHNSON & JOHNSON CONSUMER PRODUCTS	(800) 526-3967
JOHNSON & JOHNSON MEDICAL, INC.	(800) 433-5170
JONES MEDICAL INDUSTRIES, INC.	(800) 525-8466
J.R. RAND CORPORATION	(800) 526-7111
J.S. DENTAL MFG., INC.	(800) 284-3368
JUMAR CORPORATION	(800) 435-7863
JUSTI	(800) 235-4639

K

KAIBAB STARBRITE INC.	(800) 678-1162
KAUFMAN DENTAL MFG., INC.	(800) 228-0532
KAVO AMERICA CORPORATION	(800) 323-8029
KAYCOR INTERNATIONAL LTD.	(800) 323-4612
KCOMP	(800) 747-5266
KEELER INSTRUMENTS INC.	(800) 523-5620
KEITH ILLUMINATION CORP.	(800) 433-9698
KELLER LABORATORIES INC.	(800) 325-3056
KENT DENTAL INC.	(800) 345-8202
KERR MANUFACTURING COMPANY	(800) 852-0921

KETTERBACH/TEMKET, INC.	(800) 932-0038
KILGORE INTERNATIONAL INC.	(800) 892-9999
KINETIC INSTRUMENTS INC.	(800) 233 2346
KINGSWOOD LABORATORIES, INC.	(800) 968-7772
KISCO	(800) 325-8649
KLH MEDICAL, INC.	(800) 328-8884
KODAK DENTAL PRODUCTS	(800) 242-2424
KOWA AMERICAN CORPORATION	(800) 221-2076
KYOCERA AMERICA, INC.	(800) 421-5735

L

LACTONA/UNIVERSAL	(800) 523-2559
LA-MAN CORPORATION	(800) 348-2463
LA MAR INDUSTRIES	(800) 456-5558
LANG DENTAL MFG. CO., INC.	(800) 222-5264
LC DENTAL	(800) 866-6766
L.D. CAULK/DENTSPLY	(800) 532-2855
LEE PHARMACEUTICALS	(800) 950-5377
L & F PRODUCTS, INC.	(800) 526-0321
LIFECORE BIOMEDICAL INC.	(800) 787-8246
LIFE-TECH, INC.	(800) 231-9841
LIGHT-TECH, INC.	(800) 462-5542
LUXAR CORPORATION	(800) 548-1482

M

MACINTOSH COMPUTERS	(800)SOS-APPL
MACROCHEM CORPORATION	(800) 622-3685
MADA EQUIPMENT COMPANY, INC.	(800) 332-6232
MAJESTIC DRUG COMPANY, INC.	(800) 238-0220
MARION MERRELL DOW	(800) 552-3656
MARTIN MCLANE MEDICAL PRODS.	(800) 443-9421
MASEL INC.	(800) 423-8227
MASTERS SERIES VIDEO STUDY CLUB	(800) 521-8913
MATECH, INC.	(800) 292-6620
MCCLEAY DENTAL INC.	(800) 367-1993
M-DEC	(800) 321-6332
MDS PRODUCTS, INC.	(800) 637-2337
MDT CORPORATION	(800) 331-9457
MEDICAL I.D. SYSTEMS, INC.	(800) 262-2399
MEDICAL POLYMERS TECH, INC.	(800) 460-0440
MEDIDENTA INTERNATIONAL, INC.	(800) 221-0750
MEDIMARK	(800) 548-9389
MED-INDEX	(800) 999-4614
MELALEUCA, INC.	(800) 522-0700

MERCK & COMPANY	(800) 637-2579
MERITECH, INC.	(800) 932-7707
METREX RESEARCH CORPORATION	(800) 841-1428
METTLER ELECTRONICS CORP.	(800) 854-9305
MICROCOPY	(800) 235-1863
MICRODENTAL LABORATORIES	(800) 229-0936
MICRON DENTAL MFG. COMPANY	(800) 697-7726
MICRO-VAC INC.	(800) 729-1020
MIDWEST DENTAL PRODUCTS CORP.	(800) 800-2888
MILES INC., DENTAL PRODUCTS	(800) 343-5336
MILTEX INSTRUMENT COMPANY, INC.	(800) 645-8000
MINNTECH CORPORATION	(800) 328-3340
MION INTERNATIONAL CORP.	(800) 759-6466
MISSION DENTAL, INC.	(800) 323-5087
MITER, INC.	(800) 325-8566
MJR EXQUISITE IMPORTS, INC.	(800) 852-5544
M & M INNOVATIONS INC.	(800) 688-3384
MOGO, INC.	(800) 944-6646
MOORE, E.C. COMPANY, INC.	(800) 331-3548
MORACK, INC.	(800) 837-9696
MOSBY, INC.	(800) 426-4545
MOYCO INDUSTRIES, INC.	(800) 523-3676
M-R SULLIVAN MANUFACTURING CO.	(800) 456-2014
MTI PRECISION PRODUCTS	(800) 367-9290
MYDENT CORPORATION	(800) 275-0020
MYO-TRONICS RESEARCH, INC.	(800) 426-0316

N

NANO ENTERPRISES	(800) 925-8533
NATIONAL BAG COMPANY, INC.	(800) 247-6000
NATIONAL LABORATORIES	(800) 677-9218
NATURE'S WAY PRODUCTS, INC.	(800) 926-8883
NDL LABS INC.	(800) 872-1525
NEVIN LABORATORIES, INC.	(800) 544-5337
NEW IMAGE INDUSTRIES, INC.	(800) 634-7349
NEXADENTAL	(800) 437-5606
NIGHTINGALE CONANT	(800) 525-9000
NIKON INC.	(800) 645-6687
NOIR MEDICAL TECHNOLOGIES	(800) 521-9746
NORDIC TRACK	(800) 467-0494
NORTHWEST DENTAL, INC.	(800) 640-0911
NU-DENT, INC.	(800) 645-4333

O

OIS/SC ORTHODONTICS	(800) 441-7700
OMNIGENE, INC.	(800) 433-0364
OMNII INTERNATIONAL	(800) 643-3639
OMNI PRODUCTS INTERNATIONAL	(800) 777-2972
OPTICARE	(800) 223-4573
OPTIVA CORPORATION	(800) 682-7664
ORACHEM PHARMACEUTICALS	(800) 523-0191
ORAL-B LABORATORIES	(800) 446-7252
ORAL DYNAMICS, INC.	(800) 726-1628
ORAL HEALTH U.S.A., INC.	(800) 533-5069
ORALSAFE, INC.	(800) 237-8825
ORATEC CORPORATION	(800) 368-3529
OXYFRESH USA, INC.	(800) 333-7374

P

PACIFIC ABRASIVES, INC.	(800) 999-5255
PALMERO DENTAL SALES COMPANY	(800) 344-6424
PARKELL	(800) 243-7446
PATTERSON DENTAL	(800) 838-7326
PEERLESS INTERNATIONAL, INC.	(800) 527-2025
PERIOWISE, INC.	(800) 660-6466
PFINGST & COMPANY, INC.	(800) 221-1268
PHOTOMED INTERNATIONAL	(800) 998-7765
PIONEER DENTAL	(800) 325-3962
PLAK SMACKER, INC.	(800) 228-9021
PLASTODONTICS	(800) 695-2367
POLAROID CORPORATION	(800) 225-1618
PRACTICON, INC.	(800) 959-9505
PRECISION ROTARY INSTRUMENTS	(800) 762-7689
PREMIER DENTAL PRODUCTS CO.	(800) 344-8235
PREMIUM LATEX PRODUCTS, INC.	(800) 755-4588
PREVENTIVE CARE, INC.	(800) 998-2002
PREVENTIVE DENTAL ENTERPRISES	(800) 448-5089
PRN DENTAL SUPPLIES, INC.	(800) 642-8090
PRO-DEN SYSTEMS, INC.	(800) 252-5863
PRO-DENTEC	(800) 228-5595
PRODUCTIVITY TRAINING CORP.	(800) 423-2683
PROFESSIONAL ECONOMICS BUR. OF AMERICA	(800) 328-3925
PROFESSIONAL RESULTS, INC.	(800) 350-3705
PROFESSIONAL SOFTWARE SOLUTIONS	(800) 433-2409
PROFITFINDER	(800) 443-5095
PRO FLOW INC.	(800) 645-7171
PROTECH PROFESSIONAL PROD., INC.	(800) 872-8898

PSI DENTAL MATERIALS	(800) 443-5459
PULPDENT CORPORATION	(800) 343-4342

Q

QUALITY LATEX PRODUCTS, INC.	(800) 292-3273
QUALITY SYSTEMS, INC.	(800) 888-7955
QUANTUM LABS INC.	(800) 328-8213
QUICK INTERNATIONAL INC., DENTAL EXPRESS	(800) 638-6935
QUINTESSENCE PUBLISHING CO.,INC.	(800) 621-0387

R

RAMVAC CORPORATION	(800) 572-6822
R C ERICKSON & ASSOC.	(800) 477-6758
RECIGNO LABORATORIES INC.	(800) 523-2304
REGENCY DIAMOND COMPANY	(800) 669-3353
REGENT LABORATORIES, INC.	(800) 872-1525
RELIANCE ORTHODONTIC PRODUCTS	(800) 323-4348
RESEARCH INFORMATION SERVICES	(800) 235-6646
RESTORATIVE TECHNICS DIVISION	(800) 274-2230
RICHMOND DENTAL COMPANY	(800) 277-0377
R. J. LABORATORIES, INC.	(800) 825-8532
ROBELL RESEARCH	(800) 848-1800
ROB'S UPHOLSTERY	(800) 450-7627
ROCKY MOUNTAIN ORTHODONTICS	(800) 525-6375
ROWPAR PHARMACEUTICALS, INC.	(800) 643-3337
ROYDENT DENTAL PRODUCTS, INC.	(800) 992-7767
RX HONING MACHINE CORP.	(800) 346-6464

S

S & S CARPET MILLS	(800) 241-4013
SABRA-THE DENTAL PROD. GROUP	(800) 537-2272
SAFCO DENTAL SUPPLY COMPANY	(800) 621-2178
SAFESKIN CORPORATION	(800) 456-8379
SALVIN DENTAL SPECIALTIES	(800) 535-6566
SANTA BARBARA MEDCO, INC.	(800) 346-3326
SAVAGE LABORATORIES	(800) 231-0206
SAVE-A-LIFE SYSTEMS, INC.	(800) 933-5885
SCHEIN DENTAL EQUIPMENT	(800) 645-6594
SCHEIN, HENRY INC.	(800) 367-3674
SCICAN, INC.	(800) 572-1211
SCIENTIFIC PHARMACEUTICALS	(800) 634-3047
SCM MEDICAL	(800) 338-2707
SCRUBS BY DOC	(800) 325-9044

S.D.I. LABORATORIES, INC.	(800) 227-8507
SEPTODONT, INC.	(800) 872-8305
SHERWOOD MEDICAL	(800) 325-7472
SHOFU DENTAL CORPORATION	(800) 827-4638
SHOWERFLOSS, INC.	(800) 959-3567
SIEMENS, PELTON & CRANE	(800) 659-6560
SILVERMAN'S DENTAL	(800) 448-3384
SIME HEALTH LTD.	(800) 824-7463
SIMIPLE-CLEAN TRAP CORPORATION	(800) 841-3584
SIMPLEX EQUIPMENT AND SUPPLY	(800) 462-4823
SIMPLIFIED PROTECTION, INC.	(800) 800-1828
SIMPLIFIED SYSTEMS, INC.	(800) 888-0900
SKIN + CORP.	(800) 338-9909
SMARTPRACTICE	(800) 522-0800
SMITHKLINE BEECHAM	(800) 743-4014
SOFTECH, INC.	(800) 233-4998
SONEX INTERNATIONAL CORP.	(800) 633-7858
SONIX IV CORPORATION	(800) 878-2769
SOUTHERN DENTAL INDUSTRIES, INC.	(800) 228-5166
SPARTAN U.S.A., INC.	(800) 325-9027
SPECIAL PRODUCTS, INC.	(800) 538-6836
SPECIALTY MEDCO INC.	(800) 363-4568
SPORICIDIN INTERNATIONAL	(800) 424-3733
SPRING HEALTH PRODUCTS	(800) 800-1680
SPS MEDICAL	(800) 722-1529
S.S. WHITE BURS, INC.	(800) 535-2877
STAHMER, WESTON & CO., INC.	(800) 423-7188
STAR X-RAY COMPANY, INC.	(800) 374-2163
STEPPING STONES TO SUCCESS	(800) 548-2164
STERI-DENT CORPORATION	(800) 346-3368
STERI-OSS INC.	(800) 993-8100
STERI-SHIELD PRODUCTS	(800) 446-0041
STER-O-LIZER MFG. CORP.	(800) 468-8241
STIRN INDUSTRIES	(800) 245-1095
STRAUSS DIAMOND INSTRMENT INC.	(800) 982-9641
STRIATA INC.	(800) 424-2835
STRONG DENTAL PRODUCTS	(800) 648-9729
STRYKER DENTAL IMPLANTS	(800) 666-8603
SULTAN CHEMISTS, INC.	(800) 637-8582
SULTAN DENTAL PRODUCTS, INC.	(800) 238-6739
SUNBEAM-OSTER	(800) 528-7713
SUPER TOOTH PRODUCTS, INC.	(800) 522-7883
SUTER DENTAL MFG. CO., INC.	(800) 368-8376
SYTAR SYSTEMS, INC.	(800) 877-9827

TAK SYSTEMS	(800) 333-9631
TALLADIUM, INC.	(800) 221-6449
TANAKA DENTAL	(800) 325-5266
TARA CROWN, INC.	(800) 523-8272
TECH CHEM INC.	(800) 852-5641
TECHNICRAFT INDUSTRIES, INC.	(800) 677-8786
TECNOL, INC.	(800) 826-5763
TEKSCAN INC.	(800) 248-3669
TELEDYNE WATER PIK	(800) 323-6650
TEMREX	(800) 645-1226
TETRAHEDRON, INC.	(800) 336-9266
TEXCEED CORPORATION	(800) 344-1321
THE DENTAL RECORD	(800) 243-4675
THE DIAL CORPORATION	(800) 660-2018
THE HYGENIC CORPORATION	(800) 321-2135
THM BIOMEDICAL INC./OSMED	(800) 327-6895
THOMPSON DENTAL MFG. CO.	(800) 622-4222
TIDI PRODUCTS, INC.	(800) 225-8434
TILLOTSON HEALTHCARE CORP.	(800) 445-6830
TIME DENTAL PRODUCTS	(800) 441-5107
TP ORTHODONTICS, INC.	(800) 348-8856
TRESCO, INC.	(800) 669-4823
TRI HAWK CORPORATION	(800) 874-4295
TROLLPAST INC.	(800) 537-8765
TROPHY U.S.A.	(800) 642-1246
TULSA DENTAL PRODUCTS	(800) 662-1202
TUTTNAUER USA COMPANY, LTD.	(800) 624-5836

ULTRADENT PRODUCTS, INC.	(800) 552-5512
UNICEP	(800) 354-9396
UNION BROACH CORPORATION	(800) 221-1344
UNITED SERVICE DENTAL CHAIR	(800) 328-9689
UNIVERSAL IMPLANT SYSTEM, INC.	(800) 394-4442
UPJOHN COMPANY	(800) 253-8600
USA DENTAL PRODUCTS, INC.	(800) 228-9021
U.S. DENTEK	(800) 433 6835
U.S. GYPSUM	(800) 621-9622
U.S. PHARMACOPEIA	(800) 227-8772

V

VANIMAN MANUFACTURING CO.	(800) 826-4626
VAN R DENTAL PRODUCTS, INC.	(800) 833-8267
VARI-X	(800) 421-6841
VERATEX CORPORATION	(800) 521-2640
VFS SYSTEM - PATIENT VIEW	(800) 283-7843
VIC POLLARD DENTAL PROD., INC.	(800) 235-1849
VIDENT	(800) 828-3839

W

WAGGONER DENTAL MANUFACTURING	(800) 433-0894
WALL STREET CAMERA	(800) 221-4090
WARNER-LAMBERT COMPANY	(800) 223-0182
WEISSMAN TECH. INT'L., INC.	(800) 323-3136
WESTERMAN ENTERPRISES	(800) 928-9289
WESTONE LABORATORIES, INC.	(800) 525-5071
WHIP MIX CORPORATION	(800) 626-5651
WHITE BITE, INC.	(800) 231-9665
WHITE GAPS	(800) 456-2272
WHITEHALL LABORATORIES	(800) 343-0856
WIMEX®	(800) 368-6650
W. L. GORE & ASSOC., INC.	(800) 282-2182
WORD PERFECT CORPORATION	(800) 633-2509
WORLDWIDE DENTAL, INC.	(800) 328-2335
WYKLE RESEARCH, INC.	(800) 859-6641

XYZ

YOUNG DENTAL	(800) 325-1881
ZAHN DENTAL COMPANY, INC.	(800) 496-9500
ZENITH/FOREMOST DENTAL MFG. INC.	(800) 662-6383
ZEST ANCHORS, INC.	(800) 262-2310
ZEZA, INC.	(800) 527-8937
ZILA© PHARMACEUTICALS	(800) 922-7887
ZIRC DENTAL PRODUCTS, INC.	(800) 328-3899

BIBLIOGRAPHY

"A Guide to Learning Curve Technology to Enhance Performance Prediction in Vocational Evaluation," from Paul McCray, Thomas Blakemore Research Utilization Report, Stout Vocational Rehabilitation Institute, School of Education and Human Services, UNIVERSITY OF WISCONSIN-STOUT - Menomonie, WI 54751.

Best Quotations for All Occasions, Lewis Henry, 1945, Fawcett Publishing.

Clinical Research Associates Newsletter, 3707 North Canyon Road, Suite 6, Provo, UT 84604 (801)226-2121.

Marketing Concepts & Strategies, Pride/Ferrell, 8th Edition.

Peter's Quotations, 1977, Morrow Publishing.

"Pneumatic versus hand condensation of amalgam: effect on microleakage," by Kenneth W. Chapman (Associate Professor, Department of Primary Patient Care, University of Louisville, School of Dentistry, Louisville, Kentucky) and Gary A. Crim (Professor, Department of Primary patient Care, University of Louisville). QUINTESSENCE INTERNATIONAL Volume 23, Number 7/1992

Textbook of Complete Dentures, Fifth Edition, Arthur O. Rahn, Charles M. Heartwell, Jr., 1993.

The American Heritage Dictionary of the English Language, 1992 - Third Edition.

The Golden Book of Quotations, Golden Press, 1964.

The Self-Publishing Manual, How to Write, Print and Sell Your Own Book, 8th Printing, 1995, Dan Poynter.

ORDER FORM

- Fax Orders: __1 (218) 534-3949__

- Telephone Orders:
  Call Toll-Free: __1-800-450-0091__
  (Have your DISCOVER, VISA, or MASTER
  CARD ready)

- Postal Orders: SILK PAGES PUBLISHING
  7030 Gullwood Road
  Lakeshore, MN 56468 U.S.A.

PLEASE SEND THE FOLLOWING:

_____ COPIES OF

DENTISTRY: Building Your Million Dollar Solo Practice
$59.95 U.S.A. / $79.95 CANADA

I understand that I may return any books within 30 days of purchase-
for a full refund -- for any reason, no questions asked.

SALES TAX:

Minnesota residents please add 6.5% sales tax.

SHIPPING & HANDLING:

Add $2.00 for the first book and $1.00 for each additional book to the
same address.

PAYMENT:

___ Check

___ Credit Card ____ VISA ____ MASTER CARD ____ DISCOVER

Card Number: _____

Name on Card: _____ Exp. Date: _____

CALL *TOLL FREE* AND ORDER NOW!